T0319769

Neither Free Trade Nor Protection

Neither Free Trade Nor Protection

A Critical Political Economy of Trade Theory and Practice

Bill Dunn

Department of Political Economy, University of Sydney, Australia

 Edward Elgar
PUBLISHING

Cheltenham, UK • Northampton, MA, USA

Published by
Edward Elgar Publishing Limited
The Lypiatts
15 Lansdown Road
Cheltenham
Glos GL50 2JA
UK

Edward Elgar Publishing, Inc.
William Pratt House
9 Dewey Court
Northampton
Massachusetts 01060
USA

A catalogue record for this book
is available from the British Library

Library of Congress Control Number: 2014954959

This book is available electronically in the **Elgar**online
Economics subject collection
DOI 10.4337/9781783471935

ISBN 978 1 78347 192 8 (cased)
ISBN 978 1 78347 193 5 (eBook)

Typeset by Columns Design XML Ltd, Reading
Printed and bound in Great Britain by T.J. International Ltd, Padstow

Contents

Figures

Tables

Acknowledgements

Some of the ideas developed in this book were first published in an article published under a similar title in *Marxist Interventions* in 2009. Material published in *Journal of Sociology* in 2014 and in the proceedings of the 2012 conference of the Society of Heterodox Economists is incorporated into Chapter 8. I thank the referees and conference participants for their comments. I am very grateful to Frank Stilwell, particularly for his comments on earlier drafts of Chapters 3 and 8. The usual disclaimers apply. My thanks above all go to Carmen Vicos. Her support and my gratitude go far beyond the enormous help she provided with the book.

1. Introduction: contesting the conservative antinomies of trade theory

International trade matters profoundly and provokes furious controversy. The overwhelming majority of professional economists champion free trade. At the same time a vociferous minority sees free trade as unfair trade, insisting the apparent freedoms are illusory and that trade relations are exploitative.

On both sides there are powerful scholarly literatures. The theory of comparative advantage, in particular, has occupied a crucial place in the liberal canon for nearly 200 years and remains the cornerstone of mainstream international economics (Ricardo 1951; Krugman and Obstfeld 2003). It is the starting point for the World Trade Organization (WTO 2014) and the basis on which Bhagwati (2002) can dismiss opponents as impassioned but irrational. For orthodoxy, trade extends the efficiency of markets across borders. For Marshall, one of the founders of mainstream neo-classical economics, trade may even provide the very 'causes which determine the economic progress of nations' (2009: 225).

Some of the critical ideas have fallen out of fashion since the 1970s but many of the central insights are still defended, particularly in relation to persistent problems of development in the poorest parts of the world (Bracking and Harrison 2003; Bush 2004; Bieler and Morton 2014). There are powerful arguments that it is state strategies, rather than free markets, that enable some countries to escape poverty and under-development (Chang 2002). Again, several writers go further and find in trade the fundamental causes of international wealth and poverty (Emmanual 1972; Wallerstein 1974).

There is a lot at stake. Trade volumes are huge and have increased steeply in recent decades, both in absolute terms and relative to national incomes. Trade is growing in importance.

A visit to any standard textbook will confirm a simple dualism dominates the debates. Trade policy is presented as if it involved a straightforward choice between openness and closure (for example, Sloman and Norris 1999). This is not very helpful. More careful study soon reveals that even its supporters acknowledge that conventional, pro-free trade theory relies on invalid assumptions. The theoretical premises are 'relaxed' and all sorts of minor and occasional modifications and qualifications are admitted but any such amendments are seldom allowed to interfere with the confident conclusions that free trade brings mutual benefits. A variety of more or less radical critics can then have fun with the faulty assumptions of the mainstream. They can highlight examples where trade brings systematic disadvantages. Unfortunately, the criticisms too easily flip into an equally unsupported generalization that trade is injurious and iniquitous. So debates about international trade too often and too easily regress to a simplistic antagonism for or against free trade, or between market and state-led strategies.

Such binaries are misleading and conservative. If the object is depicting how the global economy actually works, rather than constructing a phantom economics for a world elsewhere, neither free trade nor protection are appropriate starting points. Free trade theory plays an important rhetorical role in encouraging a particular kind of opening, a reduction of tariffs and other barriers. But the gap between theory and a genuinely laissez-faire world never really closes. As Friedman (1962) acknowledges, there is an inherent tension between the freedom within markets and the freedom of others to restrict them. In the broadest sense, trade means an 'exchange of commodities for money or other commodities' (OED 1982). This takes place within as well as between countries. Most liberals admit that some 'market imperfections' within countries can justify state regulation. There are goods whose production is banned or whose trade is legitimately restricted. Protection of both consumers and corporate intellectual property is routinely accepted. Impeccably liberal writers from Mill (1994) to Walras (see Kolm 1968) have advocated land nationalization because of the inevitable lack of a free market. As Polanyi (2001) argues, state support is always needed to underwrite markets not just in land but also in those other 'fictitious commodities': labour and money. Free trade's most famous proponents, Smith and Ricardo, allowed many exceptions. Even the most dogmatic of contemporary free-traders would presumably baulk at the free exchange of drugs, people and nuclear weaponry (Reich 1991). So while abstract liberal theory takes support for free trade as axiomatic, this can prove fragile.

Trade openness in practice has almost always been a question of degree. All states maintain some restrictions. The phenomenal rise in trade of recent years can also be read as a process of 'managed openness' in which states continue to restrict trade in some dimensions but also to actively promote it in others (Weiss 1999, 2005). A huge quantity of trade also remains, and perhaps becomes increasingly, unfree in the sense that it is conducted within firms. Estimates for the level of this intra-firm trade vary but figures of about a third of the total are commonly cited (Held et al. 1999; Dicken 2003; Cohn 2005). This involves a transfer of goods from one place to another but with the same firm at both ends there is no market and the price mechanism operates at most indirectly. Goods cross national boundaries and appear in the trade statistics but this is not trade at all in the sense cited earlier, with no exchange of commodities for money or other commodities. Many apparently market-based relations are themselves more organized than free; also entailing significant doses of power and control. As Gereffi and his co-authors (2005) argue, the bureaucratic forms of organization within firms and pure market mechanisms really represent only two ends of a spectrum. The relations between clothing multinationals and their subcontractors are particularly well known. European supermarkets can actively control the production process deep inside African countries from which they import. Free trade was never the norm; nor is it yet (Krasner 1976).

The situation is even more straightforward on the other side of the fence. If free trade has hardly been the norm, nor has autarchy. At least since the collapse of the Tokugawa shogunate in Japan, states have not chosen isolation. The closest approximations to closure have been imposed by powerful adversaries rather than adopted as strategy. States at most employ selective protection to encourage particular industries. Rather than a simple-minded protectionism what we see instead are more usually policies of state-led development. Even the early mercantilists almost always argued for something rather qualified. Writers like Mun and Child advocated a strategic use of trade restrictions and such orientations become even clearer in later authors like Hamilton and List. Similarly, important post-World War II theorists like Prebisch and Singer proposed particular restrictions or reforms to the international trade regime rather than blanket opposition. There are occasional exceptions. In the inter-war period the Romanian nationalist Manoïlescu argued for closure (Emmanuel 1972; Brolin 2006). Emmanuel (1972) does at one point advocate autarchy, although he sees little chance of its implementation. Something similar is perhaps implicit in some of the arguments of Frank and Amin but a blanket opposition to trade is rare in theory and even rarer in practice.

There are also some striking similarities between the apparently opposite perspectives. Both traditions can be seen as descendants of the weakest point in Smith's analysis. Like both lines of his descendants, Smith's objective is precisely the 'wealth of nations'. This may seem an obvious and eminently reasonable purpose but that very obviousness is telling and it is worth reflecting on why it might be a problem. The focus on national wealth can overlook other sources or owners of wealth. Smith also tends to privilege exchange relations and market efficiency over broader economic and social questions and much of this is repeated in both sides of the subsequent trade literature.

There is, of course, an element of caricature in presenting 200 years of trade theory as a simple dualism. There are honourable exceptions. Among mainstream economists Rodrik is perhaps the most consistent in pointing out that trade need not bring the much-vaunted benefits (for example, Rodrik 2001, 2003; Rodriguez and Rodrik 2000). In later life, Samuelson (2004) similarly raised deep questions for free trade enthusiasts, as had Keynes (1973) before him. Among the critics, several dismantle the orthodoxy, without, as far as I am aware, attempting to erect the nationalist or anti-trade alternatives that will be criticized here (for example, Shaikh 1979, 1980, 2007; Deraniyagala and Fine 2001; Deraniyagala 2005). This book is indebted to the work of these and other scholars. However, they remain relatively isolated voices. The starting points of the purportedly antagonistic perspectives are usually remarkably similar. Both tend to obscure the conditions that produce trade and which make it good or bad for particular countries and for particular groups within them.

This conservative dualism of trade theory can perhaps be understood as an example of what Bourdieu (1977: 164–71) describes as *doxy* and *doxa*. The idea is that the orthodoxy (in this case liberal trade theory) and the heterodoxy (in this case mercantilist and dependency theories) between them constitute a terrain of debate or *doxy*. The sound and fury of this debate draws attention to these perspectives and effectively conceals the *doxa*. This is the universe of the unexplored, a universe that potentially includes more radical critiques which quite literally remain out of the question. For example, rival trade theories push out of sight longstanding Marxist emphases on production but also questions of trade's potential gender and ecological implications. Skocpol (1977: 1089) similarly describes a '"mirror image" trap that plagues any attempt to create a new paradigm through direct, polemical opposition to an old one … For what seems like a direct opposite may rest on similar assumptions, or may lead … around full circle to the thing originally opposed'. Apparent antagonisms can actually conceal shared convictions, which remain unchallenged (see also Lukes 1974; MacLean 2000).

This book's title recalls the long-time slogan of the 'International Socialists', who during the Cold War supported 'Neither Washington nor Moscow but International Socialism'. The point was to argue that Western capitalism and what they designated 'state capitalism' in the Communist countries were different versions of the same thing. Whatever the theoretical merits of stressing either the similarities or differences between the two sets of political economies, politically, the slogan served a useful purpose of orienting the left away from supporting either of the superpowers and towards Marx's (1974) different interpretation of socialism as working class self-emancipation. The point was to avoid arguing on a terrain of others' choosing, arguing about which superpower was preferable, rather than articulating a positive agenda. The title here suggests a similar wariness about accepting debates around trade, which limit the remit to (more or less equitable) exchange relations and frame political economy in terms of a choice between states and markets.

I am aware of an apparent irony here, that a book about trade appears to be selling a narrative which says that the importance of trade is often overstated. What I am actually arguing is that trade needs to be put in proper perspective, understood in its broader social, economic and historical context. If this book makes only limited progress towards this immense task, there are useful things that can be said and done. Of course, trade is hugely important and the critical comments are not intended to dismiss some very important arguments. Trade theories should be taken seriously but investigated critically. They should not, as too often, be imagined to capture abstract, universal truths but should be recognized as partial in two senses of the word. Trade theories are partial in articulating particular interests, but also partial in that they only capture one facet of what should properly be understood as complex social configurations. With that proviso, it becomes possible to think more critically about some of the claims being made by the different theories, to control for what they are not investigating and to question them more carefully than has often been the case.

The rest of the book is organized as follows. Chapter 2 puts trade into historical perspective, highlighting how trade relations are inextricably connected to relations of power and wealth between and within countries, are ancient but ever-changing. Findlay and O'Rourke (2007: xviii), on whose book this chapter draws extensively, write of mainstream trade theory:

> If time is brought into the theory at all, and usually it isn't, this typically takes the form of allowing countries to gradually accumulate capital, breed new workers, or become better educated as a result of the voluntary decisions of rational, free individuals. The summit of unpleasantness attainable in such models is the use of tariffs, quotas and other trade policy instruments that will benefit some individuals or groups (and possibly nations) but lower the utility of other domestic or foreign residents.

> If only life were like this ... the greatest expansions of world trade have tended to come not from the bloodless tâtonnement of some fictional Walrasian auctioneer but from the barrel of a Maxim gun, the edge of a scimitar, or the ferocity of nomadic herdsmen.

Trade has seldom been a general good or evil and usually benefits some people to the detriment of others, not necessarily in equal proportion. The history also makes clear that until quite recently, national boundaries were not clearly defined and the meaning and measures of international trade are necessarily vague. The history also helps to provide the context in which rival theories were developed. Ideas are not straightforward reflections of the social and economic condition of their authors but they cannot be understood without understanding those contexts. Smith and Ricardo were products of and spokespeople for British capitalism in its dynamic youth. Figures like Hamilton and List were avowed representatives of competing but weaker national capitalisms. Several authors in the dependency tradition might be seen in a similar light. There is not a direct personal mapping and key figures like the American Wallerstein and the Graeco-French Emmanuel attempted to speak for the anti-colonial revolts rather than their own 'national' interests, but still the hopes and possibilities of a changing world conditioned what was thought wrong and what was thought possible.

Chapters 3 to 5 look in some detail at important trade theories. The first focuses on mainstream arguments, especially comparative advantage. This is territory well covered and readers familiar with the key claims and criticisms may safely skip the chapter. However, many people are exposed to one side or the other of these debates; either failing to appreciate the theoretical power of the underlying claims of the theory of comparative advantage or the assumptions on which the case for free trade is built and the problems they entail. It is discussed, in particular, how comparative advantage assumes perfect markets, and ignores time, space and the role of money. The anti-free trade perspectives are divided into two chapters, largely for ease of presentation because there is something closer to a continuum rather than a neat separation into distinct schools of thought.

Chapter 4 looks at what might be seen as the moderate opposition, which tends to couch the problems in terms of market imperfections. It considers the long tradition of mercantilism, of trade restrictions and industrial promotion, and the ideas developed in the post-World War II period of poorer-country disadvantage and deteriorating terms of trade. It also considers 'New Trade Theory', particularly articulated by Krugman, which argues that market imperfections can be mobilized to national advantage by the governments of large, rich countries.

Chapter 5 focuses on ostensibly more radical ideas of imperialism, dependency and unequal exchange. The criticisms mentioned above, in particular on the limits of radical nationalism and the focus on exchange relations, are extended and it is argued particularly that unequal exchange provides an inadequate explanation of systemic inequality.

Chapters 6 to 9 consider evidence from the 1960s onwards and perform a series of empirical tests. In practice, free trade and protection have been rare, almost imaginary ends of a spectrum of trade policy. This variation provides a basis for evaluating many of the claims being made.

Chapter 6 considers the relationship between trade and economic growth. It confirms there are weak, positive associations between trade openness, and trade opening, and growth. There is some evidence for this in aggregate, for rich and poor countries and for large and small ones. The chapter finds little evidence that trade surpluses are conducive to growth. Indeed, until the 2000s, a negative balance seems to be associated with stronger growth. There is some indication, particularly in the 1970s, that a positive balance in primary products had a negative impact, as various theories discussed in Chapter 4 anticipate, but this is not found subsequently.

Chapter 7 looks at whether countries grow faster when they trade on the basis of 'factor endowments'. That is to say it considers the Heckscher–Ohlin theorem, one of the key corollaries of neo-classical trade theory. For each decade between 1980 and 2010 the chapter reports results that confirm quite strong and highly statistically significant associations between land endowments and the propensity to export primary products, and weaker associations between labour endowments and manufactured exports. However, to the important supplementary question whether countries do better when they trade according to the prescriptions of Heckscher–Ohlin theory, the results are much less conclusive. There was some evidence in the 1980s that, if anything, countries' economies grew more quickly when they traded according to their factor endowments but little evidence of any such association in subsequent decades. Indeed, by the 2000s, the countries that defied Heckscher–Ohlin on average grew slightly faster than those that followed its prescriptions.

Chapter 8 looks at trade and inequality within countries. It focuses on the Stolper–Samuelson theorem, an extension of the Heckscher–Ohlin theorem, which maintains that there are likely to be winners and losers within countries from both protection and trade opening. The results indicate that trade had important impacts on (in)equality but that it worked in more complex ways than identified by conventional theories. The chapter therefore considers how other economic processes might work alongside or apart from trade and it broadens the discussion to one of inequality as a complex social and political achievement.

Chapter 9 extends the investigation of changes within countries by looking at the relationship between trade opening and labour organization. In recent decades many countries experienced both an increase in economic openness and falling levels of industrial action. The chapter reports tests showing that an anticipated negative impact of trade openness on levels of industrial action only becomes apparent in the presence of an interaction term between the level of trade openness and countries' relative wealth. This indicated that the decline in industrial action tended to be stronger in richer countries that opened less and poorer countries that opened more, contrary to more simplistic interpretations of recent change. Further tests then confirm a markedly steeper downward trend of industrial action in manufacturing than other sectors. This is compatible with the greater pressure on manufacturing workers associated with that sector's greater spatial mobility. It might potentially be explained by the numerical decline in manufacturing in many countries, although there is no strong evidence of the effect being greater in richer countries where such decline is more severe. Finally, the chapter shows a significant process of 'disembedding' of the incidences of industrial action in particular sectors, notably in manufacturing, from national contexts. However, the processes of disembedding do not appear to be directly linked to countries' relative exposure to trade.

Chapter 10 takes up the historical story from the 1970s, where it was left in Chapter 2, to the crisis of the late 2000s. It confirms what several accounts have identified as a significant role played by trade and the development of global imbalances in producing the crisis (Wade 2009; Wolf 2010; IMF 2011). However, it understands these misalignments as the products of a wider restructuring in the global economy, itself the result of contested struggles and strategies adopted in response to the crisis of the 1970s.

Chapter 11 concludes that the theoretical binaries are simply not confirmed by the evidence. The weakness of the relation between the degree of countries' openness or closure and overall economic performance is well established empirically but seems to have impinged very little on trade theory. Trade is neither a straightforward good nor a bad. An overly narrow focus on trade obscures what are in some ways more fundamental social relations. Apart from anything else, capital investment and exploitation in production are themselves the crucial determinants of tradable surpluses. The importance of trade is specific, varying over time and depending on who is being considered. The generality of trade theories conceals this specific importance, notably how the systematic imbalances in the global trade regime contributed to the crisis of 2007–09.

Before going further a few disclaimers are in order. The empirical chapters use mainstream data, for example of gross domestic profit (GDP) and of trade, and should be interpreted as contributions to a critique of existing narratives rather than as providing an adequate mapping. Conventional measures are often the best available indicators of important economic facts but it should be understood that such data are inherently flawed; for convenience or for ideological reasons they ignore some activities (like housework) that add to wealth and wellbeing and include others (like rent) that add nothing. Trade data routinely suggest a global deficit, as if the Martians were engaged in unfair competition. These chapters also concentrate on merchandise trade rather than the more slippery but increasing trade in 'services'. There is much else that cannot be discussed. For example, one area where there has recently been interesting work is in the analysis of commodity chains. Selwyn (2011) describes how such accounts tend to abstract from the specifics of national political economies in which the value is being added but the considerable potential for a fruitful synthesis is not developed here. In short, there are limits to what can be achieved but it is worth trying to move forward.

2. The making of world trade

INTRODUCTION

This chapter cannot provide a sufficient history of the many hundreds of years of world trade but an understanding of the past, of how trade has changed and even meant different things, helps inform the arguments and evidence of the rest of the book.

But if history helps to make sense of theory, history itself never arrives untainted. How we write history, on which events we focus and how they are interpreted involves making choices, which are themselves informed by theory; or too often informed by unacknowledged prejudices. History, as Cox (1981) says of social theory more generally, is always for someone and for some purpose and this chapter uses history to make several arguments.

The history here contests a pervasive narrative of the gradual triumph of free trade, the market and what Smith calls commercial society (Heller 2011). It becomes obvious that international trade precedes modern capitalism by several millennia while the concomitant rise of trade and capitalism hardly involved laissez-faire. The history reminds us that trade is an active process. While the traders themselves are intermediaries who seldom warrant a mention in modern textbooks or contemporary discussions, they are hard to miss in any serious narrative, for example in the Dutch VOC (East India Company) and the British East India Company or the Atlantic slave ships of the seventeenth and eighteenth centuries. Time and again it becomes obvious that trade involves relations of power. So the history challenges the conventional narrative of trade conducted at 'arm's length' by rational, utility-maximizing actors.

The history also underlines trade's interdependence with other social process, not least with power in production and in the state. It is impossible to answer debates about trade's relative importance with precision but considering its role, for example in the establishment of capitalism in Europe, the industrial revolution and the long, post-World War II boom, can temper some rather categorical contemporary judgements about the gains from trade, made by conventional theories of comparative advantage, or for example of the losses from unequal exchange.

At the start of the story there were no 'nation states' as we understand them today and patterns of production and ownership have been repeatedly transformed. As will be discussed in Chapter 7, there is much to recommend the mainstream Heckscher–Ohlin theory of trade based on 'factor endowments' but it is worth asking exactly how the factors were inherited. As Marx said in 1848 (1977: 269): 'You believe perhaps, gentlemen, that production of coffee and sugar is the natural destiny of the West Indies. Two centuries ago, nature, which does not trouble herself about commerce, had planted neither sugar-cane nor coffee trees there.'

European colonization transformed the land, and transported the capital and the labour. The point is a broader one, that often we need to go deeper to understand the historical and social meaning of trade, to ask what constitutes trade, what is being traded and why.

The remaining five sections of this chapter progress in rough chronological order, beginning with trade during the many centuries before Europe came to dominate the rest of the world; then considering trade and the rise of capitalism in Europe; trade, slavery and the industrial revolution; the era of British free trade and imperialism (and free trade imperialism) before finally turning to the post-World War II economy. Chapter 10 resumes the narrative in the 1970s, after the theoretical interlude in the next three chapters and empirical investigations that follow.

WORLD TRADE BEFORE EUROPE'S RISE

Even a brief survey of trade over the millennia prior to Europe's dominance reinforces a picture of trade, wealth and power and their dynamic and changing relationships.

Rosenberg's recent work (2006, 2009, 2010) on uneven and combined development emphasizes that even prehistoric 'societies' were involved in networks of social interaction at continental distances. I put the word 'societies' in scare quotes to make the point that it only really makes sense to conceive society as a differentiated whole; not as discrete entities involved in arm's-length transactions. Already in ancient times, there were more or less dense flows of goods, people and ideas. Some of these flows were freer than others. Some faced considerable physical and social obstacles. Over time, more or less effective boundaries could be created around nodes of relatively greater density both to establish forms of rule within them and to protect against outsiders. Rosenberg is precisely developing a theory of the origins of states and international relations, so these comments are not intended to downplay states' historical or contemporary practical importance. They should guard against seeing the emergent boundaries as absolute, and of thinking of political economy in specifically national terms. They support a social-ized understanding which sees states 'more as strategies in social struggles than as preordained facts' (Augelli and Murphy 1993, p. 139). The relation between internal and border-crossing activities is dynamic and changing.

Mann (1986) makes a powerful case that the emergence of the first civilizations or empires of domination – in Mesopotamia, in Egypt, in the Indus Valley and in Shang China – arose at least in part because of their relative isolation. But this was never absolute. These civilizations were seldom self-sufficient and crucial materials like timber and metal ores were often scarce. Military expeditions or trade, and the two were not necessarily neatly delineated, were needed to acquire them. So, for example, ancient Mesopotamia imported timber, stone, gold, silver and copper. As early as the fifth millennium, seashells from the Indian Ocean 1500 km away were to be found in Syria, and obsidian (a volcanic rock useful for early tools), whose nearest source was 600 km away, was found in the upper Tigris (Curtin 1984). Ancient Egypt imported wood and metals but also medicinal oils, ivory, silver, precious stones, spices and perfumes. It exported grain, linen, wool, vegetable oils and papyrus. Later Mediterranean empires like Phoenicia and Athens would rely essentially on trade. The home states and their immediate hinterlands did not produce enough food for what became large urban populations (Heaton 1948; Woolley 1963).

Trade took many different forms, some involving no market exchange at all, others interesting mixtures of monetary and power relations. Trade and piracy, with the distinctions between them often blurred, were already extensive in the prehistoric Mediterranean. In ancient Egypt, trade became largely a monopoly of the Pharaoh, but it was then Lebanese merchants who brought timber to Egypt in return for craftwork (Pareti 1965; Curtin 1984). Both the Roman and Chinese empires operated internal systems of tribute. We might think of Rome as successfully running trade deficits for centuries, only partly offset by the provinces' consumption of Italian wine, oil, metalware and pottery. At the same time freer trading relations prevailed beyond the empire, which paid for Indian spices, especially pepper, Chinese silks and Arabian incense, but also ointments, drugs, cottons, metalware, precious stones, dyes, horses, parrots and wild animals for the circuses (Heaton 1948). China's external relations, at about the same time, were a bit different. Its 'barbarian' neighbours were formally held in tributary relations. Even fierce northern nomads paid China tribute, but this could be conveniently reciprocated by 'gifts', whose total value amounted to as much as 7 per cent of imperial revenue (Curtin 1984). Phoenicia and later Carthage developed as trading empires, beginning a long tradition, later continued by Venice and Genoa, of port cities as seats of power and in which merchants themselves became rulers (Pareti 1965; Curtin 1984; Held et al. 1999).

Many other trades reached out far beyond the support provided by home states. Numerous cities encouraged and protected foreign merchants settling within them and as such became the institutional basis for securing trade. 'As early as the twenty-fourth [*sic*] century BC ... Mesopotamian merchant colonies were established in the heart of Asia Minor' (Woolley 1963: 449). By 300 BC Greek traders were operating far beyond Europe, reaching India, which in turn traded extensively with China (Held et al. 1999). Rome established trading colonies in India and Africa as far south as Zanzibar, while Indian merchants settled in Burma and China and at least as early as 300 BC, Chinese ships traded in Malaya and barbarian ships in (designated) Chinese ports (Curtin 1984). Chinese 'port cities attracted large communities of foreign merchants, mainly Arabs and Persians' (Findlay and O'Rourke 2007: 63).

Thus, well before the Christian era, there was extensive trade across Eurasia and much of Africa. Chinese sources have the first Romans coming from the sea but the Silk Road established regular links before the first century BC (Curtin 1984). Transcontinental trade, by various routes, would never disappear but its scale and economic importance would change over the centuries. Land routes could be displaced by improvements in shipping and navigation, knowledge of the trade winds and the introduction of the compass. The relative costs of transport and production changed the sort of goods that it was worth transporting over long distances, while trade also rose and fell with wider economic and political fortunes. Figure 2.1 depicts the (necessarily approximate) average per capita wealth of Western Europe, Western Asia and China in the years 0, 1000 and 1500. Rome's wealth puts Europe slightly ahead of most of the rest of the world at the dawn of the first millennium. A thousand years later, Europe had fallen behind Asia and the Islamic world (Maddison 2003). Five hundred years on, Western Europe had again crept ahead, Western Asia fallen back. Long before the first of these dates, the regions were in contact and their development connected.

By the end of the first millennium, the Islamic world was the richest, at the economic and geographic centre, and the only region trading directly with each other area of the known world. Among other things, it imported slaves and swords from Western Europe; slaves, furs and silver

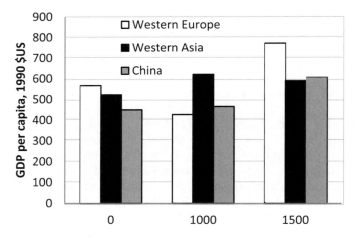

Source: Maddison (2003).

Figure 2.1 *GDP per capita in Western Europe, Western Asia and China; 0, 1000 and 1500 AD*

from Eastern Europe; paper, silver and slaves from Central Asia; gold, slaves (again), ivory and rice from sub-Saharan Africa; pepper, spices, silks, teak and textiles from South Asia; spices and perfumes from South East Asia; and, finally, silk and porcelain from East Asia. In turn it exported (or re-exported) pepper, spices, textiles, silk, silver, salt, manufactures, swords, horses, iron and gold (Findlay and O'Rourke 2007). The 'simultaneous power of the Abbasids and the Tang made it comparatively easy for long-distance traders to make the whole journey across Asia and North Africa' (Curtin 1984: 105). For centuries, these regions would possess products Europeans wanted but would struggle to obtain through free trade (Findlay and O'Rourke 2007; Maddison 2007). Already during China's Northern Sung dynasty (960–1126), iron and steel output and employment 'was far in excess of anything obtained before England in the eighteenth century' (Findlay and O'Rourke 2007: 65). Extensive trade and tribute operated through 'force ... and by monopoly advantages' (Wallerstein 1974: 15). However, the Chinese also traded extensively with regional neighbours and beyond, the traders were typically private but controlled and supported by the government (Curtin 1984). The most famous of the merchants, an Arab called Pu Shou-keng, who was superintendent of maritime shipping at Quanzhou, would surrender to the Mongols in the thirteenth century.

Findlay and O'Rourke (2007) then describe the achievement, between 1250 and 1350, of a 'Pax Mongolica' extending across most of Eurasia. The intensified interaction is also attested by the rapid spread of the plague, which in turn contributed to the empire's decline (Bentley 1993). Mongol decline, as theories of hegemonic stability (discussed below in relation to Britain and the US in the nineteenth and twentieth centuries) would anticipate, led to a decline in trade. The roads closed and the supply of precious goods to the West, like Chinese silks, dried up. In the East, the decline of trade was short-lived. Early Ming China attempted to eliminate private trade but to extend the tributary system, particularly at sea (Bentley 1993). The age of commerce in South East Asia started a century before the arrival of Vasco de Gama, with the Muslim admiral Zheng He undertaking the greatest series of trading voyages from 1405 (Findlay and O'Rourke 2007). Conveniently for the Portuguese, the Ming then turned their back on overseas contracts after about 1430, but Findlay and O'Rourke suggest 'Asia, not Europe, still dictated the pace of intercontinental trade' (2007: 141). As late as the seventeenth century, in China, Zheng Chenggong or Coxinga (1623–62) maintained 8000 ships and 170,000 troops and made an annual profit from the Japanese trade of 20 tonnes of silver (Findlay and O'Rourke 2007). However, European growth and wealth was already starting to outstrip that in other parts of the world. Europe would greatly extend its lead over subsequent centuries but it was already inching ahead.

The changing hierarchies of wealth are worth noting, not least in terms of arguments, discussed in Chapter 5, that trade inequalities simply beget ever bigger inequalities. The future reversal of fortunes becomes completely inexplicable. The interaction of trade and the broader political economy is much too complex to be reduced to such simple formulae.

TRADE AND THE RISE OF CAPITALISM

Europe did come to dominate the rest of the world, decisively so by the nineteenth century, a process discussed in this and the next section. This section revisits but cannot resolve some well-trodden debates about the role of trade in the rise of capitalism. It becomes apparent that even if trade is seen as both a necessary solvent of feudalism and ingredient in the establishment of capitalism it was not sufficient. As already seen, trade had been present in several parts of the world for millennia without producing anything like the societies that finally emerged in Europe. There is a danger (exacerbated by its brevity) of this account being taken as 'Eurocentric'. There is necessarily a European focus in discussing how

Europeans achieved pre-eminence but nothing should suggest that Europe was bound to dominate or that the processes being described were either somehow uniquely European or inevitable. It was Europe, or perhaps better Western Europe or even a small corner of North West Europe, that rose. This rise was at the same time, albeit to a degree that remains in dispute, a global process. Europeans came to dominate, but in dynamic relations with the rest of the world, which was never merely a passive recipient of Europe's exploitation or beneficence.

Pirenne argues that Europe's decline after the collapse of the Western Roman Empire was substantially caused by the closure of Mediterranean trade routes with the rise of Islam. The revival of trade with the crusades was then crucial to Europe's recovery (Heller 2011). Sweezy (1976) revives Pirenne's ideas of the importance of trade to the rise of capitalism. Now couched in Marxist language, he argues that feudalism was essentially stagnant until it was broken up by the external force of trade. For Sweezy, as for Pirenne, the lords' personal consumption was the only motive force for feudal expansion and as such inherently limited (Banaji 2011). Increasing merchant activity and wealth gradually undermined the old sources of power and old mode of production. Merchants brought the goods and innovations to Europe from the non-European world and these increased agricultural productivity. The rise of commerce also encouraged moves away from agriculture. For example, it made sense to buy handicrafts from specialist artisans who could make them more efficiently than manorial serfs (Sweezy 1976).

Brenner (1976) posits an alternative 'political' interpretation of feudalism's collapse and capitalism's rise based on the outcomes of struggles within European countries (see also Wood 2002). Peasant success, particularly in France, won individual gains and peasant freedom. Lordly success in Eastern Europe imposed a second serfdom. More ambiguous outcomes in Britain limited lordly power while also denying moves to peasant self-sufficiency and independence. Commercial farming, peasant inequalities and ultimately the rise of a dispossessed proletariat grew. Brenner is explicitly and successfully contesting demographic arguments that see population pressures as responsible for feudalism's collapse. It was always, also, a social and political process. However, one important problem is then that it is possible to regress the question to ask why peasants were more successful in some places than others. At least part of the explanation seems to lie in what they were doing; for example, commercial wine-growing areas of France were particularly well organized (Hilton 1985). Trade comes back to the centre of the story.

Wallerstein gives the trade-based account a slightly different emphasis. He insists that the processes in Eastern and Western Europe should be understood together. Wallerstein sees the second serfdom as 'capitalist in origin' (1974: 91). Two forms of social system cannot exist side by side and the apparently feudal and capitalist constituted a single economic entity. Eastern Europe would become the food supplier to an industrializing West.

Wallerstein (1974) also ties Europe's rise to its exploitation of other regions through trade. The Portuguese navigations and then particularly the 'discovery' and exploitation of the New World become crucial. The brutal Spanish conquest of the Americas looted gold and mined silver, often with forced labour (Heller 2011). The wealth soon left Spain, despite strict restrictions and severe penalties, entering the rest of the continent. This new money financed Asian imports and freed commercial activity within Europe. It had an inflationary effect, destabilizing existing sources of wealth (and power) and, probably most fundamentally, began to set labour to work. For Wallerstein (1974) it was therefore European political power that was able to enforce unequal economic relations. The Spanish conquest was enabled by its military, and particularly naval superiority, even as Europe was still retreating in the face of the Ottomans. Findlay and O'Rourke substantially agree, claiming that 'politics ... determined trade' (2007: xix).

However, some significant qualifications to this narrative of trade and power seem in order. Firstly, as Brenner (2006) argues, commercialization was ubiquitous. Trade, organized on broadly capitalist principles, had developed in many places, including but far from exclusively in ancient Europe, without leading to the establishment of a capitalist society. Neither trade itself, nor American gold and silver were sufficient to establish capitalism. Trade was also intrinsic to the feudal world. Without it, lords would have been bereft of arms, jewels, wine and anything but the crude clothes made by their tenants (Bloch 1965). England already imported more than a gallon a head of French wine in 1242 (Heaton 1948). The feudal estates, in turn, sold foodstuffs, raw materials and various manufactured products (Findlay and O'Rourke 2007). Copper, iron, tin, timber, hides, tar, wool, dyes, millstones, fish, salt, beer and grain were all widely traded in feudal Europe. If much of this was 'domestic' rather than international trade, it is worth repeating that at this time there were hardly separate national economies in the modern sense. There was also, already, substantial medium and, as above, long-distance exchange even at continental distances, particularly in items with a high ratio of value to weight such as spices, silks, furs and slaves (Findlay and O'Rourke 2007). None of this produced capitalism.

Among other things, successful merchants could buy their way into the feudal ruling class, as they did most conspicuously with the purchase of noble titles in France. The structures of feudalism may have been relatively rigid but this was not absolute, as the whole practice of knighting makes clear (Bloch 1965). Within Europe, many of the trading centres rose and fell; the Champagne Fairs reached their height in the mid-thirteenth century, the Hanseatic League a century later. These disappeared, not without trace but without in themselves producing capitalism. There seems a particular danger of reading back Europe's success from what we now know to have happened. There is at least a problem of timing. The crisis of feudalism and the second serfdom in Eastern Europe occurred centuries before anything approximating an industrial export economy would develop in the West. There was still a considerable gap from the conquest of the Americas to Europe's decisive transformation and industrial revolution of the nineteenth century. As Banaji (2011: 92) puts it: 'If, as Sweezy argued, the market was a factor of feudal disintegration, it could become so on the basis of the specific laws of motion of feudal economy, and only in the long run.'

Second, Dobb (1963), to whom Sweezy is himself responding, rejects the idea of a stagnant feudalism. Dobb's views have subsequently been nuanced but it seems to be generally accepted that the growth of trade stemmed at least as much from evolution within the existing social system rather than trade inducing change from outside. Trade remains a vital part of the picture as a vehicle for technological diffusion and advance but its role becomes less prominent (Harman 1989; Heller 2011).

This hints at a problem with Wallerstein's reading, stressing the centrality of political power as the basis of exploitation and trade. It is a welcome reminder of the relevance of power and military strength, taboo subjects to academic economists (Raffer 1987). It is plausible to argue that it is political forms (the relative coherence of the European states) and trading relations that meant these had a particular influence beyond Europe's overall economic capacity. Politics and economics, trade and production, can never be reduced to each other, each has its own distinct moment. But they are not separable and it does seem that Europe already possessed certain prior productive advantages. Minimally, these were necessary in shipbuilding and arms but as noted above, although much smaller than it would become over the next five centuries, Europe was already establishing a more general economic lead. Europe itself was, of course, highly differentiated and the productive core shifted with regions rising and falling. Italy, Germany and Holland each left its mark on the next but it was only in Britain that capitalism became firmly established (Heller 2011).

The story of conquest and retreat is an ancient one. The crusades were indeed substantially commercial wars fought by, and at least financed by, Genoa, Venice and other trading states attempting to establish themselves in the Middle East. Rather than simply restoring trade, which had continued between the Islamic world and Christian Europe, even against papal bans, it was West Asia's already existing wealth and importance that made its trading centres so attractive (Heaton 1948). Portugal's first Indian Ocean empire similarly accessed existing sources of wealth and production in Asia. Its naval superiority won it pre-eminence within the Indian Ocean trading networks but its success owed more to charging the opposition protection money than to lowering prices through any productive innovation (Heaton 1948). Only 470 ships returned to Portugal from the East over the entire period from 1500 to 1634. Most of the Portuguese trade consisted of carrying Asian goods to Asian destinations (Curtin 1984). At that time 'the European tail was not yet wagging the Asian dog' (Findlay and O'Rourke 2007: 157). It seems entirely possible that Portugal's Indian Ocean empire, like the Islamic and Chinese ones before it, might have come and gone without producing capitalism as we know it (Rosenberg 1994). Indeed, Portugal's dominance did soon recede. More efficient Dutch competitors moved in. They had a more profound effect not just enriching themselves but now also transforming production in their colonies. For example, the Dutch established a monopoly of nutmeg and clove production on Malaku, Banda and the Andaman Islands (Curtin 1984): 'In 1621 they killed or enslaved almost all the nutmeg producers on the Banda islands and replaced them by Dutch planters and slave workers who delivered their whole crops to the VOC' (Maddison 2007: 132). Not just the brutality, but also the transformation they brought, was more profound.

Domestic development also does much to explain the supersession of the Portuguese in the Indian Ocean by the Dutch and then the British. Dutch 'fluitschips' were cheaper to build and operate and helped establish Dutch dominance of the carrying trade, first in Europe but soon beyond (Heaton 1948). The 300 Dutch ships in the East and West Indies in 1634 were a small part of the total fleet of 4300, most of which were involved in fishing and in trade in the Baltic and Mediterranean (Findlay and O'Rourke 2007). The Dutch VOC was still controlled by the government but was also a much more commercially oriented business concern. It came to dominate European imports of Japanese copper, silk and porcelain, Chinese silk, green tea, pottery, tin, lacquerware, Indian cotton, peppers, silks and saltpetre, Javan and Arabian coffee, and Malay tin and spices (Heaton 1948). Still the Dutch faced fierce rivalry in the Indian Ocean up to the second half of the eighteenth century, notably

from the much less well-known Bugis, a diaspora trading people of
Sulawesi origin (Curtin 1984). Europeans still remained a relatively and
small contested presence in Asia.

The British in turn supplanted the Dutch. At one level this was simply
a military victory, the Royal Navy supported the East India Company,
even as it grew more slowly out of private funds. However, Britain's
more lasting success owes much to the specifics, including the size, of its
domestic political economy, which had a 'more solid core than that of
Holland, which depended on imported materials and on *entrepôt* characteristics which could be duplicated or dispensed with' (Heaton 1948:
321). The Dutch and British economies were also secured by political
transformations and policy interventions. The countries were home to the
first great 'bourgeois' revolutions. The English Revolution swept away
attempts by the Stuarts to restore the guild system and helped establish
conditions for private property and freer markets at home even as they
deepened the monopolistic international trade practices. The state continued to support the chartered companies that took responsibility for
particular trades and it established the Navigation Acts, which banned
foreign vessels from colonial ports and allowed them into English ports
only to sell their own national products, not those of third parties.
Mercantilist restrictions of trade were extended, for example with bans
on wool exports, while woollen and other manufactures were encouraged
(Heaton 1948).

The Dutch and British imperial experience contrasts with European's
conquest of the western hemisphere. Precious metals enriched the
Castilian state but neither Portugal or Spain became rich. There was an
insufficient economic base to support manufacturing and instead, in
Spain, the rise of commercial sheep farming turned 'gold into sand'
(Polanyi 2001: 36; Anderson 1979; Raffer 1987). Despite its colonial
monopoly, Spanish products were displaced in South American markets
by textile and other manufactures from Italy, Holland and England
(Findlay and O'Rourke 2007). Meanwhile, the colonies employed
import-substituting practices. Vine production in Peru displaced Spanish
imports. As important as gold and silver might initially have been, by the
late 1650s cochineal exports from the Americas accounted for 42 per cent
of total exports, surely reflecting, rather than causing, Europe's economic
growth. Imports of cod, and then the slave products of tobacco and cotton
would have a more profound effect on Europe's economy (Findlay and
O'Rourke 2007).

European capitalism emerged within a network of international trade
and probably could not have done so without it (Wood 2002) but trade
was far from a sufficient condition. For many centuries the changes being

wrought were gradual. Neither the economic or political transformation should be seen as setting a fair course for global capitalism. European growth was still fragile. By 1700, Western Europe's average gross domestic profit (GDP) per capita had reached almost $1000, on a par with modern Burkina Faso (Maddison 2003).

TRADE, SLAVERY AND THE PEDESTAL OF THE INDUSTRIAL REVOLUTION

It is possible to make some similar points with regard to New World slavery and the slave trade. The trade, surely the epitome of unfree trade, brought vast profits, which funded early British industrial capitalism and its infrastructure. The key textile industry relied on slave-produced cotton. A powerful case can be made for Marx's claim that 'the veiled slavery of the wage-labourers in Europe needed the unqualified slavery of the New World as its pedestal' (1976: 925). Williams (1964), Solow and Engerman (1987) and Blackburn (1988, 1997), among others, subsequently re-articulate this thesis that slavery made capitalism. However, it was obviously not a sufficient condition for industrial capitalism. In earlier times, and in other countries at the same time, slavery did not have the same impact.

Blackburn's (1997) account describes slavery as a form of 'primitive accumulation'. The scale of the horror and of the profits was huge. Between 1600 and 1800, Findlay and O'Rourke (2007) conservatively estimate 287,000 Africans were transported to mainland America and 2,045,000 to the Caribbean. Others suggest much higher numbers. Heller writes that 'by the eighteenth century the total reached no less than 6,130,000' (2011: 168). Blackburn (1997) reports the British alone landing 1.5 million slaves in the last 46 years of the trade to 1807, at an average price of £42 and a total profit of over £4 million. Less well remembered than slavery, between 1600 and 1800, 'no fewer than 75%' of over a million European migrants were themselves 'indentured servants or convicts' (Findlay and O'Rourke 2007: 231). Money poured back to Britain, directly financing industrial firms and infrastructure like canal-building projects but also helping to keep interest rates low.

Slavery and the 'triangular trade' produced profits and markets at each of its points. Initially, landing parties might simply kidnap Africans but, for the most part, slaves were bought on the African coast, sometimes for substantial sums and typically with European-made goods. For example: 'On one occasion a woman changed hands for a gallon of brandy, six bars of iron, two small guns, a keg of gunpowder, and two strings of beads, while a man cost eight guns, a wicker-covered bottle, two cases of spirits, and twenty-eight cotton sheets' (Heaton 1948: 244). The African slave sellers were not, for the most part, fobbed off with a few trinkets. As demand rose and slavers bled the supply, the price of slaves increased by about two and a half times in the second half of the eighteenth century, at the same time increasing the demand for European products (Findlay and O'Rourke 2007). Across the Atlantic, the slave colonies provided important markets, protected by the Navigation Acts (Blackburn 1988). There is some controversy about the importance of these markets, because, for example, the colonies largely grew their own food rather than relying on imports. Nevertheless, North America received about 15 per cent of all English exports in 1700 and this jumped to 33 per cent of the total and 16-fold in volume over the next 75 years (Heaton 1948). British export-oriented industries like iron and cotton, in particular, took off (Blackburn 1997). Sugar and tobacco were exported back to Britain, before cotton became so important in the late eighteenth century. Raw cotton exports from the US rose from 189,000 pounds in 1791 to 21 million pounds in 1801 and to 93 million pounds in 1810 (Findlay and O'Rourke 2007). Slave traders and slave owners made huge profits late into the eighteenth century. The slave trade and slave products became integral to the economies on both sides of the Atlantic.

What is missing from this narrative is why slavery should have such strong effects in Britain, and at most only weaker ones elsewhere. Portuguese and Spanish companies initiated the European transportation of slaves to the Americas without producing comparable growth in those countries. Britain's mercantilist policy based on 'settler colonies, capitalist slavery and economic nationalism' (Heller 2011: 159) also had Portuguese, Spanish and French precedents. The Spanish economy effectively regressed; those of Portugal and France grew more slowly than the British. Britain's rise therefore remains a 'puzzle' for trade-based explanations (Findlay and O'Rourke 2007).

Ideas of slavery providing a pedestal or of primitive accumulation allow that something more dynamic was then built on their basis. At the beginning of the period, Britain's role seemed set as an exporter of a little wool. What seems truly different was the way the wealth bled out of the slave trade and slavery stayed within Britain and was invested productively in what would become the Industrial Revolution. There was already something of a 'mass' market for tobacco and sugar imports. Wallerstein is a major proponent of the importance of colonialism to Europe's growth but he acknowledges that the integration of production of commodities for 'daily use' was key (1974: 302). Britain's local consumption contrasts with more diverse French colonial exports, which included larger quantities of cacao, coffee and indigo as well as sugar. The smaller domestic market for these meant that many of them were then exported within Europe (Blackburn 1997). The merchants amassed wealth but in the absence of particular institutional frameworks and relations of production, this did not lead to capitalism. Slavery fuelled Britain's industrialization but did so in the context of an already growing and commercialized economy (Brenner 1977; Crouzet 1990).

Industrialization then quickly enabled a much more asymmetric international division of labour within Europe and beyond (Findlay and O'Rourke 2007). In particular, it reduced the cost of making cotton yarn by 90 per cent between 1779 and 1812. 'It provided Europe at last with a commodity which could be shipped in vast quantities to the Orient' (Heaton 1948: 491). Previously, it had been difficult to find anything to sell in return for precious Asian products.

Europe's trade with the rest of the world increased more quickly than production between 1500 and 1800. A narrative of trade-led growth is just about sustainable. However, both growth rates were still very low by modern standards. Even at the end of the eighteenth century, most of the European economy was rural and the main power sources were firewood and draught animals (Crouzet 1990). Trade represented about 1 per cent of global GDP in 1820 (Findlay and O'Rourke 2007). It was only in the nineteenth century that the Industrial Revolution and global trade would explode.

BRITISH FREE TRADE, IMPERIALISM AND ITS OPPONENTS

The nineteenth century witnessed a more decisive transformation. By 1913, trade reached 8 per cent of global GDP (Findlay and O'Rourke 2007). Britain became the champion of free trade. Its own trade increased dramatically, by 1840 accounting for almost a third of the world total. For Britain, trade had become essential. In 1800 it could just about feed itself. By 1914 it imported half its food, as well as a vast array of raw materials (Heaton 1948; Kenwood and Lougheed 1992). Other European countries remained only more or less willing to open their borders in the face of British competition. However, more optimistic accounts see Britain leading others in its wake, providing hegemonic stability and the basis for peaceful global prosperity (Kindleberger 1973). There is some truth in this narrative of trade liberalization and growth but it should be stressed that any free trade regime was equivocal, short-lived and confined to Europe.

The era of British 'hegemony' saw increased trade and, for a decade or two in the third quarter of the century, substantial reductions in intra-European barriers. Total trade jumped especially quickly between 1840 and 1870 (Kenwood and Lougheed 1992). From the late eighteenth century, British political economists had argued for free trade, or at least a relative freeing of trade. The Corn Laws, protecting agriculture, were abolished in 1846, although this left many tariffs in place. The Navigation Acts were repealed in 1849. France and Britain signed the Cobden–Chevalier Treaty in 1860, reducing French duties on British manufactures to a maximum of 30 per cent and reducing British tariffs on French wine. A series of other agreements saw much of Europe reducing its trade barriers. This did not last long. By 1879 Germany under Bismarck and the 'alliance of iron and rye' moved quickly against free trade, imposing particularly heavy duties on agricultural imports. France abandoned the Cobden–Chevalier Treaty in 1892. The Méline tariff raised manufacturing duties to 24 per cent on the basis of negotiation with other countries but also gave substantial subsidies to domestic producers, notably in shipbuilding (Foreman-Peck 1983).

The US stands out both as the fastest-growing economy and as a consistent opponent of free trade. British colonial policy in America had systematically prevented the development of local manufacturing, with laws against textile manufacturing and iron working, even bans on the transport of hats between provinces and on the emigration of skilled craft workers (Emmanuel 1972; Chang 2002). After a period of modest restrictions in the early years of the republic, by the early 1800s high tariffs became the norm. Tariffs also raise revenue, often more politically acceptable than direct taxation, and customs revenues comprised as much as 89 per cent of US Federal receipts in 1821 (Caves et al. 1993). Southern plantation owners, selling cotton to Britain, typically supported free trade but northern industrial interests won out, decisively in the Civil War, and strongly protectionist policies prevailed. The McKinley and Dingley tariffs of 1890 and 1897 further raised levels to an average of 57 per cent (Foreman-Peck 1983). The rise of industry elsewhere cut Britain's lead and by 1913 its share of world trade was down to (a still remarkable) 19 per cent (Kenwood and Lougheed 1992).

European trading relations with the rest of the world also remained less than free and equal. In India, Britain continued to extract the traditional tributes. The Opium Wars, fought as late as 1839 and 1857, imposed a version of free trade, to be sure, but hardly one entered into freely by the Chinese, or bringing mutual benefits. The East India Company assumed monopoly export rights of opium exports in 1773 and, by the 1790s, 2000 chests of Indian opium (each of 149 pounds) went to China each year. The number rose over subsequent decades to 3800, 4400, 11,400 and 24,300 by the 1830s (Findlay and O'Rourke 2007). Chinese tea came to Britain in return. Elsewhere, British mass production undercut potential competition, reducing prices if not necessarily improving quality. 'Livingston was surprised to learn that English iron was labelled "rotten" by Africans in the nineteenth century because local iron was of a much better quality' (Raffer 1987: 135). However, its lower prices meant Britain would tend to favour an open 'free trade imperialism'. This could still involve coercion towards the locals but it would also be challenged by other European powers as direct colonialism took off.

The gap between Europe and the rest of the world increased. Findlay and O'Rourke (2007) suggest that India and China in particular experienced substantial deindustrialization between 1750 and 1914. The effects of imperialism and deepening integration into a global market were uneven and much disputed. Developing country exports as a whole had fallen to about 3 per cent of the world total by 1870 but then rose to 8 per cent by 1913. However, this was produced particularly by increasing demand for food and raw materials (Findlay and O'Rourke 2007). Plantation economies expanded in Latin America, the Caribbean and parts of Asia. Increased competition between these regions also drove down prices (Kenwood and Lougheed 1992). At the same time, the apparent gains experienced by Britain and other European powers did not mean a universal ransacking of poorer countries, which did obtain cheap manufactured goods in return (Amin 1974). Although the gaps between rich and poor countries increased, many poorer countries were also industrializing and growing. Findlay and O'Rourke (2007) argue that rather than being strict alternatives, primary production was 'crowded in' by manufacturing.

The importance of trade for the core is similarly disputed. Many European countries without formal empires grew at least as quickly as the leading imperialist powers. This is not to reject ideas that economic motives lay behind the expansion of European interests around the world, merely to acknowledge that, like any venture, the gains from trade and imperialism can be uncertain while the industrial revolution within Europe and North America went far beyond primitive accumulation and by this time the dynamic sources of growth lay substantially at home.

By World War I, capitalism had long been illiberal. Leading states protected domestic markets while they carved up the globe into formal and informal empires. The war ended any delusions of laissez-faire capitalism. International trade plummeted and countries came off the gold standard. France and Britain, in particular, ran up huge debts to the US.

Post-war recovery would be on a much less open basis. Accumulation was primarily intensive, more labour-intensive than capital-intensive, and economic growth outstripped the trade growth with barriers remaining high. However, trade remained important and trade asymmetries became a major contributor to the breakdown of 1929 (Dunn 2014a). Alone among leading economies, the US consistently ran trade surpluses, balanced by gold inflows that in turn encouraged low interest rates and rapid growth. Elsewhere, most obviously in Britain, there was much less of a roar to the 1920s. Britain returned to gold in 1925 with the pound at the pre-war level. This strong pound policy was supported by financial interests but it also helped foreign investments, much more prominent from Britain than other countries (Webber and Rigby 1996). It also kept the price of food and raw materials imports relatively low. The still important textile industry relied on imported cotton and could ill-afford to pay more for its US supplies. Britain was also relatively protected by the surpluses it ran with the 'sterling bloc' countries, including colonies and dominions whose currencies rose along with Britain's. However, exporters in general suffered from what had become an overvalued currency. Britain's trade position deteriorated, gold flowed outwards, the economy stagnated and Britain struggled to pay its wartime debts to the US. Meanwhile, France grew by an extraordinary 7 per cent a year between 1918 and 1929 (Maddison 2003). Coming off gold allowed an inflationary strategy, which could both pay the state's own domestic debts and allow wage gains to be inflated away. France finally rejoined the gold standard in 1928 at a fifth of the pre-war level. Correspondingly, cheaper exports further undermined British competitiveness as France achieved substantial manufacturing trade surpluses and moved close to an overall balance (Foreman-Peck 1983). France had less difficulty than Britain paying its debts.

As the US economy boomed and its surpluses grew, money flooded in. Interest rates stayed low, in part at least because rises would have put still more pressure on Britain and its ability to pay its debts. Increasingly, as Wall Street soared, it encouraged speculation far beyond the rapid growth in the broader economy. The bursting of the bubble and the Wall Street Crash of 1929 reflected and then greatly exacerbated a downturn in production in the US, which quickly spread around the world. The inward spiral of international trade saw prices collapse, particularly for agricultural products (Kindleberger 1973). Rising formal trade barriers were now accompanied by competitive devaluations as countries came off the gold standard. By 1931, even Britain abandoned gold and trade openness (Kenwood and Lougheed 1992).

Falling trade and competitive devaluation are usually interpreted as having at least exacerbated the downturn. However, there is some ambiguity, particularly for poorer countries. Import substitution initially appeared successful in Latin America. Developing countries certainly did relatively well compared with the developed during the great depression. Findlay and O'Rourke make this a broader point, maintaining that 'tariffs were *positively* associated with growth across countries in the interwar period' (2007: 467). Keynes (1973) suggested that national strategies of development were at least possible but most states continued to adopt cost-cutting policies at home while seeking foreign markets. As rich countries put up barriers, colonial markets abroad became relatively more important, at least contributing to the renewed drive to war (Findlay and O'Rourke 2007; Tabb 1999).

US HEGEMONY AND THE POST-WAR BOOM

By the end of World War II, the US had clearly proven itself the leading national economy. This pre-eminence changed US attitudes towards trade. Particularly in terms of its economic size, the case for US hegemony seems much stronger than for earlier British (and for some accounts Dutch) versions. However, trade was only a small proportion of US GDP and its exports represented only 11 per cent of the world total in 1948 (UN 1962), much lower than Britain in its nineteenth-century heyday. The US also had little formal empire although troops remained in occupation of the defeated powers and America retained bases in many allied countries. Trade opening remained contested, unsurprisingly also given the apparent success of past protectionist policies. However, more outward-looking US interests won out and major conferences, dominated by the US, established the basis for a more internationalist order.

The US and the dollar became the explicit axes of the global economy. The 1944 Bretton Woods Conference established an international financial system, which allowed dollars to be trusted 'as good as gold' as stores of value but also used as a means of circulation, overcoming the limits of gold, which had plagued the inter-war period. The dollar was fixed against gold, at $35 an ounce, with other currencies pegged against the dollar, adjustable but with International Monetary Fund (IMF) agreement, also reducing the prospects of a repeat of the competitive devaluations of the 1930s, after gold was abandoned. Influential interpretations see financial stability then enabling increasing trade openness and US 'hegemony', thus securing international capitalist prosperity (Kindleberger 1973; Gilpin 1987, 2001).

Bretton Woods also created the IMF and World Bank (conveniently headquartered in Washington, DC) with voting by contribution, which initially gave the US alone an effective veto. Britain remained a valued junior partner but its debts and subordination to the US were now greater than ever (Helleiner 1993; Hudson 2003). The IMF provided funds against temporary balance of payments problems and oversaw the system of currency pegs. Keynes' plans for an international currency and a symmetrical system, which would have disciplined both trade surplus and deficit countries were rejected. Instead, deficit countries would be expected to cut imports and increase exports, towards which currency devaluation might contribute. Surplus countries, of which the US was initially the major instance, had no parallel obligation to increase imports or restrict their exports. Bretton Woods also allowed, but did not impose, capital controls. The US would not implement them, as American representatives made clear from the start. American capital had most to gain from free movement across borders.

Proposals for an International Trade Organization, drafted by the US, were rejected by Congress. A much looser framework of trade rules, not requiring Congressional approval, was negotiated and came into force in 1948 as the General Agreement on Tariffs and Trade (GATT). Among other things, this explicitly allowed imperial preferences. Voting was 'one country, one vote' rather than by shareholding, as at the IMF and World Bank. Developing countries soon had a majority. Special quantitative and other restrictions were allowed and negotiations to reduce barriers stalled. Rich countries sought consensus rather than votes, while poorer ones tended to organize instead under the umbrella of the UN and its Commission on Trade and Development, founded in 1965 (Narlikar 2003, 2006).

The most conspicuous divide was between East and West. Although it participated in the original conference, the USSR and its allies remained outside the Bretton Woods framework. An alternative Council for Mutual Economic Assistance (COMECON) was established in 1949. Trade relations between Eastern bloc countries remained very unequal, with the USSR producing the absolute majority of the output. It initially extracted reparations from East Germany but, among other things, fixed commodity prices would later mean that (compared with Western market prices) the USSR effectively provided its allies with subsidized fuel (Foreman-Peck 1983). The USSR also decided countries' respective roles in a division of labour, with Romania, for example, relegated to the role of producer of basic manufactures. These were not closed economies. Trade within the bloc increased faster than the global average and exports to the rest of the world also increased not only absolutely but from 3.1 to 4.0 per cent of the world total between 1948 and 1959 (UN 1962).

Relations between the rich and poorer countries also changed. The old empires could potentially have shut out the US, which broadly encouraged (non-communist) decolonization. The US was in a stronger position than Britain in the nineteenth century to maintain 'free trade imperialism' and many newly independent countries became open to US business. Poorer countries provided many necessary resources, particularly oil, but also minerals that richer countries lacked but on which they were dependent (Magdoff 1969). A high proportion of US foreign investment was directed towards mining and oil (Hummels and Stern 1994). However, the share of world exports of non-oil-exporting poorer countries fell from 24 per cent of the total in 1948 to just 12 per cent in 1968 (Rangarajan 1984). Many poorer countries, even those not explicitly siding with the East in the Cold War, adopted strategies of state-led development including relatively restrictive trade policies. Many of them experienced unparalleled economic growth, even as aggregate gaps between rich and poor countries widened. At a global level, trade and investment were increasingly concentrated among rich countries.

The global economy trebled in size between 1950 and 1973, an annual growth rate of almost 5 per cent (Maddison 2003). In many ways 'Fordism' or 'Keynesianism' achieved growth on an intensive basis; intensive both in the sense of deepening capital accumulation but also in the sense of deepening agglomeration economics and growth within existing locations. For theories of hegemonic stability this was alternatively a Pax Americana, in which the US encouraged others into openness – and bore the costs in policing the system. The tariffs of leading countries dropped substantially and trade openness now increased, even faster than the rapid economic growth. Trade quite plausibly contributed to the success of the international system but the rise in trade to GDP ratios was quite small for most countries. Globally, this ratio rose from about 6 to 8 per cent of GDP between 1950 and 1970, rather more slowly for the US, Britain and France, considerably quicker for Japan and (West) Germany.

Trade does seem to have been particularly important for these fastest-growing economies. Japan and Germany, encouraged by the occupying authorities, both adopted anti-Keynesian domestic policies, in which 'sound' money was prioritized and domestic demand lagged behind growth. Demand shortfalls could potentially be met by exports. The reasons for Japanese and German 'catch-up' are complex and contested. In many respects, both national economies were more managed, less liberal, than those of the US or UK, and their subsequent faster expansion has plausibly been attributed to this as much as to orthodox monetary policy (for example, Hutton 1995). Among other things, their unusual position in the Cold War, and lower levels of arms spending, also allowed higher levels of productive civilian investment and spending on research and development (Harman 1984; Archibughi and Michie 1997). By contrast, Krugman (1994) sees 'catch-up' as a more or less natural process. However, the institutional structures at least supported this and the stable Bretton Woods monetary system encouraged an export orientation. The trade story seems stronger in Germany where surpluses grew and the share of exports in manufactured output jumped steeply from 8.3 to 24.2 per cent between 1950 and 1974. Exports accounted for over 40 per cent of crucial goods like cars and machines at the end of this period (Brenner 1998). Japanese trade volumes were relatively lower and it would not be until the 1980s that its trade surpluses represented anything close to 1 per cent of its GDP. What is clear is that with rapid growth, both German and Japanese productivity gaps with the US narrowed and the Bretton Woods system translated these straightforwardly into lower relative export prices.

Japanese and German growth epitomized the unevenness of the system and at least contributed to its demise. Exports increased and both countries began to run surpluses with the US. Germany agreed modest revaluations in 1961 and 1968 under US pressure but neither country had much incentive to re-value their currencies and decrease their competitive position. Conversely, it was not possible for the US to devalue because the system was based on the gold–dollar link. The US trade surpluses peaked around 1960. With foreign aid, investment and military commitments, by the 1960s overall balance of payments deficits started growing and dollars began to accumulate outside the US.

Instead of gradual adjustments, asymmetries deepened and the dollar glut mushroomed. The quantity of circulating 'Eurodollars' reached 70 billion in 1970, beyond US gold reserves that had more than halved from $25 billion in 1950. The gold could only be claimed by 'official non-residents', and it was allied governments who held most of the dollars and, in the context of the Cold War, they could be lent upon. But the French began demanding gold and the market price rose above the official one of $35 an ounce (Cerny 1993; O'Brien and Williams 2004; Allen 2005). On 15 August 1971 Nixon suspended dollar–gold convertibility, also introducing tariffs pending devaluation. After two years of attempts to cobble together an alternative arrangement, the Bretton Woods system was abandoned. The value of the dollar fell. The end of Bretton Woods was initially read as evidence of US relative decline and the end of its hegemony (Kindleberger 1973). The US economic lead and its share of global exports had dwindled over the previous 25 years. By the following year the world economy entered its first major post-war recession. The abandonment of gold has alternatively been interpreted as an effective competitive strategy. Other states would continue to hold dollars as a reserve currency, giving the US the same privileges of seigniorage without even a nominal claim to American gold (Gowan 1999; Hudson 2003). The important consequences of the crisis of the 1970s for the international trade regime will be explored in Chapter 10.

CONCLUSION

This chapter has made no attempt to provide a comprehensive history. Perhaps most egregiously, it has offered no discussion of the extensive trade networks in early Africa or pre-Colombian America. Some excellent general surveys are available (Curtin 1984; Findlay and O'Rourke 2007). Even the summary discussion above makes clear that trade has ebbed and flowed, not only in its level but also in terms of how it was conducted, the importance of particular trade routes, the sorts of commodities exchanged and trade's relation with other political and economic processes. Trade is also a story of power. There are many ancient cases of trade bringing mutual benefits and of individuals, cities and societies enriching themselves and leading wider processes of development. However, for most of the history discussed here, the lines between honest trade and piracy and plunder were not clearly drawn. As Curtin (1984) remarks, thieves and merchants shared a common god in Hermes and patron saint in Nicholas. The sheer variety of forms should warn against any simple theory capturing the essence of such a range of complex and contested processes.

3. Free trade theory and its critics

INTRODUCTION

This chapter concentrates on pro-free trade arguments, particularly the theory of comparative advantage. The theory shows that countries can potentially gain from trade. In the simplest examples it demonstrates that both of two parties can benefit from trade even when one of them is absolutely more efficient at producing both of two goods. Much, much more is often claimed of the theory. A leading textbook informs its readers boldly: 'Free trade brings benefits to all nations. This theme forms the foundation for any basic discussion of international trade' (Caves et al. 1993: 199). However, as the chapter shows, the theory of comparative advantage is insufficient to support the weight it is asked to bear as either a description or a justification of real-world trade practices.

This chapter has six substantive sections. It first discusses Smith, who is usually seen as providing the basis of modern trade theory. It argues that Smith's work hardly justifies his appropriation by the modern pro-trade enthusiasts. As the section following on from it articulates, Ricardo is more clearly a proponent of free trade and the elegance of the theory of comparative advantage bears repetition. The subsequent four sections then critically evaluate the Ricardian foundations of pro-free trade theory. It is argued, respectively, that the theory ignores market imperfections, time, space and the role of money and credit. Each of these areas produces potentially fatal problems for the basic theory.

More intelligent economists recognize some of the problems and 'relax' the assumptions made in the most basic models. They would no doubt feel the objections in the second half of the chapter to be misplaced. However, the more sophisticated models are still typically presented as modifications of the original. It is hard to avoid thinking of Ptolemaic astronomy and epicycles, introducing an ever more convoluted intellectual architecture to avoid critical reflection on the underlying principles.

As the title and overall rationale of this book should make clear, the criticisms of pro-free trade arguments do not imply an embrace of protectionism, as is all too often implied. To suggest these are the only alternatives is an intellectual sleight of hand, which, diverting attention to the follies of a largely imaginary opposition, prevents proper critical scrutiny of important but problematic ideas.

ADAM SMITH: THE MISUNDERSTOOD MERCANTILIST?

Smith is typically presented as the founder of 'modern' mainstream economics. Friedman proudly sported his Adam Smith Club tie. If people know one thing of Smith it is usually that he celebrated the 'invisible hand' of the free market. He was actually a much more complex thinker than this implies.

Smith was not primarily a trade theorist. This is evident from the ordering of the *Wealth of Nations* alone. Trade only makes its substantive appearance with the fourth of five 'books' (Smith 1999). However, it is reasonable to see what Smith says in support of trade as following from his starting point in the first book on labour as the source of value and the virtues of the division of labour (Smith 1997). Famously, Smith describes a pin factory and provides some (unlikely) numbers of the potential gains. He argues that splitting the process of making even such a simple commodity into its constituent parts greatly improves productivity. Each worker becomes a specialist in a particular trade, specialization involves saving time otherwise lost moving between different jobs, while machinery is more easily applied to more simple tasks. Smith acknowledges that such specialization could cause the workers intellectual damage but believes that in material terms the division of labour brings great benefits. The first chapter of the *Wealth of Nations* ends by celebrating the achievements of European civilization; so great that the wealth of a European prince might not exceed that of a frugal peasant by more than the same frugal peasant's income exceeded that of an African king.

When his writing turns to trade, Smith's position is qualified. He contrasts productive expenditure on 'additional stock of materials, tools, and provisions' with unproductive expenditure on 'foreign wines, foreign silks, &c.' (1997: 391). This brings him close to the ideas of industrial promotion of his mercantilist opponents. His criticisms of monopolies and the guild system and of the relation between town and country even anticipate elements of arguments of unequal exchange (Raffer 1987; Brolin 2006). Smith has been claimed as a supporter of extensive, not minimal, state intervention (Heilbroner 1997) and even characterized as a 'misunderstood mercantilist' (Reinert and Reinert 2005). It is at least clear that his support for trade was conditional.

Smith himself reserves a particular scorn for mercantilism but his reasons are revealing. He particularly mocks the association (which he finds in Locke and Mun) of wealth with gold and silver. He also opposes the mercantilist emphasis evidenced in the title of Mun's book *England's Treasure in Foreign Trade* (Smith 1999: 11):

> The inland or home trade, the most important of all, the trade in which an equal capital affords the greatest revenue, and creates the greatest employment to the people of the country, was considered as subsidiary only to foreign trade. It neither brought money into the country, it was said, nor carried any out of it.

Smith regards the productive, commercial economies within countries, not trade between them, as the greatest source of the *Wealth of Nations*. Shortly after the above-quoted passage comes Smith's famous reference to the invisible hand. This too is worth quoting at length (Smith 1999: 32):

> As every individual ... endeavours as much as he can both to employ his capital in the support of domestic industry, and so to direct that industry that its produce may be of the greatest value; every individual necessarily labours to render the annual revenue of the society as great as he can. He generally, indeed, neither intends to promote the public interest, nor knows how much he is promoting it. By preferring the support of domestic to that of foreign industry, he intends only his own security; and by directing that industry in such a manner as its produce may be of the greatest value, he intends only his own gain, and he is in this, as in many other cases, led by an invisible hand to promote an end which was no part of his intention.

This famous defence of free markets and the gains attendant on selfish individualism expressly supposes a preference for domestic over foreign products. Only exceptionally do the gains from trade outweigh this natural prejudice.

When the gains from trade are sufficient, they should be encouraged and Smith argues that 'if a foreign country can supply us with a commodity cheaper than we ourselves can make it, better buy it of them with some part of the produce of our own industry employed in a way in which we have some advantage' (1999: 33). He mocks the idea of making wine in his homeland (1999: 35):

> By means of glasses, hotbeds, and hot walls, very good grapes can be raised in Scotland, and very good wine too can be made of them at about thirty

times the expense for which at least equally good can be brought from foreign countries. Would it be a reasonable law to prohibit the importation of all foreign wines merely to encourage the making of claret and burgundy in Scotland?

This is the essence of what has been called 'absolute advantage', in which trade is based on each party sticking to what it does best. It is a fairly obvious idea but a powerful one. There are many goods that it would be difficult or impossible to produce domestically and which a country needs to import. The limits of the Scottish weather or of fossil fuel reserves under particular territories remain very real. Such strictly natural factors are, of course, exceptional and the recurring presence of wine and grain in the examples justifying trade becomes suspiciously unrepresentative.

Smith (1999) also allowed exceptions, where trade should be restricted. These included industries needed for national defence. Smith supported the Navigation Acts, allowed for retaliation against foreign protectionist policy and thought that where domestic industry was taxed, foreign imports should be taxed equivalently (1999: 41–3). He also maintained that capital needed to adjust gradually to new competition so, in rather sharp contrast to some precipitous recent restructuring, 'changes of this kind should never be introduced suddenly, but slowly, gradually and after a very long warning' (1999: 49). Smith is also sensitive to internal differences within countries and believes that complete freedom of trade is a utopian fantasy because 'the prejudices of the public, but what is much more unconquerable, the private interests of many individuals, irresistibly oppose it' (1999: 48).

The fifth and final book of the *Wealth of Nations* moves back from trade to the 'Sovereign or Commonwealth', including a discussion of how the state should develop the economy through public works and public institutions. Smith's support for trade, and even for free markets more generally, is therefore again qualified. It is also clear that Smith, like his mercantilist opponents, is explicitly suggesting strategies to enrich 'the Commonwealth'. For Smith this means Britain. He is writing at the very start of the Industrial Revolution but Britain already had something of an economic lead. It is therefore Britain's manufactures that could find an absolute advantage in international markets, while the costs of raw materials and food, and therefore wages, could be reduced by foreign imports. Smith also believes that workers are free to move and that they will tend to migrate to more developed countries (Darity and Davis 2005), to their own and those countries' advantage. There are thus many aspects to Smith's optimistic vision. He supports a freeing of international trade but does not give it a particularly prominent place in augmenting the nation's wealth.

RICARDO AND COMPARATIVE ADVANTAGE

Ricardo's overall worldview was more pessimistic. Like Smith, he begins with labour but believes that wages, or the natural price of labour, provides only enough for subsistence and to perpetuate the labours' race (Ricardo 1951: 93). It is in Ricardo, not Marx, that we find something close to an 'iron law of wages'. Ricardo agreed with Malthus, his friend but otherwise often intellectual opponent, on the relentless pressures of demography. More optimistically, Ricardo accepts 'Say's Law', which predicts that markets will work, or 'clear', efficiently. The usual formulation is that supply creates its own demand. Among other things, this predicts full employment and this is important to the discussion of foreign trade and the theory of comparative advantage, which come immediately after the chapters on wages and profits.

The theory is rightly famous. The World Trade Organization (WTO) tells us that it 'is arguably the single most powerful insight into economics' (WTO 2014). The WTO highlights Samuelson's response to the challenge 'to "name me one proposition in all of the social sciences which is both true and non-trivial"' (WTO 2014):

> Samuelson's answer? Comparative advantage.
>
> That it is logically true need not be argued before a mathematician; that it is not trivial is attested by the thousands of important and intelligent men who have never been able to grasp the doctrine for themselves or to believe it after it was explained to them.

The theory argues that it is in countries' interest to specialize even when they have only a relative or comparative advantage, not simply when they have an 'absolute advantage', as in Smith. Countries do not necessarily have to be more efficient than their trading partner in one line of business and less efficient in another. It also pays to specialize and trade where countries enjoy only relatively greater efficiency, where there are varied differences between lines of business across countries, even where one country is absolutely more efficient than the other. As Samuelson's comment suggests, this is much less obvious.

It is worth re-stating Ricardo's own example, which is couched in terms of respective quantities of work. Ricardo compares cloth and wine production in Portugal and England, making the assumption that Portugal can produce both commodities with less work than can England. Ricardo articulates a labour theory of value, so prices simply reflect amounts of work. The example also ignores (or abstracts from) any capital expenditures. Therefore, if England produces a certain amount of wine with the labour of 120 people and a certain amount of cloth with the labour of 100, while Portugal can make the same quantities with the work of just 80 and 90 people, respectively, the relative difference is much greater in wine than in cloth. It will pay both countries to specialize accordingly (Ricardo 1951). Table 3.1 provides a summary.

Table 3.1   Ricardian comparative advantage

	Wine	Cloth	Total
Before trade and specialization, total work			
England	120	100	220
Portugal	80	90	170
With trade and specialization, total work			
England		2×100	200
Portugal	2×80		160

Each country saves on its total labour and, overall, less work produces the same total amount of wine and cloth. The assumption of full employment allows that this labour is freed to produce more wine or cloth or any other useful good. The argument simply requires two sets of relative differences, between countries and between the productivities of different industries.

The theory is sometimes usefully illustrated with homely or non-economic examples. Krugman and Obstfeld (2003) describe Babe Ruth's rational decision to concentrate on slugging rather than pitching a baseball, despite being one of the best pitchers in the league. Conversely, if, as John Lennon said, Ringo Starr was not even the best drummer in the Beatles, we are nevertheless invited to assume that the relative difference in their guitar playing was greater and that the band's familiar line-up made sense.

Modern trade theorists abandon the labour theory of value for a cost-of-production approach, with actual costs weighed against 'opportunity costs'. Also usually eschewing the wine for a more austerely acceptable 'corn' or 'food', the argument can be couched in terms of 'production possibility frontiers', and represented graphically. So any country can devote its resources to the production of 'corn' or 'cloth' or to some combination of the two, as in Figure 3.1(a). It is possible to produce combinations of corn and cloth inefficiently, to the 'left' or 'below' the curve of Figure 3.1(a) but it is impossible to produce more, to produce in combinations to the 'right' or 'above' the curve. The maths is simplified if the line, which in the jargon continues to be called a 'curve', is instead drawn straight as in Figure 3.1(b). Then all that is needed to make the argument is a second line with a different slope, representing the production possibility frontier of a second country, as in Figure 3.1(c). The first country is relatively more efficient at cloth production, the second at corn. The first can sell the newcomer some cloth to get more corn than it could have made, and vice versa. Some territory to the right of both countries' curves is filled, marked as 'A' and 'B' in Figure 3.1(c). For both countries, the production possibility frontier is extended.

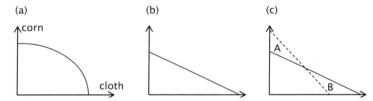

*Figure 3.1   Comparative advantage, graphical representation of two
          countries – two commodities production possibility frontiers*

This example assumes countries of similar total output (the area under the original curves is the same). However, the argument only relies on the slope of the lines. Clearly, a smaller country could supply only a part of the output of a larger one. Jamaica can supply only a part of the United States' agricultural demand, but it still makes sense both for the US to buy some food cheaper than it could grow it and for Jamaicans to buy some US-made cars rather than trying to establish their own industry.

The extension of the argument to a world with many countries and many commodities complicates the mathematics but the same principles apply, at least as long as there are as many commodities as countries.

An example with two countries but several multiple commodities allows a simple presentation in monetary terms. In the spirit of *comparative* rather than absolute advantage, Table 3.2 assumes that the home country is never absolutely more efficient but that the ratios of productivity in six industries vary from 1 through to 2 in regular, 0.2, increments. The implication of this is that the home country is poorer and workers are lower-paid (Krugman and Obstfeld 2003). If wages are

Table 3.2   Comparative advantage with two countries and many commodities

Commodity	Home			Abroad		
	Work	Quantity produced	Cost/ Price per unit	Work	Quantity produced	Cost/ Price per unit
Before specialization, work, production and price						
A	2.0	1	1.33	1.5	1.5	1.0
B	1.8	1	1.20	1.5	1.5	1.0
C	1.6	1	1.07	1.5	1.5	1.0
D	1.4	1	0.93	1.5	1.5	1.0
E	1.2	1	0.80	1.5	1.5	1.0
F	1.0	1	0.67	1.5	1.5	1.0
Total	9	6		9	9	
After specialization, work, production and price						
A				2.77	2.77	1.0
B				2.77	2.77	1.0
C				2.77	2.77	1.0
D	2.91	2.08	0.93	0.69	0.69	1.0
E	3.32	2.77	0.80			
F	2.77	2.77	0.67			
Total	9	7.62		9	9	

two-thirds the level in the foreign country, the prices of the goods can be expressed in relative money terms. By assumption, each country consumes an equal mix of products, so before trade and specialization they would also produce the quantities shown. This implies that the home country would devote unequal amounts of work to each activity. The numbers suggest that the home country, although still less efficient in terms of work required, has a comparative advantage in products D, E and F, the foreign country in A, B and C. Different scenarios are possible in terms of just how the work of producing goods at the margin might be distributed. The foreign country has the larger economy because of its greater efficiency so here it retains some production of good 'D' where it appears not to have a comparative advantage. The home country is not of sufficient size to produce everything in D, E and F for both countries, if consumption is to continue in the same ratios. The price would presumably settle somewhere between 0.93 and 1.0. The example nevertheless again shows more of each commodity in the world than before specialization and that each country can gain from trade. In this (optimistic) scenario, the home country has increased its output by 27 per cent.

The elegant simplicity of comparative advantage has surely contributed to its enduring appeal. It is, of course, a highly abstract model. This is not necessarily a problem. Theory requires abstraction and is always imperfect. However, there are many reasons to believe things may not work so neatly in practice. Frank claims to have 'identified over thirty underlying assumptions each of which is historically and empirically unfounded and several of which are mutually contradictory' (1978: 94). He does not condescend to detail these. However, Dunkley (2004) provides a 15-point list and Sheppard (2005) one of seven 'hard core' assumptions. These points are telling enough and are incorporated into the first three thematic discussions that follow, on market imperfections, time and space. The fourth section discusses money and credit. For all its elegant simplicity, there are serious limitations to comparative advantage, requiring careful thought about the assumptions being made and the purposes to which it is put.

MARKET IMPERFECTIONS AND REAL COMPETITION

The idea of market imperfections is very general and encompasses the themes of time, space and money discussed below. This section identifies several specific areas where markets are imperfect. The absence of small-country terms of trade, full employment, utility maximizing consumers with uniform preferences and market efficiency all potentially undermine the optimistic picture of mutual gains.

The theory of comparative advantage is perhaps the most important insight of what is usually termed 'classical political economy' incorporated into the 'neo-classical' tradition that developed from the 1870s and became modern mainstream economics. Keynes (1973) dubs both Ricardo and the later writers 'classical' precisely for their shared assumptions of market efficiency. It becomes particularly important for the neo-classical models to assume perfect competition. The relevant agents are all rational, self-interested individuals, they are fully informed and none of them has an influence over the total market, which is assumed to operate independently of state or societal influences (Sheppard 2005). Firms are assumed to freely enter markets. There are no profits. There is no power and no possibility of losers in a free market. With more or less reflection, this is carried over into trade theory. Friedman (1962) points out that competition, as the word is understood in plain English, means almost the opposite of what economists take it to mean in terms of a bloodless adjustment of prices. The plain language is often closer to the political economic reality, which can be an inelegant affair involving state and corporate power where there is no guarantee that the most 'efficient' in terms of work or price will prevail. There is no guarantee that saving labour and reducing costs will not translate, among other things, into higher unemployment and reduced levels of economic activity. Moreover, there are many reasons to assume that the smaller and weaker will be disadvantaged.

The heroic leap from individuals to countries as the unit of analysis requires, among other things, 'small-country terms of trade'. Just as any individual is assumed to lack market power, the output or purchases of any one country should not influence the overall price. In the jargon, each producer is a price 'taker'. In practice, the exports and imports of large countries often represent a huge proportion of global trade for particular commodities. In recent years, China's exports have clearly affected world prices and undercut those of many competitors. Large countries are typically better able to support 'their' firms, while smaller countries are more likely not only to be price takers but to become completely specialized and thence more vulnerable to market distortions or simply to market volatility. Countries cooperate and international cartels can fix prices. The oil-exporting countries' organization, OPEC, is the most well known of these cartels. Large corporations can also have a considerable degree of monopoly or monopsony power. New technology firms like Microsoft and Apple, but also industrial giants like Boeing and Airbus and retailers like Walmart, stand out. Their power to manipulate markets is sometimes exaggerated but few people would imagine that commodities like oil, aircraft or computer software are bought or sold in perfectly competitive markets. Even if we ignore overt forms of power and coercion and assume that countries do freely choose to trade and expect some benefit, all this means that any gains might be shared very unevenly.

Unequal class relations involve particularly egregious market imperfections and (perhaps for that reason) seem to remain off-limits for respectable trade theory. International competitiveness might be established precisely by cutting wages or driving workers harder through extra economic coercion rather than by efficiency. But there is a more general sense in which economic relations are inherently coercive. In a society in which workers need employment to provide for their most basic needs, the idea of 'free' labour markets is always misleading. A key aspect of this, which strikes most modern readers of Ricardo, is the reality of unemployment, not as an aberration or temporary fluctuation, but as an ongoing structural feature of almost all national economies. Ricardo's original formulation of comparative advantage envisaged equal levels of production being achieved by a reduction of work. The potential for any such efficiency gains to simply allow firms to reduce employment is all too real. This might be dysfunctional from the perspective not only of the workers themselves but also of national economies whose output suffers. It can, however, be very useful to firms as a means of maintaining labour discipline and keeping wages low. As Bowles and Boyer (1990) argue, in labour markets, quite contrary to orthodox economists' assumptions, capitalism works only when markets fail to clear. Were there no threat of unemployment, workers could bid up wages, would feel less constrained to work hard and profits would evaporate. The implications for labour of trade are complex, as will be discussed in Chapter 8, but there is already a sense in which efficiency is accrued at workers' expense.

If we do assume full employment and that specialization creates more output rather than less work, another, equally dubious, assumption is required to ensure that all the extra goods produced will be consumed. What Dunkley (2004) calls the assumption of the 'good consumer' requires that, just as much as firms strive to maximize their output, people simply want to maximize their input. At the very least, this consumption maximization requires an implausibly neat symmetry between the increases in wealth of the importing countries and the increasing supply of producers. It seems quite possible to imagine, for example, the Portuguese still finding uses for English cloth long after the English were thoroughly satiated on Portuguese wine. Even orthodox assumptions of a declining marginal propensity to consume identify different slopes to the demand curves for different goods (Jevons 1965), which then come into tension with assumptions of smooth adjustments to equilibrium if countries are also specialized in particular lines of industry.

The theory of comparative advantage requires that consumer preferences are the same across countries. If tastes differ, different demand structures produce higher relative prices for particular commodities in one country than another. This in turn implies that the country that is the more efficient producer might still end up importing (Caves et al. 1993). Tastes do vary, for all sorts of social and psychological reasons, but – most fundamentally for a narrowly economic analysis – they vary because consumption patterns change with income. Changes in wealth alter the demand structure, the relative consumption of wine and cloth and machinery. This eats away the foundations of the theory of comparative advantage, which precisely assumes that countries will have different income levels.

Finally in this section, it is pertinent to note that the existence of externalities makes assumptions of market efficiency unsustainable. Mainstream economics acknowledges that 'externalities' exist whenever goods and bads are hard to keep within private enterprise. Some externalities might be positive, involving industry innovation. In that case, one firm's activities generate unpaid-for benefits for other firms. This again produces reasons why large countries, which remain diversified, might do better than smaller ones that become completely specialized. There are also important negative externalities worth mentioning in this context, particularly those concerned with environmental degradation (Dunkley 2004). In this case, the production or consumption of any one economic player has negative 'spillovers' adversely affecting the well-being of others. In practice, trade often involves situations, in which countries, or the firms within them, specialize not because they are more efficient but because of essentially political decisions, different legislations, such as laws rejecting certain technologies, perhaps because they damage the environment or the workforce. For example, US semiconductor firms moved offshore at least in part because of lower environmental standards. Countries might find their comparative advantage in exhaustible resources, in draining their oil or logging their rainforests. In the words of US Treasury Secretary Summers, 'the economic logic behind dumping a load of toxic waste in the lowest wage country is impeccable' (cited in Kovel 2002: 76).

There are many other possible market imperfections. It is also worth noting that the focus on efficiency excludes all sorts of 'non-economic' but important social processes from the theory. The market is itself an imperfect mechanism for realizing all sorts of social objectives. For example, more rewarding but less efficient work, achieved through a less thorough division of labour, or because of a preference for locally made products are simply not entertained.

STATIC AND DYNAMIC GAINS (OR LOSSES) FROM TRADE

The theory of comparative advantage is essentially static, depending on one-off gains from specialization. Dynamic changes, some of which can themselves by fostered by trade, can have much greater effects in practice. These too might bring substantial benefits and enhance the case for trade openness. However, some of the dynamic effects potentially undermine any static gains and therefore render the argument for comparative advantage more fraught.

Most estimates reckon the likely gains from comparative advantage as small. For example, the estimated 'dead weight' losses from having trade restricting tariffs 'rarely exceed 2 or 3 percentage points' (Deraniyagala and Fine 2001: 810). Gains of such magnitude are worth having, no doubt, but might temper some of the bolder enthusiasm noted above of this being the most powerful insight economics has to offer. It is also worth emphasizing that because it is the one-off act of specialization that produces the gains, the theory of comparative advantage cannot support a presumption that open economies (countries that retain a given level of trade) should then grow more quickly than closed economies. To justify such bolder prognoses, free trade supporters would have to look elsewhere.

Claims of even one-off gains become potentially complicated if there is the possibility of economies (or diseconomies) of scale. In the jargon, the theory relies on constant technology and unchanging production functions. Ricardo's examples assume that output is doubled by doubling the amount of work. This, of course, is unrealistic. Darity and Davis (2005) suggest that already in Smith's analysis, it was recognized that the differences between agriculture and industry meant that an increased international division of labour implied widening inequality (see also Ros 1987). There will often be economies of scale, so that doubling the inputs into production would result in more than twice as much being produced. More likely, the same English cloth factory might run a second shift, for example, rather than needing to double in size. There might also be 'external' economies of scale, with spillover effects between firms, perhaps through the development of a larger pool of skilled workers, supplier industries or the use of common infrastructure. In Portuguese viticulture, as in agriculture more generally, there seems more likely to be diseconomies of scale. This was important in Ricardo's (1951) descriptions of declining marginal utility, although it does not feature in his account of trade. The best grape-growing slopes are already cultivated and more production will push the winemakers onto poorer land, probably also further from their vats. Who gains from these changes is not clear. It is the English who economize most on work, while the Portuguese savings now look less secure. But (with a Ricardian labour theory of value) this might alternatively mean that the relative price of English products comes down, to the advantage of the Portuguese. We would need to know something more about money and exchange rates to know who benefits most, and even to be sure that both parties will actually gain.

This can be seen in 'Graham's paradox', established for over 90 years but usually hidden from students of economics. Graham (1923) and Viner (1965) use a simple example of wheat and watch production but the point can be made by sticking with the familiar wine and cloth. For the sake of a simple numerical example, a 'unit' of each commodity is taken to be produced in the specified number of day's work and each country to have a supply of one million days labour: see Table 3.3. Therefore, before trade, we have Ricardo's case, with Portugal producing considerably more than England. If the respective price of the goods lies somewhere between 120/100 and 80/90, both countries will gain from trade. For simplicity, assume the prices are equal: one unit of wine is traded for one unit of cloth. At such a price it would pay both countries to trade. They therefore begin to specialize. If there are even modest diseconomies of scale in wine production, the English, by producing less wine, produce it more efficiently in terms of cost per unit produced. The Portuguese, producing more, do so less efficiently on average. Conversely, economies of scale in cloth production mean more production in England and less in Portugal. A situation of partial specialization with such changes is shown in Case II (Table 3.3). The pattern of comparative advantage is as before. The range of prices at which it would pay both parties to trade has narrowed somewhat but 1:1 still pays. Therefore, trade is still likely. Now assume England exports 2500 units of cloth and imports 2500 units of wine. England can now consume 4773 units of wine and 5394 of cloth, Portugal 5833 and 5133, respectively. In these examples England's 'GDP' has grown from 9167 to 10,168 and Portugal's contracted from 11,806 to 10,965.

Viner (1965) takes the case to near-complete specialization and the situation then becomes starker. (As below, once specialization is complete it becomes impossible to make assumptions about relative prices, which creates problems of its own for comparative advantage.) The point is nevertheless already clear at this situation of partial specialization at which Graham (1923) leaves it. Dismissing the likelihood of economies of scale, Viner goes on to reject the thesis as 'little more than a theoretical curiosity' (1965: 481). Here it has largely remained as a 'paradox', apparently absurd in confounding the expectation of mutual gains. Of the few subsequent references to Graham, a large proportion have come from proponents of New Trade Theory, discussed in the next chapter, who, since the 1980s have recognized the importance of scale economies. But the story of mutual gains has long been undermined.

Table 3.3   Graham's paradox

	England			Portugal		
	Days' work	Output per day	Output	Days' work	Output per day	Output
Case I: before specialization						
Wine	500000	1/120	4167	500000	1/80	6250
Cloth	500000	1/100	5000	500000	1/90	5556
Consumption			9167			11806
Case II; with partial specialization						
Wine	250000	1/110	2273	750000	1/90	8333
Cloth	750000	1/95	7895	250000	1/95	2632
Consumption after trade						
Wine	2273 + 2500 =		4773	8333 − 2500 =		5833
Cloth	7895 − 2500 =		5395	2632 + 2500 =		5132
			10168			10965

The static character of the theory of comparative advantage also discounts learning effects and technological innovation. That trade can foster such processes can be interpreted as a strong argument in its favour. For example, imports from more developed countries can provide a source of technological innovation in poorer ones (Yanikkaya 2003). The history discussed in the previous chapter identified how trade could be crucial to technological diffusion and growth. However, this immediately qualifies the story of advantages gained through specialization and introduces a series of potential problems for the theory.

First, it is quite plausible that the English winemakers will be forced to 'shape up' by their Portuguese counterparts and learn better ways of production from them. It is less obvious how, having followed the prescriptions and specialized, English cloth makers will learn from foreign winemakers. Competition drives specialization, but the process of specialization undermines competition. In the examples above, price competition between countries produces a more efficient overall division of labour but, once countries have specialized, there is little or no competition.

Second, if technological innovation becomes a key variable, there may be strong grounds for protection and state support for national systems of innovation. What is internationally inefficient at one time might be improved upon (Dunkley 2004). Historically, England was not always a cloth maker and if it had just specialized in those activities it conducted at some earlier time it would never have become one. The US too, was an agricultural exporting country until late in the nineteenth century. The more general point is that static models cannot capture how differences at any one time, which determine a country's specialisms, might cease to be valid if specialization were delayed. At the very least, dynamic changes imply that countries overcome any momentary comparative disadvantage.

Third, changing productivity within countries (as in Graham's paradox but for whatever reason it occurs) will change the likely pattern of winners and losers. There is a range of possibilities depending, for example, on where the gains are achieved within national economies and what effect this has on exchange rates. Hicks (1953) suggests that uniform increases in productivity in country A mean that its greater wealth increases the demand for country B's products, so even as international inequality increases, some part of the improvement with 'slop over to B' (1953: 124). However, the picture is different if productivity improvements are uneven. Innovation in A's export sectors cheapen its products, to B's further advantage, while innovation in non-export sectors which compete with imports from B, work to B's disadvantage.

Recalling the market imperfections discussed above, one further relevant aspect of dynamic change is how comparative advantage assumes that capital moves costlessly and instantly from one activity to another. In practice, of course, there are inevitably adjustment costs associated with specialization: ripping up the vineyards, demolishing the unwanted factories and then establishing them elsewhere. Smith thought any changes should be implemented gradually, particularly because of the difficulties of changing business for 'the undertaker of a great manufacture' (1999: 49). Even orthodox economic accounts admit that the costs of reallocating resources should be subtracted from any gains from trade (Caves et al. 1993). Implicitly, at least, comparative advantage requires a constant re-switching. So, for example, Portugal's winemakers might face renewed competition from one sort of grape and one sort of wine to another, so their vineyards also now have to be uprooted. As productivity and wage rates elsewhere change, any country's 'correct' production and market niche alters. The banana plantations become uncompetitive, as many Caribbean Islands found to their cost. Theory tells us that there is something else to do with a country's resources, but it is seldom obvious just what.

In short, trade takes place in a dynamic and changing world while the theory of comparative advantage is static. The conventional theory's ability to capture the impact of changes or to guide policy becomes profoundly questionable.

SPACE, DISTANCE AND NATIONAL POLITICAL ECONOMY

Just as the theory of comparative advantage is atemporal, so it is also aspatial. 'Transport costs are either ignored, or treated as an exogenously given barrier to trade; space is Newtonian rather than a social construct' (Sheppard 2005: 155). In reality, geography impinges on trade relations in important ways. Even in the nineteenth century, the Atlantic voyages required to transport Ricardo's two commodities were hardly trivial. Despite much hyperbole over the 'death of distance' and deterritorialization in the recent literature on globalization, there is little evidence that the work or costs involved in moving most goods and services diminish to zero. This is essentially a practical, empirical matter, which supporters of trade would acknowledge needs to be weighed against the gains. However, it means that 'access to markets' will have semi-natural elements, which might disadvantage certain countries, such as inland Africa and Asia (Smith 1997; Darity and Davis 2005). Place matters, so that trade is likely to look different for different countries, for Austria and Vanuatu. Transport and communication efficiencies vary between activities and can often be changed by policy.

Once we enter the real world of international relations, as the perspectives discussed in the next chapter emphasize, there are many reasons to question ideas of voluntary, 'arm's-length' trade between nations. There are many cases of direct or indirect coercion. The restructuring of indebted countries in the 1980s is discussed in Chapter 10. As discussed above, economic competition itself coerces. Building a war chest of foreign currency reserves against potential free-market speculation can impose a similar logic to that of International Monetary Fund (IMF)-sponsored structural adjustment. It induces countries to trade, but to export more than they import, and as such defies ideas of trade as a voluntary, barter-like exchange.

National borders continue to matter but these are social constructions, not the neat containers of economic activity that much of economic theory takes them to be. Ricardo (1951) not only posits the ease of capital relocation within countries but also contrasts this with the difficulties of moving across national borders. There are necessary assumptions. Were capital (and land and labour) within a country not 'given' it would become impossible to talk of choices between different uses, and the supersession of one line of business by another more in line with the country's comparative advantage. An open global economy makes these assumptions all the harder to sustain as workers migrate in their millions and capital flows accelerate, but they have always been problematic. Portugal did specialize, but the English bought the Portuguese vineyards (Frank 1978). Meanwhile, the textbooks can slide effortlessly from acknowledging capital movements to telling us that they too 'lead to gains from trade that can make consumers everywhere better off' (Krugman and Obstfeld 2003: 637). The claims of gains from trade are now extended to capital mobility even as that capital mobility pulls the conceptual rug from the claims of gains from trade. Frank's dependency views see capital export as part of a process through which the core exploits the periphery but they also imply that any gains might be sent away from rich countries.

There are epistemological problems in assuming that the logic of mutual gains achieved by self-interested individuals through acts of truck, barter and exchange apply equally to nation states in the global economy. It is reasonable to assume that, if it were a free decision, individuals would not trade unless they perceived some benefit in doing so. Unfortunately, nation states are not like individuals, neither having interests nor being capable of making rational decisions on the same bases. States simply do not possess utilities in the same sense that neo-classical economics maintains they are held by individuals; states do not experience pleasure and pain. A series of more or less plausible conceptual leaps are required to assume that additions of material or monetary wealth amount to the same thing and to justify extrapolating the presuppositions of an individualist economic orthodoxy. Of course, states are not unitary actors and it is seldom states themselves that engage in trade. Particular government bureaus or departments might perhaps do so but it is more likely to be firms that trade; firms whose attachment to the national interest is likely to be at best conditional.

The theory of comparative advantage assumes 'lump sum' compensation, an implausible national unity that depicts countries as homogeneous entities (Dunkley 2004). In a sense this is just another instance of market imperfections and is exemplified by the discussion of unemployment above. Firms and individuals may save rather than spend their income or send it overseas. Once we recognize that countries are internally divided, even if we posit net national gains, there is no reason to assume that everybody benefits. As will be discussed, particularly in Chapter 8, mainstream trade theorists since Stolper and Samuelson (1941) acknowledge this. It has, to say the least, interesting implications for the 'liberal' arguments. There are many possible scenarios in which trade, even where it involves net national gains, might be against the interests of the majority of the people. Meanwhile, as above, within countries, capital is heterogeneous and there are many obstacles to its movement. There are costs and time lags associated with switching production from one industry to another. Conversely, there are likely to be spatial and thence national interdependencies between economic sectors (Sheppard 2005). Ripping out one sector because it does not fit the country's static comparative advantage might also have negative spillover effects.

THE ECONOMY IS INESCAPABLY MONETARY

Several aspects of a monetary economy undermine the assumptions of comparative advantage. The textbook models begin with trade as a barter-like process (see, for example, Caves et al. 1993). For the purported mutual benefits to be achieved in practice requires some big assumptions about money and finance in the international economy (Shaikh 1979). The possibilities of saving, or having a 'liquidity prefer-ence' rather than immediately reinvesting, or of sending money across national borders have been mentioned above. Baiman (2010: 433) argues that, with some plausible assumptions about consumer preferences, 'Ricardo's story is mathematically overdetermined' and the mutually beneficial free-trade equilibrium disappears. Two further points will be made here, both reiterating the importance of time.

First, Shaikh considers the role of debt and debt repayment, illustrating this in a situation where the international economy uses commodity money, as it did with the gold standard. It would be quite consistent with Ricardo's labour theory of value to posit an equal quantity of gold as the product of an equal quantity of work. Shaikh (1980) then adds to Ricardo's familiar pre-specialization depiction of England and Portugal some prices of their products. This now implies that Portugal's absolute advantage in both lines of business means that initially its products are cheaper and it outsells its English competitors and successfully exports both its products to England. Initially, England can sell nothing in Portugal and it runs a trade deficit, which is to say that money (gold) flows in the opposite direction.

For Ricardo, as for subsequent quantity theories of money, this brings about a fall in the prices in England until at some point the relatively cheaper cloth is sold into Portuguese markets and the happy patterns of specialization are established. It is likely that the flow of gold will change prices in the direction suggested. But this is not all that happens.

Shaikh (1980) suggests (following Marx) that the outflow of gold from England will also determine the supply of loanable capital within England, tending to raise interest rates. This will be partially offset by the diminished scale of cloth and wine production, which decreases the borrowing demand, but this will only be partial as long as there is some bias toward local production. The increased borrowing costs will constrain investment and production of other commodities. In net, 'the drain of bullion will lead to lower bank reserves, curtailed production, and a higher rate of interest' (Shaikh 1980: 38). Portugal experiences the opposite effect. The low rates of interest and excess of loanable capital boost local production. They also make lending to England attractive. In doing so, the balances seem to be restored but the money is lent, at interest, and so eventually returns, in greater quantity, to Portugal. The trade imbalance is maintained by the persistent flow of gold in the opposite direction.

If we have commodity money this cannot continue indefinitely. Even with fiat money there is likely to be a less well-defined limit determined by the confidence of currency and bondholders. There must eventually be a collapse in the value of the English currency. Again, conventional theory would see this restoring trade balances as currency depreciation restores English competitiveness. However, it also means England can afford less because it has become poorer and therefore there is also a fall in the level of trade (Shaikh 1980). Portugal gains while England loses. As a consequence, Shaikh insists (1979: 301): 'It is *absolute* advantage, not comparative, which rules trade.'

Incorporating money and foreign exchange rates with a sensitivity to time discussed above introduces a further series of complications. Falling foreign exchange values are expected to improve export competitiveness, limit imports and improve the trade balance. But this does not happen immediately. The textbooks acknowledge 'J-curve' effects, involving a mild dip before the improvement. In the short term, falling currency values mean that the terms of trade fall. Supply and demand do not adjust instantaneously, so exports earn less and imports become more expensive. The balance of trade deteriorates. Only after an indeterminate period are producers able to respond, to utilize their new competitiveness. Similarly, the downward pressure on demand and imports will vary, consumption of essential food supplies and industrial inputs falling only over time.

Three things stand out from this. First, the timing is uncertain. As seen in the early 2000s, the US dollar and the US trade balance could fall together for many years. Second, there is little theoretical reason to expect the total 'recovery' to be greater than the initial fall. Much will hang on elasticities of supply and demand of the particular commodities. It may not be the case that there is a sufficient increase in demand, say for the now cheaper potatoes, to outweigh the lower price per sack. Nor might producers be able to increase supply to match any extra demand. Third, even if the recovery is rapid and export performance improves, this is based on falling terms of trade and at least some degree of national impoverishment. This, of course, has been one of the criticisms of IMF structural adjustment policies; that trade and trade surpluses allowed creditors to be repaid but did little for national development. A reciprocal set of observations might be made about currency revaluation and improving terms of trade. There seem likely to be winners and losers within countries but the net effects on national income are hard to anticipate.

CONCLUSION

Comparative advantage is a powerful theory, which has occupied a central place in economic thinking. It provides reasons to expect mutual gains from trade, even in situations where it might seem counter-intuitive. The less efficient can have something to offer to the more efficient and the more efficient something to gain by trading with the less efficient.

However, there are many problems with the theory. It assumes perfect competition based on the action of rational individuals and is ill-equipped to deal with the realities of national, corporate and class power. It is static, predicting one-off gains but saying nothing about dynamic effects, which for good or ill, might be more important. It is aspatial, ignoring the complexities of geography, national boundaries and national interests, while the picture of mutual gains can also be questioned once attention is given to the operation of the monetary economy.

Mainstream trade theorists acknowledge many of these points and the next chapter looks in more detail at several perspectives that incorporate the reality of imperfect markets. Some of the problems have been acknowledged more cursorily, or dismissed as minor quibbles and curios (Sheppard 2005). The problem, however, remains that even where there is a relatively thorough acknowledgement and engagement with the challenges, these are typically seen as requiring minor adjustments to comparative advantage, as involving exceptions rather than invalidating the general claims. However, 'we cannot dismiss the proposition that some of these assumptions are "critical", in the sense that current theoretical deductions no longer hold once those assumptions are modified' (Sheppard 2005: 155).

Once again, questioning the dominant theory does not imply a rejection of trade. Nor does it mean abandoning attempts to understand it. Back in 1963 Balogh wrote (cited in Raffer 1987: 276):

> On the contrary: the failure of empty generalities, the exposure of the grand abstract designs and diagrams as signifying nothing, depicting non-existent relations; the recognition of the historical uniqueness of macro-economic problems, all this increases the need for careful and detailed economic analysis, for the painstaking investigation of each case and its peculiarities.

There are alternative ways of looking at trade.

4. Market imperfections and state strategies

INTRODUCTION

This chapter considers several perspectives that are critical of the dominant free trade narrative. They recognize that markets are imperfect and consider the consequences. There is no single, simple theory here, like comparative advantage, but a series of propositions about how trade is often an inelegant business, involving change over time and asymmetries of power and wealth. The chapter discusses three influential and in some respects overlapping schools of thought, before making some general criticisms.

The next section discusses mercantilism, a longstanding and diverse tradition in favour of policy interventions in trade as part of broader strategies to build national economies. The section discusses the mercantilist tradition before Smith and the influential responses to classical political economy, coming particularly from Hamilton in the US and List in Germany. The second substantive section discusses ideas that poorer countries suffer structural disadvantages and deteriorating trading conditions. It begins with the theories of Singer (1950) and Prebisch (1950), considers other ideas of poorer-country disadvantage and goes on to discuss how even in a supposedly liberalizing world, trade remains an organized and managed activity. The chapter then introduces New Trade Theory (NTT), and suggests that (consciously or otherwise) this appropriates some of the insights of the poorer-country perspectives, of systematic power and disadvantage, to identify how large, rich countries can use asymmetries to their advantage and gain through trade restrictions. The final comments suggest that among other things, eminently sensible observations about market imperfections lead many apparent critics either to seek to lessen these by making the world more liberal, a perspective that converges with the mainstream, or to utilize power asymmetries to national advantage rather than genuinely challenging them. These perspectives also often exaggerate the capacity and benevolence of state intervention.

It might be preferable to re-order the presentation, to bring NTT closest to the mainstream ideas discussed in the previous chapter and put some of the more critical ideas closer to those of the radical dependency theorists discussed in Chapter 5, with which, in some respects, they converge. However, with this warning, the continuity and intellectual development of the ideas suggests the chronological ordering. The final section stresses that the ostensibly different views have some important similarities.

MERCANTILISM

As discussed in the previous chapter, Smith's attitude towards trade often conflicts with the claims of his putative followers but he does deride the mercantilists. Book IV of the *Wealth of Nations* begins by caricaturing the mercantilist position and the 'popular notion' (1999: 5–6): 'That wealth consists in money, or in gold and silver [...] A rich country, in the same manner as a rich man, is supposed to be a country abounding in money; and to heap up gold and silver in any country is supposed to be the readiest way to enrich it.'

This desire for money underpins strategies to encourage exports and limit imports. Smith acknowledges occasional nuance in writers like Mun, for whom money could leave if it bought goods that brought back more in the future; like the 'husbandman in seed-time' but the mercantilist end remains the same, to accumulate money. This amounted to a simple-minded Midas fallacy (Reinert and Reinert 2005). For Smith, 'it would be too ridiculous to go about seriously to prove that wealth does not consist in money, or in gold and silver; but in what money purchases, and is valuable only for purchasing (1999: 14). Smith's attack seems to have had a lasting effect. The *Oxford English Dictionary* defines mercantilism as an 'old economic theory that money is the only form of wealth' (OED 1982: 633). An influential modern textbook sees mercantilism today as 'an economic philosophy and practice of government regulation of a nation's economic life to increase state power and security. Policies of import restriction and export promotion ... follow from this goal' (Balaam and Veseth 2001: 464).

There is some truth to Smith's criticism. Early mercantilists did sometimes simply associate wealth and money, although even their fiercest critics admit these were exceptions (Heckscher 1955b). Mun advocates a range of strategies. For example, 'it will not increase our treasure to enjoy the Merchant that exporteth Fish, Corn or Munition, to return all or part of the value in Money' (1959: 38). Later mercantilist writers reach conclusions that appear to anticipate Smith. For Childe, money was only a commodity and so its export too could be to national advantage (Schumpeter 1986). As discussed in the previous chapter, Smith's criticisms of Mun's emphasis on foreign trade rather than domestic sources of growth also make rather salutary reading for some modern trade enthusiasts.

Early mercantilist practices were diverse but almost always involved more than attempts to increase the national bullion hoard. Heckscher (1955a) understands mercantilism as the period of state-building practices eventually superseded by liberalism. At least as early as the fourteenth century, this included efforts to overcome feudal disaggregation and internal division and to develop national industry. England's King Edward III attempted to establish a local cloth industry against more efficient continental producers and apparently only wore English cloth to set an example (List 1983; Chang 2002). Effective industrial policy in England would only really begin under the Tudors in the sixteenth century, when the accompanying trade strategies included restrictions of wool exports and the encouragement of raw materials and machinery imports, and the immigration of skilled craft workers. The same themes were repeated well into the eighteenth century. The king's address to parliament in 1721 reiterated 'that nothing so much contributes to promote the public well-being as the exportation of manufactured goods and the importation of foreign raw material' (cited in Chang 2002: 21). Similar policies were attempted elsewhere. Reinert and Reinert (2005: 9) see the Dutch in the sixteenth century trying to avoid the decline experienced by Spain and again recognizing that some activities, particularly manufacturing, brought bigger gains than others. Significantly, the Dutch also saw economic development as a synergic process with different activities strengthening each other. By the seventeenth century, France under Louis XIV and Colbert, his minister of finances, had become the mercantilist archetype. This involved 'building manufacturing and infrastructure, facilitating internal trade, and attempting to recreate, on a national level, the synergies that earlier observers ... had confined to city-states' (Reinert and Reinert 2005: 13). Both the early theory and practice prioritized building industry rather than achieving an overall balance-of-payments surplus.

Two final things about the discourse are worth noting. First, the term 'mercantilism' often seems like a linguistic anomaly. Literally the policy of merchants, it is now associated with state-centred as opposed to market-based practices. As seen in Chapter 2, it was, of course, states that stood behind and enabled the success of the early European merchant companies. If trade today is seldom so directly state controlled, many of the perspectives discussed below continue to identify how trade remains an organized rather than free market process. List (1983) makes almost the opposite criticism of his free trade opponents; their pre-occupation with buying at the best price is a merchant's prejudice, which ignores broader, longer-term economic objectives. The word mercantil-ism therefore reminds us that belief in a sharp dichotomy between state and market is a rather recent construction and a potentially unsatisfactory one.

Second, for all the ferocity of avowedly liberal criticisms, the basic identification of trade surpluses as good and trade deficits as bad remains remarkably pervasive. Building surpluses need not reflect a simple-minded miser's appetite for gold, as mercantilism's critics have been keen to depict. An influx of money could stimulate the country's internal economy and raise the level of employment (Keynes 1973). Such concerns, of course, might seem irrelevant for orthodoxy, for which money is neutral and unemployment simply assumed out of existence. However, mainstream authorities, in both news media and policy circles, usually share the normative judgement. Even the language of surpluses and deficits is revealing. Only if we reverse Smith and insist that wealth consist in 'money, or in gold and silver; and not in what money purchases' are such prejudices obviously justified.

By the time of the classical political economists, Britain had estab-lished its economic lead. Its industry had little need of protection and its industrialists championed free trade. Landowners and farmers would continue to resist but 14 years after the Great Reform Bill of 1832 increased the franchise, the Corn Laws banning grain imports were finally abolished. Over the following years, Britain would move towards something close to free trade. By this time, the main sites of practical and intellectual opposition had shifted to Britain's competitors.

Most familiar in an American context is Hamilton's 1791 *Report on the Subject of Manufactures*. Even before this, the American Revolution embodied opposition to the trade policies of Britain that had stifled industrial development within the colonies and prohibited the local colonial authorities from using tariffs (even as these still predominated in Britain) (Chang 2002). Meanwhile, the colonists were charged duties, which went to the British authorities, most infamously and provocatively in the Tea Tax. At least in part, the revolution was a revolt against such impositions. Washington's inauguration wearing a suit of homespun cloth echoed the point made four centuries earlier by Edward III (List 1983).

Hamilton was an important figure in the early republic. As the title suggests, his report is concerned primarily with how the US should develop industry and Hamilton proposes a range of measures for achieving this. The report is far from simply a tract about trade. It does begin (to risk anachronism, Hamilton precedes Ricardo by a generation) by rejecting America's static comparative advantage as an agricultural producer but trade policy is then only reintroduced towards the end of the report as part of a broader industrial strategy. Compared to agriculture, industry would increase the division of labour (which of course was also the starting point of Smith's political economy), extend the use of machinery, increase employment (especially of women and children), promote immigration, furnish a greater scope for the diversity of talents and dispositions, afford more ample and various fields for enterprise and secure the demand for agricultural products (Hamilton 1792). Hamilton acknowledges there would be temporary costs, well compensated by future gains. He antici-pates 'infant industry' arguments, sometimes admitted even by modern economics textbooks as 'having some general validity' or a 'germ of truth' (Sloman and Norris 1999: 506; Caves et al. 1993: 224). American indus-tries needed particular encouragement because of 'the fear of want of success in untried enterprises, the intrinsic difficulties incident to first essays towards a competition with those who have previously attained to perfection in the business to be attempted' but also in retaliation because 'foreign nations second the exertions of their own citizens' (Hamilton 1792: 27). Modern versions describe how an industry might initially lack economies of scale, workers with the necessary experience, specialist suppliers and access to finance, available to established foreign competi-tors. However, with initial support, an industry could become competitive and even the basis of a country's trade specialization. Besides the narrow economic benefits, for Hamilton 'every nation ... ought to endeavour to possess within itself all the essentials of national supply. These comprise the means of subsistence, habitation, clothing and defence' (1792: 47).

Hamilton was substantially defeated during his own lifetime. The US did not initially adopt a federal tariff system and when it did so, after 1789, tariffs remained modest until the war with Britain in 1812. Subsequently, US policy became much more restrictive with manufac-tured goods subject to about 35 per cent tariffs after 1816, rising to 40 per cent by 1820 (Chang 2002). American trade barriers would remain high for more than another century.

Debates over trade and industrial development would continue to divide US political economy. Broadly, northern industrialists wanted protection from European competitors. Writers like Carey and Clay extended the Hamiltonian tradition making arguments for the harmony of interests between national agriculture, manufacturing and commerce. Southern plantation owners typically supported free trade, wanting to sell tobacco and particularly cotton to the bigger and expanding European markets (Rogowski 1989). There were exceptions. Fitzhugh, from the perspective of the US South, insisted that voluntary and apparently mutually beneficial exchanges within the US disadvantaged that region (cited in Brolin 2006: 43):

> To them it is cheaper at present, to exchange their crops for manufactures than to make them. They begin the exchange, and they learn to rely more and more on others to produce articles, some of which they formerly manufactured, and their ignorance of all, save agriculture, is thus daily increasing.

Fitzhugh, an openly racist supporter of southern slavery, is interesting in this context both in arguing that the inequalities are not intrinsically international and in that his opposition to trade anticipates many subsequent ostensibly radical arguments.

Within Europe too, Britain's lead nurtured economic and intellectual grounds for criticisms of free trade. List's *National System of Political Economy* is best known. He too suggests that regulating trade might be necessary to develop industry. List is very clear that 'import duties should not be levied in the hope of enticing specie into the country ... This is a discredited part of the mercantile system' (1983: 36). He supports the freeing of trade within Germany and the Customs Union or *Zollverein*. He also supports the idea of free trade in some possible future 'cosmopolitan economy' where between equal parties it might indeed bring mutual benefits. However, in the unequal real world, free trade would benefit England while (List 1885: 130–1):

> European Continental nations would be lost as unimportant, unproductive races. By this arrangement it would fall to the lot of France, together with Spain and Portugal, to supply this English world with the choicest wines, and to drink the bad ones herself: at most France might retain the manufacture of a little millinery. Germany would scarcely have more to supply this English world with than children's toys, wooden clocks, and philological writings, and sometimes also an auxiliary corps, who might sacrifice themselves to pine away in the deserts of Asia or Africa, for the sake of extending the manufacturing and commercial supremacy, the literature and language of England.

List noted how Britain had practiced mercantilism until it established its economic lead. Only then, in a much-repeated metaphor, did it attempt to 'kick' or 'throw away the ladder' by which it had climbed to dominance. Britain wanted to deny potential competitors the same policies, the better to sell its industrial products into their markets and the cheaper to buy their raw materials. Instead, countries like Germany should follow Britain's lead. List was perhaps a European rather than simply German nationalist and encourages 'a world of a united centre engaged in exploiting the "barbarian and half-barbarian peoples or those with receding cultures"' (cited in Raffer 1987: 18).

When List was writing, Prussia and then the German Zollverein were only moderately protectionist. Europe was moving towards freer trade and this would accelerate until sharply reversed by Germany under Bismarck in 1879. It is sometimes claimed that Bismarck kept a copy of List's work on his desk (Henderson 1983). As seen in Chapter 2, the retreat from free trade, except within the colonial empires, continued into the next century. The effects on the global economy of greater trade restrictions remain controversial, although global growth rates do not appear to have changed dramatically. It is clear that during this period the US and Germany caught up and in many respects now overtook Britain (where opposition to free trade again became louder). In 1879, German and US gross domestic profit (GDP) per capita were, respectively, 60 per cent and 85 per cent of British levels. By 1913, the figures had risen to 74 per cent and 108 per cent (calculated from Maddison 2003). At least for the US and Germany, industry-building strategies and trade restrictions appeared to work.

The subsequent 30 years were uniquely grim. Two world wars, the Great Depression and the rise of fascism saw much of the optimism of the previous century evaporate. The inward spiral of trade after 1929 has reasonably been seen as a part of the decline (Kindleberger 1973) although post-war free trade interests in the US may have exaggerated protectionism's responsibility (Strange 1996). The decline of trade was more consequence than cause of the depression. Of course, there were now feedback mechanisms as markets everywhere collapsed. Almost everywhere trade barriers remained high. Nationalist sentiments grew. Emmanuel suggests that, in Romania, Manoïlescu 'alone tried to undertake the defence of long-term protectionism' (1972: xix). However, under various guises, more restrictive trade practices and national economic planning became the order of the day.

Only after World War II would the now dominant US become relatively free trading. This was indeed still only a relative change. As mentioned in Chapter 2, Congress vetoed the formation of an International Trade Organization. Average US tariffs remained about 14 per cent in 1950 and the export to GDP ratio was only about 3 per cent (Held et al. 1999; Chang 2002). However, US industry, in particular, now had clear economic advantages over potential competitors and little to fear from trade openness. The focus of anti-free trade perspectives shifted southwards.

CRITICIZING SYSTEMIC ASYMMETRIES AND MARKET IMPERFECTIONS

The Prebisch–Singer thesis is usually taken as the claim that the terms of trade of primary products tend to decline relative to those of manufactured goods (Brolin 2006). This is indeed Singer's (1950) key claim. Prebisch (1950) agrees it is the lot of poor countries (in Latin America in his study) to export primary products but his analysis stresses the character of the economies rather than the nature of the products. Prebisch's views, in turn, shade into broader ones of poorer country disadvantage and dependency discussed in the next chapter. This section begins by considering Singer and the specific claims of changing terms of trade for primary products, then discusses other reasons for expecting poorer-country disadvantage and then, more broadly still, looks at some of the many respects in which, despite recent 'liberalization', trade remains an imperfect and managed process.

The claim of declining terms of trade inverts Ricardo (1951: 97):

> From manufactured commodities always falling, and raw produce always rising, with the progress of society, such a disproportion in their relative value is at length created, that in rich countries a labourer, by the sacrifice of a very small quantity only of his food, is able to provide liberally for all his other wants.

For orthodoxy, faster productivity growth in industry should lower the relative prices of manufactured goods (Prebisch 1950). Empirically, it has long been clear that this does not happen. Over the course of the twentieth century the decline in the terms of trade of primary products has been estimated as amounting to 53 per cent (Ocampo and Parra-Lancourt 2010; see also Cypher and Dietz 1998 and Todaro and Smith 2009). The trajectory was uneven. The thesis is therefore far from unambiguously true. Important exceptions include gold and oil but there have been numerous variations over time and between commodities. Primary prices rose in the nineteenth century and again at the start of the twenty-first. The falling prices of a few important commodities could also dominate the statistics (Ross 1999). 'Kindleberger … at one point questioned not only the empirical validity, but the whole concept of commodity groups allegedly sharing either price or income-elasticities' (Brolin 2006: 124). Emmanuel sees the fall in primary products' terms of trade as an 'optical illusion' which does not apply when rich countries like Sweden and Canada export primary products (Kindleberger 1956; Emmanuel 1972). Most commentators do accept a general empirical tendency towards falling relative primary prices but it is important to distinguish some quite distinct claims.

Singer, a German Jew who escaped from Nazi Germany in 1933, became a student of Keynes at Cambridge and remained an academic in Britain. Keynes's influence on Singer's 1950 paper seems clear, notably in its understanding of each national economy as a whole, not merely the sum of its parts. Singer starts by acknowledging that export-oriented primary producing sectors in developing countries could be the most capital intensive and efficient within those national economies. However, it does not follow from this that such sectors were 'good' for the national economies. First, foreign ownership of capital in export sectors meant these often remained apart from the internal economic structures. Dualist economies tended to develop. The static comparative advantages export industries might bring, meant foregoing the cumulative gains from more integrated industrial development; a point echoing earlier mercantilist claims and developed further particularly by Hirschman (1958). Of course, foreign firms also repatriated profits, not allowed by Ricardo's model but an intrinsic part of corporate behaviour in the twentieth century. Secondly, while recognizing there was an unprovable counter-factual involved, Singer (1950: 476) contrasted the apparent efficiency of export sectors not only with the existing economies but also with opportunities lost:

> The tea plantations of Ceylon, the oil wells of Iran, the copper mines of Chile, and the cocoa industry of the Gold Coast may all be more productive than domestic agriculture in these countries; but they may well be less productive than domestic industries in those countries which might have developed if those countries had not become specialized to the degree in which they now are to the export of food and raw materials.

In terms of the core claim that the terms of trade of primary products tend to fall relative to those of manufactured goods, Singer begins by noting this as 'a matter of historical fact' (1950: 477). He argues that in industry technical gains tend to lead to an increase in income whereas in agriculture they tend to lead to a fall in price. The principal mechanism is that demand for food and some raw materials do not rise in proportion to real income. Demand is relatively 'inelastic'. Like individuals, as societies become richer they demand relatively less food and raw material and more manufactured goods.

Singer also notes the role of technical progress and the production of synthetic alternatives to primary commodities, a point that would be further developed by Dos Santos (1970) and Robinson (1979). Rubber provides the classic example. Others have developed longer lists of factors determining elasticities including country substitution, commodity substitution, recycling and the weaker position of the sellers compared to larger, more powerful buyers (Raffer 1987). Most of these also work against poorer countries and primary products.

Singer also sees foreign trade as more significant for poorer countries not only in relation to GDP but also, especially, relative to the margins over subsistence. Although his core argument is secular not cyclical, Singer also notes that poorer countries are more vulnerable to fluctuations. There is then also a 'curious ambivalence' whereby cyclical upturns raise commodity prices providing the means for importing capital goods and industrializing but remove the incentives to do so, while falling prices sharpen the desire but remove the means (Singer 1950).

Prebisch's (1950) argument is conceptually quite different and based on 'imperfections' in labour markets rather than commodity markets. His argument also draws explicitly on Keynes, but now particularly identifying the absence of full employment and perfect competition among workers as the fundamental flaws in comparative advantage. Labour organization in democratic, rich countries means that workers not only enjoy rising wages in response to tight labour markets and low unemployment during boom times, but they are substantially able to cling on to these gains in downturns. There is a ratchet effect on wages with firms able to pass on the higher costs as higher prices. Trade unions are therefore primarily responsible for rising rich-country prices. This contrasts with the situation in poorer countries where unions typically remain outlawed and where there is a ready flow of workers from the countryside. Wages stay low. As a result, poorer-country prices tend to fall relative to those in rich countries. Their terms of trade deteriorate. In later work, Prebisch (1959) incorporates the role of 'monopolistic pricing' and contrasts competitive primary-product markets with oligopolistic ones for finished goods. However, the fundamental problems are the differences in labour markets between rich and poor countries.

Although the starting point is not in the character of the products, the solution still lies in industrialization: 'Greater productivity in industry gradually spreads to other activities, which are thereby obliged to use more capital, per capita, in order to achieve the increase in productivity without which they would be unable to pay higher wages' (Prebisch 1950: 44). Unfortunately, any attempt to overcome the problems through such industrialization confronted systematic obstacles. How should it be financed? 'Voluntary savings are not sufficient to cover the most urgent capital needs' (1950: 5). Meanwhile, an environment of dollar scarcity and falling gold reserves, which had developed since the 1920s, induced Latin American countries (like others) to depreciate their currencies, further worsening the terms of trade and making it harder to fund investment. Prebisch, more than Singer, was particularly interested in cyclical effects. Anti-cyclical policies that develop industry require 'a reduction in the coefficient of imports for current consumption' (1950: 53, Prebisch 1971). This does not mean a country should reject trade but adapt imports to the needs of industrialization 'sacrificing part of its exports in order to increase industrial production as a substitute for imports' (1950: 45).

Many other accounts of poorer-country disadvantage followed Singer and Prebisch's early work. Not all of these focused directly on trade while by the late 1960s many also took inspiration from more radical and Marxist theories of imperialism and dependency (discussed in the next chapter). One trade dilemma already implicit in Prebisch is that money matters and that the effects of changing currency values depend on specific elasticities. A falling currency would be expected to increase export volumes but worsen the terms of trade. What this means for exports in price terms and for real incomes is hard to predict. A rising currency will improve the terms of trade but can undermine markets. What became known as the 'Dutch Disease' outlined how natural gas discoveries and exports increased the value of the guilder, which undermined the competitiveness of Dutch manufacturing, from which capital and labour was also drawn away (Ross 1999). The potential impact on resource-rich poorer countries seems all the greater. At the very least, it became clear that countries apparently abundantly endowed with natural resources did not thereby become rich. There is something closer to a 'resource curse' (Sachs and Warner 1995b). This can be read in liberal terms, conveniently shifting the blame back onto the poorer-country governments and their distortion of free markets. Abundant resources encourage rent-seeking behaviour and corrupt government rather than productive investment (Ross 1999). Others continue to blame foreign investment and exploitation (Bush 2004). Successive depletions involved in resource extraction have been particularly powerfully demonstrated in relation to very poor areas like the Brazilian Amazon (Bunker 1984). In various ways it becomes clear that a static comparative advantage in primary products provides insufficient grounds for trade-based prosperity.

More broadly, the Keynesian tradition developed important criticisms of mainstream economics, underpinned by a recognition that markets were imperfect. Several of the criticisms of comparative advantage noted in the last chapter follow from this; among other things it is necessary to acknowledge the role of market power, space, time and money. Rich countries are in stronger positions of monopsony and monopoly, as buyers and sellers of commodities. Just as monopoly allows firms to raise prices at a national level, tariffs could have the same effect of improving the terms of trade (Kaldor 1940). Smaller, poorer countries are more likely to be price takers. The role and cooperation of large, rich country multinational corporations producing tropical foodstuffs within poorer countries also helps keep prices down (Robinson 1979). Sweezy sees the price discrepancies caused by monopoly as escaping 'any general rules' (quoted in Shaikh 1979: 297) and the criticisms could not produce an elegant, easily digestible formulation to compete with comparative advantage but they provide many reasons to be cautious about free trade.

Keynes himself has a somewhat ambiguous and changing attitude towards trade, reflecting the fact that his analytical priorities lay elsewhere, particularly with achieving full employment (Eichengreen 1984). In the *General Theory*, Keynes (1973) emphasizes the role of the balance of trade and the effect of this on money and interest. He explicitly recalls the earlier mercantilist tradition to argue that bringing money into the country stimulated economic activity. The relation is not a necessary one, in India an abundance of money failed to stimulate investment. However, in general, Keynes believes that 'a favourable balance, provided it is not too large, would prove extremely stimulating; whilst an unfavourable balance may soon produce a state of persistent depression' (1973: 338). He is cautious about practical policies, and agrees there are potential gains from an international division of labour 'even though the classical school greatly overstated them' (1973: 338). However, the importance of time and money undermined orthodox assumptions of equilibrium and a barter-like balance. Many later Keynesians advocated rather thorough-going industrial policy and economic planning. Trade policy was often subordinate to this but many of the Keynesian insights had implications for trade. The importance of economies of scale and of different 'production functions', different ways of producing similar goods in different countries, undermined the assumptions of comparative advantage (as discussed in the last chapter) and meant there was much that states could do to foster growth (Kaldor 1989).

The problems identified by Prebisch, Singer and others encouraged many poorer countries in their pursuit of industrialization in the post-World War II period. Prebisch himself became an influential figure as director of the UN Economic Commission for Latin America and subsequently secretary-general of the United Nations Conference on Trade and Development (UNCTAD). Many Latin American and Caribbean countries but also many newly independent states in Africa and Asia, including India, Ghana, Pakistan, Indonesia, Nigeria and Ethiopia adopted versions of what came to be called import substitution industrialization (ISI) (Stiglitz and Charlton 2005: 19). This could encompass a range of strategies and, it should be stressed, was never simply a general protection.

As will be discussed in Chapter 10, the ideas of ISI fell from favour after the Latin American debt crisis of the early 1980s. The contrasting success of the Asian 'Tigers' (South Korea, Taiwan, Singapore and Hong Kong) was held out as demonstrating that free trade represented a better option for poorer countries. What quickly became clear was that export-oriented industrialization, particularly as it was practiced in Korea and Taiwan, had little to do with free trade and looked much like ISI (Wade 1990; Amsden 1992). Prebisch's UNCTAD had after all included in its proposals 'a universal desire of increased exports (industrial ones in particular)' (cited in Brolin 2006: 106). State-led strategies had preceded opening, while the continued commitment to export promotion itself defied principles of free trade. If Hong Kong perhaps came reasonably close to the free trade ideal, the support and privileged access that all four of the Tigers enjoyed to US and Western markets as front-line states in the context of the Cold War also meant that they were unlikely to provide a model for others to follow. Again, the experience of successful Export-Oriented Industrialization confirmed rather than refuted the fundamental asymmetry of the global trading system.

Market imperfections and asymmetries continued to remain a source of conflict and contest, even as more and more countries became open to trade. While the success of the Tigers and subsequently of other countries, particularly in Asia, makes clear that increasing trade and economic development are perfectly compatible, critics could still identify many respects in which trade openness and free trade were not equivalents. It is impossible here to describe the many ways in which increasing trade involved what Weiss (1999) terms 'managed openness'. However, it is worth briefly noting a few elements: international organization, enduring interventions by nation states and the role of multinational corporations. All of this contrasts with notions of free trade and free markets based on price signals automatically adjusting supply and demand.

The World Trade Organization (WTO) has received most attention, as will be discussed in Chapter 10. It celebrates a fairly substantial reduction of tariff levels but continues to reinforce, even deepen, many asymmetries in the trading system. Large rich states can dominate the proceedings, from agenda setting to the dispute settlement mechanism and the ability to enforce sanctions. Among other things, poorer countries complain that the WTO fails to reduce rich-country support and protection of agriculture. The declared universalism of the WTO also sits uncomfortably with the numerous regional and preferential trade agreements; many of which have also been criticized as disadvantaging one or other of the participants. Smaller and poorer countries do not deal with the US as equals. The supra-national bodies like the WTO but also the IMF and World Bank add an extra layer of governance and constraint, rules which member countries are supposed to follow.

However, despite the WTO there are numerous things that states, particularly the more powerful ones, continue to do: imposing import quotas, currency manipulations, providing government support to local industry, encouraging popular support for local over foreign products, imposing customs regulations, and using health and safety regulations to restrict imports. On the other side of the coin, states also continue to promote exports, providing export subsidies, export credit guarantees, and legal and technical assistance. There are many reasons why states can and do still intervene in trade. All this contrasts with important arguments that states are losing power (Frieden 1991; Strange 1996) and acclamations of the triumph of liberalism and the free market (Friedman 2000).

If states have lost power it is primarily to giant corporations. The top 500 have been estimated as controlling 70 per cent of world trade and in some sectors a handful of firms could dominate almost completely (Sikka and Willmott 2010). Large proportions are conducted within corporations (Dicken 2003). Among other things, there is much scope here for firms to use 'transfer pricing' to manipulate the declared values of the goods they move across borders in order to reduce their tax liabilities. Shocking examples include toothbrushes sold at $5655 each, plastic buckets for $973, fence poles for $1854, apple juice at $2052 a litre, a pair of tweezers for $4896 and toilet paper at $4121 a kilo, and alternatively, prefabricated buildings at $1.20 and bulldozers at $383 each (Buckman 2005; Sikka and Willmott 2010). Many nominally market-based, intra-firm relations, are also pervaded with power, such as when particular goods production is outsourced to captive suppliers (Gereffi et al. 2005). An emerging school of value-chain analysis usefully maps the series of unequal trade relations involved in producing many commodities (Selwyn 2012). Corporate power goes beyond any ability to manipulate markets. Understandably, corporations lobby in their own interests and have influence within many states. At the very least, the resources spent on lobbying for sectional interests are a waste from a national perspective (Caves et al. 1993), but the outcomes seem eminently likely to drive national economies away from any theoretical ideal position of comparative advantage. Corporations are also effective lobbyists of international institutions, both directly and via their respective governments, notably in the way pharmaceutical companies achieved the WTO's understanding of intellectual property protection (Sell 2000).

In short, enduring asymmetries of wealth and power leave difficult questions about the basic premises of conventional trade theory and claims that voluntary opening implies that national economies will benefit. It is reasonable to assume that somebody was winning from the increases in trade but reasonable to ask, and often hard to theorize, just who that was.

NEW TRADE THEORY

The absence of genuinely free markets has been embraced by some modern trade theorists who show that countries can maximize their gains by policies other than free trade. Reinert and Reinert see the system of good and bad trade of the early English mercantilists as 'completely in line with Paul Krugman's trade theory ... based on increasing and diminishing returns' (2005: 13–14). While it is therefore easy to see NTT and particularly its strategic implications as modified versions of arguments about how rich countries can kick away the ladder, they represent a substantial theoretical improvement on the atemporal and aspatial world of the theory of comparative advantage.

As noted in the previous chapter, it has been widely remarked that neo-classical economics in general and the theory of comparative advantage in particular are essentially static. Ignoring time means that orthodox arguments overlook dynamic changes and that following current comparative advantage can therefore involve foregoing greater future gains.

Criticisms of the aspatial character of neo-classical economics tend to be less pronounced than those of its atemporality and Krugman is innovative in also pinning his trade theory onto a broader attempt to incorporate geography. What he says, at least in principle, initially applies as much within countries as between them. Krugman starts with geographical and temporal unevenness, noting and explaining local sites of particular industries. A longstanding geographical tradition has identified why localization should occur, pooling workers with specialist skills, providing non-traded inputs and technological spillovers (Krugman 1993: 50): 'Localization will tend to occur unless the cost of transporting intermediates are particularly *low* compared with those of transporting final goods.' Moreover, and in contrast to so much pop globalization theory, localization will tend to be deepened by improvements in transport and communication technologies as the gains from economies of scale from producing in one place outweigh the savings in producing near final markets. Krugman highlights how this creates the possibility of feedback or, after Myrdal, 'circular causation' (Krugman 1991). The concentration of industry tends to be self-sustaining (Krugman 1993). Even within countries, rather than there being a single set of factor endowments, population can 'start to concentrate and regions to diverge; once started, this process will feed on itself' (Krugman 1991: 487).

By incorporating economies of scale and how they bring efficiency gains, Krugman (1979, 1990) shows that it may make sense for countries with the same factor endowments to trade with each other. Rather than both of two countries having two small industries (say making both jam and marmalade) there are efficiency savings in having large-scale production with single industries (jam in one country and marmalade in the other). Helpman (1981: 306) extends these arguments emphasizing monopolistic competition: 'country size matters. Other things being equal, the larger country has a lower relative price for the good produced with economies of scale.'

The possibilities for large countries, in particular, to shift the character of their economies and the terms of trade in their favour are considerable (Krugman 1990: 3): 'It is possible (not certain) that such tools as export subsidies, temporary tariffs, and so on, may shift world specialization in a way that is favourable to the protecting nation.' The use of tariffs can then make rational the production of importable goods, which may lead to dynamic gains (Caves et al. 1993). One simple example is that by protecting domestic markets, the local firms' sales can be increased and those of foreign competitors decreased. The locals make efficiency gains and can then compete more effectively, abroad as well as at home (and the protections can be lifted). Import protection ends up as export promotion (Krugman 1989). Oligopolistic rivalry can also make sense wherever there are few firms in the market. 'Then reciprocal market invasions can represent threats and counter threats between rivals' (Caves et al. 1993: 188). Orthodoxy maintains that the 'world would be better off without monopolies, but most countries are happy to maximize their own incomes by using any monopoly power they may possess' (Caves et al. 1993: 241).

By the same token, if a country fails to innovate, it may lose its industry to a country that began with similar factor endowments. In a dynamic world it also becomes at least possible for a country to suffer an absolute as well as relative decline (Krugman 1990). Again, this is not fundamentally new. As the discussion in the last chapter established, for Graham in the inter-war period it was already clear that if assumptions of constant returns are dropped, there can be a decrease in welfare (Raffer 1987). Even mainstream textbooks can conclude that 'the analysis indicates that the importing country should probably consider restricting imports whose foreign suppliers possess monopoly power' (Caves et al.

1993: 246). However, NTT developed using the formal mathematical models of the mainstream, provided further reasons for expecting international trade to be uneven and contested and for expecting large, rich countries to do best.

DILEMMAS OF THE OFFICIAL OPPOSITION

Most of the perspectives discussed in this chapter might be described as the official opposition to free trade. They point out that free trade is not the norm in practice and that the theory of comparative advantage therefore provides an inadequate basis to support unqualified trade opening. The case is convincing. However, it can be seen as the 'official' opposition because, however discontent some of the contributors can sound, the apparent radicalism often collapses rather tamely.

One strand of argument, recognizing the structural asymmetries in the global economy and the unfree nature of trade in practice, sets as its objective the establishment of more symmetrical and freer practices. Birdsall warns against protectionism as a 'tempting and dangerous' remedy (1998: 84). Oxfam (2002) criticize the WTO and rich countries' hypocrisy for demanding poorer countries open their borders while allowing agricultural subsidies. They then demand restitution though genuinely free trade. This is broadly the argument that has been made by, or on behalf of, many poorer countries at the WTO. The enduring agricultural tariffs and agricultural subsidies of the rich world represent an unfair obstacle to poorer-countries' trading in precisely those goods where they have a comparative advantage. Such arguments converge with mainstream writers like Bhagwati (2005), who is critical of particular existing institutions but withering in his condemnation of opponents of comparative advantage. Even in the unlikely event of successful institutional reform, the underlying problems with the theory, addressed in the last chapter, and most of the asymmetries in the global economy, discussed in this, would remain in place.

The alternative horn of the dilemma, grasped most decisively in rich-country proponents of NTT, is that the asymmetries of the system should be embraced and applied to the theorist's own country's advantage. This has also been the essence of many of the poorer-country critics. Although they start from the position of 'follower' countries, they aspire to become like those they criticize. List is probably the most obvious example.

It was noted above that for List, his desire for Germany and perhaps other European countries to catch up did not extend to the 'barbarian' peoples, whose colonization he supported. Marx is withering in his scorn; the German internationalist is perhaps particularly hostile to what he sees as a narrow German nationalism. Apart from accusing List of misrepresenting his intellectual foes (including Smith and Ricardo) and plagiarizing his predecessors (in particular the Napoleonic French writer Ferrier) Marx sees List as an 'idealizing philistine' (2006: 3; 15):

> What then does the German philistine want? He wants to be a bourgeois, an exploiter, inside the country, but he wants also not to be exploited outside the country. He puffs himself up into being the 'nation' in relation to foreign countries and says: I do not submit to the laws of competition; that is contrary to my national dignity; as a nation I am a being superior to huckstering ... Thus the German philistine wants the laws of competition, of exchange value, of huckstering to lose their power at the frontier barriers of his country!

Marx thought it impossible for Germans to free themselves from English domination abroad unless they also freed themselves from the domination of industry and competition at home. The young Marx still remains very respectful of classical political economy and, it would transpire, he greatly underestimated the potential for German national development. His fundamental critique of the strategies nevertheless retains considerable power (Marx 2006: 10): '[The German] bourgeois now hopes to become rich mainly through "protective tariffs", and ... protective tariffs can enrich him only insofar as no longer Englishmen, but the German bourgeois himself, will *exploit* his *fellow-countrymen*, indeed exploit them even more than they were exploited from abroad.'

As above, the US and Germany succeeded on the basis of something less than free trade and they too then kicked away the ladder. Most poorer countries did not close the gap, let alone leapfrog the earliest industrializers. Capitalists within them could nevertheless continue to demand protection in the name of national interest. Arguments for such policies might then be better interpreted as supporting capitalists in developing countries rather than national, let alone universal, interests. List and many of his subsequent followers have been remarkably complacent about the state as the agent of effective reform (Selwyn 2009). State capacity and interests might both reasonably be questioned.

It may seem unduly harsh to include consistent critics like Singer in the same discussion. He should at least be absolved from narrowly championing the interests of his own country's rulers. However, the policies of ISI, which can reasonably claim to have taken inspiration from them, often involved rather brutal developmental practices. Amsden's (1992) work on Korea seems particularly useful here. It was less trade than the ability of the Korean dictatorship to impose extraordinarily long and harsh working conditions that was the fundamental basis of growth (see also Chang 2007). Of course, Korea had no monopoly on dictatorial governance and many other repressive regimes failed to grow. Extreme domestic exploitation is not a sufficient condition but may quite possibly be a necessary one. Such ideas found favour in a climate of anti-communism but they were also of a piece with broader strategies of national development which became pervasive and in which states claimed, and were too readily believed, to adequately represent 'the people'. In the context of the Cold War the export of Keynesian ideas has itself been interpreted as an achievement of US imperialism (Hirschman 1989).

For many states during the Cold War there was, of course, another attractive, state-centric developmental model. While Western capitalism suffered the Great Depression, Soviet Communism appeared to prosper, and then to see off Hitler's invasion, all with lower levels of trade. By the 1960s, it was not only self-proclaimed communist regimes like China and North Korea that had adopted five-year plans, but also countries as varied as Argentina, Ethiopia, India, Malaysia and South Korea. Few of these approached Stalin's USSR for brutality but they reflected the powerful appeal of state diktat as an effective alternative to markets and free trade as a means of achieving growth. Critics of international inequality and international asymmetries could often be remarkably nonchalant about inequalities at home.

Prebisch's career seems salutary. He first came to prominence as an economic advisor to the conservative Argentinean government of General Uriburu after 1930 before being converted to Keynesianism later in the decade. Despite the conversion, he was excluded from office in Argentina under Peron, returning only once Peron had been overthrown in 1955. Rather than boosting industry, the plan he then produced recommended price changes in favour of agricultural producers: 'Even General Aramburo did not dare execute the wage-reductions proposed by Prebisch' (Brolin 2006: 106). Brolin (2006) also suggests Prebisch's ideas were informed not just by the mercantilist tradition in general but by important figures like Manoïlescu and Sombert, who joined the Romanian Iron Guard and the German Nazi Party, respectively. Prebisch was hardly the uncompromising radical he is sometimes portrayed as.

This is not to suggest that repressive domestic policies are a necessary consequence of these criticisms of free trade. Indeed, Prebisch's arguments about low wages in poorer countries could be taken as a powerful argument for raising them. Keynesian accounts, like Singer's, stress the importance of developing domestic markets rather than exports and might well be taken to imply welfare-enhancing developmental strategies. The logic of NTT is similarly to expand domestic markets, although this might now mean increasing international inequalities. This simply re-iterates that there is nothing inherently radical or left wing in opposing free trade. It is at least as likely for regimes to pursue repressive domestic policies to achieve growth while restricting trade as while embracing it. Having recognized that the world does not trade freely, there is a real dilemma onto one of the other horns of which many critics fall; join with the orthodox chorus insisting that it should trade freely, or try to position one's own country (and one's own rulers) in the best exploitative position.

CONCLUSION

At their best, the criticisms of free trade discussed here take us away from the narrowest dualism, refusing to accept the simple antinomies for or against trade. For the mercantilists and many who followed, it was industrialization that mattered and trade policies flowed from this, rather than the other way round. Successful industrialization had historically been achieved by countries with selectively high trade barriers and there were good reasons for expecting this, and for free trade to exacerbate patterns of international inequality. Prebsich and Singer similarly high-light important ways in which poorer countries or those exporting primary products might be disadvantaged. As later chapters will discuss, the evidence is often rather mixed but there are good reasons for expecting markets to be imperfect and outcomes to diverge from the happy picture of mutual gains predicted by the theory of comparative advantage. New Trade Theory indeed makes it clear that restrictions of trade can also be used by large and powerful countries to enhance their position. Neither free trade nor opposition to it is inherently egalitarian. Inequalities in the international trade regime also hang on questions, typically hidden by mainstream accounts, questions of money, investment and capital mobility. History and geography matter. Some of these insights are developed further in the more radical critiques discussed in the next chapter, some of which also struggle to shake off the limitations of the national perspectives and the unsatisfactory opposition of states against market.

5. Marxism, trade and the limits of radical nationalism

INTRODUCTION

This chapter considers a range of broadly Marxist perspectives on trade. This book is informed by Marxism and sympathetic to an understanding of trade as inextricably linked to questions of power and exploitation. However, there are significant problems with some of the most influential accounts, beyond which a properly critical political economy therefore needs to go.

The next section briefly discusses Marx. Trade relations could be important for Marx but, at least methodologically, they played a subordinate part in his analysis of capitalism. The following section discusses Marxist theories of imperialism as they were developed in the early years of the twentieth century. These early theories had the great merit of applying Marxist ideas to the concrete questions of their day but leave unresolved problems and followers have subsequently seized on some of their weaker points. The chapter then discusses the theory of unequal exchange (UE), particularly as it was articulated by Emmanuel (1972). This postulates a systematic transfer of value, impoverishing the periphery and enriching the core. Emmanuel sees the process driven primarily by higher wages in the core and higher exploitation in the periphery. The penultimate section considers broader ideas of dependency and world-systems theory (WST), which incorporate UE into a bolder and historically richer understanding of global capitalist development in which the power of core states play a vital causal role.

The final section develops some criticisms, mainly 'internal' Marxist criticisms. It is argued in particular that unequal exchanges are entirely possible, even likely, but they inadequately explain international inequalities and that claims for the extraordinary power of labour are implausible. This weakens WST, which also leaves the power of nation states substantially unexplained. The theories too often imply a structural determinism and exaggerate the role of trade in explaining the wealth and poverty either of nations or within nations. Critical trade theory needs a deeper engagement with, and integration into, a more general analysis of capitalism and its changing and contradictory dynamics. Without addition, ideas like UE provide interesting hypotheses but not general truths.

MARX'S METHOD AND THE INTERNATIONAL ECONOMY

Marx says relatively little about trade. His best-known comments come from an 1848 speech. He is withering towards crude enthusiasts (Marx 1977: 269): 'If the free-traders cannot understand how one nation can grow rich at the expense of another, we need not wonder, since these same gentlemen also refuse to understand how within one country one class can enrich itself at the expense of another.'

Marx is bitterly hostile to Britain's imposition of the opium trade on China and of slavery and the slave trade. The cotton factories of Manchester hung not just on the destruction of local textile manufactures in India but on the import of slave-produced cotton. Engels also notes the hypocrisy of Britain's rise to industrial and free trade pre-eminence. Tariff protection, the wars against the French Revolution, English men-of-war, the secession of South American colonies and the conquest of its own empire helped secure England's monopoly. 'England thus supplemented the protection she practiced at home, by the Free Trade she forced upon her possible customers abroad' (Engels n.d.: 233). All this anticipates many of the criticisms discussed in the previous chapter.

However, Marx remains a qualified supporter of free trade, reserving a particular scorn for the intellect and politics of List. He sees the protecting system as conservative and free trade as destructive but in the positive sense of breaking down nationalism and hastening social revolution (Marx 1977: 270). However, Marx never provides a definitive theoretical statement on trade and says little enough that he can be claimed by both supporters and trenchant critics. Marx's relative neglect can be read as a reflection of the times in which he wrote. Trade had ceased to be a source of major social and political controversy in Europe after the British Corn Laws were repealed until Germany's retreat from openness in 1879, shortly before Marx's death.

There are also methodological reasons for Marx's relative taciturnity. His discussion of the method of political economy in the *Grundrisse* (1973: 108) posits an 'obvious' ordering of the levels of analysis:

> (1) the general, abstract determinants which obtain in more or less all forms of society … (2) The categories which make up the inner structure of bourgeois society and on which the fundamental classes rise. Capital, wage

labour, landed property. Their interrelation ... (3) Concentration of bourgeois society in the form of the state ... (4) The international relation of production. International division of labour. International exchange. Export and import. Rates of exchange. (5) The world market and crises.

This is not the place for an extended discussion of Marx's method. The schema above was a 'back-of-the-envelope' formulation (Rosenberg 2008) in what were unpublished manuscripts. *Capital* remained incomplete at Marx's death. Despite some controversy (Lapides 1992), it never systematically ventures beyond the second analytical level (Rosdolsky 1977). It makes scattered references to trade but essentially treats the world as one giant, national economy. The anticipated further volumes on the state and, most relevant here, those on trade and international relations and on the world market and crises remained unwritten.

THEORIES OF IMPERIALISM

The analyses of imperialism that were developed in the early years of the twentieth century have the great merit from a Marxist perspective of applying a general analysis of capitalism to new specific circumstances. This generation of Marxists could not ignore capitalism's international dimensions as the colonial projects and inter-imperialist competition intensified. The early theories broadly see imperialism as flowing from capitalism's expansionary dynamic, described by Marx and Engels (1965: 37): 'The need of a constantly expanding market for its products chases the bourgeoisie over the whole surface of the globe. It must nestle everywhere, settle everywhere, establish connections everywhere.'

They were explaining a new era of colonial rivalry and conquest, although formally independent countries could be understood under the same rubric. Much of South America, for example, was seen as an informal colony of Britain. Without attempting a systematic review (see Brewer 1990; Callinicos 2009) there were important variations on the theme, and importantly for the discussion here, significant differences in the roles ascribed to trade.

Luxemburg (1963) develops what is often called an under-consumptionist reading of accumulation. Capital's extraction of profits and drive to accumulate constantly confronts a limited demand, precisely because that same exploitation limits workers' wages. The only solution was to find markets outside capitalism. With productivity increasing but purchasing power at home limited, at least for most of the population, 'every foreign market opened defers the social problem' (Luxemburg

1963: 246). For Luxemburg, as for later theorists, notably Wallerstein (1974), this need to continually draw on an 'outside' is an inherent feature and limit of capitalism. What Brewer (1990) terms a second line of argument, in tension with the first, also saw imperialist rivals drawn into struggle for cheaper labour and raw materials.

This second line of argument was developed by Luxemburg's contemporaries. Hilferding, Lenin and Bukharin attach particular significance to the development of a new stage of capitalism dominated by monopoly. Of particular interest here, Hilferding (1981) identifies how monopolies support protective tariffs, allowing them to increase prices in their home markets. With the domestic market cornered, increased output and economies of scale allow them to produce more cheaply and sell profitably, even if cheaply, into foreign markets. The potential was greater for monopolies with large home markets than for those in small countries, which therefore tended to be free-trading (Brewer 1990). Hilferding supports free trade and opposes these policies but it is notable how his ideas anticipate key discoveries of New Trade Theory (NTT) discussed in the previous chapter.

Building on Hilferding, Bukharin (1972) identifies apparently contradictory processes of internationalization and nationalization as the expansionary drivers. Again, the theory stresses the development of monopolistic cartels, combining industrial and financial capital. They come to dominate national economies, within which they overcome competition, and drive expansionary state policy, carving up the world into rival blocs. This depiction of giant trust formation was probably always more accurate for Germany than for the major imperialist powers, Britain and France, but it plausibly links changes in state policy with the transformation of economic interests (Brewer 1990). Trade itself plays little role for Bukharin, although he stresses the importance of imports of raw materials and food. As with some later Marxist theories of imperialism, the qualitative importance of particular imports escape quantitative measures (Magdoff 1969).

Lenin's (1975) analysis of imperialism, drawing heavily on that of the liberal (proto-Keynesian) Hobson, again describes the limits of domestic demand but also an increasing unwillingness of capitalists to invest within their domestic economies. Within Britain, monopoly increased the profit share and concentrated it in fewer hands (Hobson 2007). This led to a vicious cycle of increased saving, limited domestic investment, exacerbating a lack of demand and increased saving. From this stemmed the 'economic tap root of imperialism'. Capital export was the only outlet. Hobson opposes this as bad for democracy, bad for the colonized people and bad for Britain's reputation. Despite being against the national interest, elite groups, particularly in finance, benefited and were in positions of power to influence the state and popular opinion. Hobson nevertheless remains optimistic that the narrow interests of particular capitalists could be overcome, with redistribution increasing home markets and national economic growth. Lenin is more sanguine about the prospects for reform, expecting states to continue to back their capitalists. This fed the ultimately devastating drive to carve up the world and finally towards war. Lenin (1975) identifies specific advantages derived from trade, particularly cheap raw materials, but, following Hobson, it is capital export that is most important. The idea that capital continually needs to dispose of a surplus, either of goods or capital, would later also be crucial to ideas of monopoly capitalism (Baran 1957; Baran and Sweezy 1968) and, drawing on them, for Amin's (1974) interpretation of unequal trading relations. The relationship between the imperial powers and their colonies was clearly exploitative and Lenin rejects the qualified support that Marx offered to free trade; although he continues to believe that imperialism brought development and ultimately grounds for socialist revolution even in the colonized areas.

Significantly for what follows, Bukharin and Lenin also outline what they see as the consequences within the major imperialist powers. They are retrospectively explaining the outbreak of World War I but also accounting for the acquiescence of the social democratic parties in the leading countries. Bukharin finds in the state capitalist trusts and their exploitation of colonial workers a rational basis for 'a momentary interlinking of the interests of capital and labour' (1972: 163). Lenin (1975) also thinks that gains from empire provide crumbs which buy-off sections of the labour aristocracy within the metropolitan countries, giving them an interest in national imperial expansion rather than proletarian internationalism. This idea is problematic. Imperialism is simultaneously generated by limited demand, itself substantially caused by low wages, but is then the cause of wage rises.

An almost diametrically opposite Marxist reading of imperialism sees it as predicated on the tendency of the rate of profit to fall and capital's need to offset this. There is not too much profit, and the need to squander it elsewhere, but too little. Marx does suggest that foreign trade can counteract such a tendency (1981: 344–7). Amin later invokes such a law, even asserting its compatibility with the Luxemburg and monopoly capital theses of rising surpluses, indeed seeing them as expressions of the same thing (1974: 590). The interpretation of Marx's 'law' is much contested and beyond the scope of the discussion here (see Fine and Harris 1979). However, a 'softer' version of this thesis that the search for profits underpinned imperialism, seems altogether plausible. A stress on profits removes the apparent teleology and functionalism of under-consumptionist interpretations and a specifically Marxist understanding of imperialism would not need a claim that capitalism could not survive without imperialism, only that the interests of capitalists in leading states pushed them in pursuit of profits wherever they could be found, including into previously unconquered territories and into competition for those territories already captured by others (Brewer 1990).

The effects of imperialism on both the metropolitan powers and the colonies were sufficiently ambiguous to leave room for controversy. Imperialism exploited the colonies but also led to 'development' of a sort, as it spread capitalist accumulation. Imperialism in general and trade in particular were clearly important to Britain in its dynamic industrializing age and beyond (Hobsbawm 1969). However, as seen in Chapter 2, other countries traded less and European trade with colonies in Africa and Asia was a small part of the total in the early twentieth century. After World War II, many former colonies won independence with the US, encouraging decolonization. Capitalism would thrive despite the retreat from empire. However, it soon became apparent that some similar economic relations remained fundamentally in place. Economic integration was still pervaded with relations of power. An 'imperialism of free trade' (Gallagher and Robinson 1953) could continue with fewer gunboats and occupying armies.

The early Marxist theories of imperialism usefully attempted to apply a Marxist analysis to their changing world. They anticipate key claims made by later theorists of dependency and unequal exchange; of capitals' need to draw on an outside, the importance of monopoly forms and the opposed interests of workers in the core and periphery. But if they provided imperfect theorizations of the early twentieth century, their insights should be applied to a different world with even greater caution.

UNEQUAL EXCHANGE

According to Frank, Emmanuel produced the 'first serious and path-breaking analysis of unequal exchange ... which advances an alternative to, rather than merely criticises, the 150-year-old Ricardian theory of comparative advantage' (1978: 105). Many antecedents for the theory of UE have been claimed, from the physiocrats and early mercantilists (Brolin 2006). Emmanuel himself acknowledges debts both to earlier Marxists and to Prebisch. Much of his argument stems from the rejection of two simple premises made by Ricardo.

First, as seen in Chapter 3, Ricardo's theory assumes that the factors of production are immobile between countries. Emmanuel insists this is invalid for capital but that it does hold for labour. Capital mobility then means that rates of profit tend to equalize between countries in the same way they do within them, while there is no such equalization in rates of wages and exploitation.

Second, there is no reason to assume that workers are paid subsistence wages. For Emmanuel, workers' organization in rich countries and relative wage differences with the periphery then take on a central explanatory role. This has obvious debts to Prebisch, discussed in the last chapter, but where Prebisch depicts changing wages and terms of trade over time, in his still essentially neo-classical analysis, there cannot be an intrinsic inequality; 'fair' prices at one level, 'unfair' prices at another. Unequal exchange requires some underlying property whose exchange is unequal (Brolin 2006). Therefore, UE is more or less ruled out by definitional fiat in neo-classical economics and it is dismissed for the same reason even by radical Keynesians like Robinson. For Marxists, such an underlying property is available in the notion of value as a property more fundamental than price. Emmanuel himself becomes slightly ambiguous, accepting that the 'transformation problem' undermines Marx's arguments and switching to more orthodox interpretations of wages and productivity, even at one point arguing that 'I do not believe in absolute value' (Emmanuel 1972: 326). Others have developed theories of what they still term 'unequal exchange' without a labour theory of value (Sau 1978; Gibson 1980; Baiman 2006). However, without value or some equivalent criterion, the concept quickly loses its distinct critical purchase. If there is only price, what you pay is what you get. Unequal exchange requires at least some underlying measure and what follows stays close to Marx's categories.

Early versions of UE were developed by the 'Austro-Marxists' Bauer and Grossman in the early twentieth century and based on variations of the organic composition of capital (OCC) (Emmanuel 1972; Sau 1978; Brolin 2006). These depict UE in a 'broad sense' as a consequence of what Marx sees as normal processes within a capitalist economy. Only labour produces exchangeable value and surplus value. However, competition means that there is a redistribution of the social surplus. So if rates of profits are to be the same, a capitalist sector spending proportionately more on constant capital (c), machinery and raw materials and so on, than on wages or 'variable capital' (v), receives part of the value formed elsewhere. Economic sectors with a low OCC transfer value to those with a higher OCC. For example, Table 5.1 shows a simple two-sector economy. In the first sector 120 (say $120 thousand) of constant capital is spent or 'transferred' to the finished product in a given period, and 40 is spent on wages. In the second sector, less (just 60) is spent on constant capital for the same wage bill. Rates of exploitation are assumed to be the same because we have free labour where workers can move from one job to another. Therefore, in both sectors, 40 of necessary labour produces the same quantity of surplus value (s), again say 40. However, inter-capitalist competition means that there is a tendency for rates of profit, the amount actually received relative to costs, to be equalized. Capitalists are rewarded not according to the amount of value produced by their own (workers') activities but take their 'fair share' of the value produced over the whole economy. So the total of 340 in this example is distributed in the ratio 160 to 100. The products sell not at their values but at the prices indicated. So, in this example, a value of 9 is transferred from the lower to the higher organic composition department. With some reasonably plausible assumptions about the nature of agricultural production compared with manufacturing, assumptions that Marx (1981) indeed makes in his discussion of rent, this presents us with a first version of UE. According to Bauer: 'The capitalists of the more highly developed region thus do not only exploit their own workers, but also always appropriate a part of the surplus value that has been produced in the less developed region' (cited in Brolin 2006: 55). This has important political consequences. It explains how, within the Austro-Hungarian Empire, a poorer, more agricultural, Czech region opposed German domination and why German workers opposed Czech migrants to German (Bohemian) towns. So, as it would later for Emmanuel, the theory provides a rational basis for workers' chauvinism (Brolin 2006).

Table 5.1   Unequal exchange in a broad sense

	c	v	c + v	s	Total value	Total price	Profit	Value 'unequally exchanged'
I	120	40	160	40	200	209	49	+9
II	60	40	100	40	140	131	31	−9
					340			

It is worth cautioning that the assumptions of different capital compositions may be plausible but they are not obviously or universally true. Modern agriculture can be very capital intensive. Primary production more generally, notably in mining and oil extraction, can undoubtedly be highly capital intensive, even 'ultramodern' and highly productive (Amin

1974: 57). As suggested at the outset, this transfer of value is also seen by Marxists as a general feature of capitalism, occurring between all economic sectors. There is indeed no reason to imagine flows of value stopping at national borders but this would be as part of a constant swirl between sectors and regions.

Emmanuel discusses this first or 'broad' meaning of UE and continues to maintain that 'non equivalence in the strict sense, is characterized by differences in both wages and organic composition' (Emmanuel 1972: 160). However, Emmanuel's subsequent 'narrow' argument based on wages is substantially different and discrete. It is worth emphasizing that within a Marxist framework, exploitation has a specific meaning in terms of the rate of surplus to necessary labour time, so the manifestly worse conditions in poorer countries do not in themselves mean greater exploitation. Unlike Ricardo, Marx is clear that wages need not be at a subsistence minimum. They are socially determined. However, Marx usually assumes that workers are paid the value of their labour power. The 'trick' of capitalist exploitation is that while paying the full value for labour power, hidden processes of exploitation in production make workers work longer and harder than is necessary to just reproduce that value. In *Capital*, Marx broadly analyses the economy as if it were a single country so that rates of exploitation would be the same everywhere within it. Emmanuel quotes Marx, saying that 'in a given country, at a given period, the average quantity of the means of subsistence necessary for the worker is also given' (1972: 91). However, the level of exploitation is not constant over time and not predetermined. For Emmanuel, once labour is immobile between countries, we should expect international variation. Wages are higher and exploitation is less in the developed countries and this becomes the crucial, independent, variable.

Rates of surplus value between countries are 'institutionally' different (Emmanuel 1972: 64). There is some precedent for this in Marx and a short chapter (22) in volume I of *Capital* on 'National Differences in Wages' (Marx 1976). In any case, Emmanuel (1972: 49) notes that workers in the core have won high wages while those in the periphery have not: '[W]e can date the beginning of this differentiation from the beginning of large-scale trade-union struggle in the industrialized countries, that is roughly, from the 1860s.' Emmanuel dates the immobility of labour somewhat later (1972: 46): 'From 1850 to 1914 ... workers were [broadly] free to move about the world.' Outside its European heartlands, in the US, and to a lesser extent Australia, the availability of land provided an outlet for settlers, which allowed them to avoid low-paid wage-labour through independent farming. Elsewhere, peripheral wages were low because of the original standards of living of the immigrants, and kept that way through the transplant of 'clerico-feudal structures'. Again, in contrast to the US and Australia, wage competition was also greater because of the survival of the native populations. Part of the costs of reproduction was covered by the family or clan, involving a transfer of value from the 'non-economy' to the economic or productive sphere (Raffer 1987; Brolin 2006). Labour's immobility means that wages diverge between countries (Emmanuel 1972). Firms in high-income countries can pass on the costs, as higher prices, to low-wage importing countries. Meanwhile, the value produced in low-wage economies flows to high-income importers. Unlike labour, capital is now unconstrained: 'If it were, the comparative-costs theorem would rule, but given international mobility of capital this theorem can no longer be applied' (Raffer 1987: 31).

On this basis Emmanuel posits wages as the primary cause of the differences as between 'a certain category of countries' (1972: xxxi, 47). Unequal exchange can be measured as the difference between the prices of goods and what they would be, given equal wages. This is not an argument about the types of products, whether they are manufactured or primary. Emmanuel notes that Canada, Sweden, Denmark, New Zealand and Australia all export primary products successfully. Meanwhile (taking what now look like less satisfying examples, given that for Emmanuel low wages preclude development), Spain, Italy and Japan are poor but industrialized countries (Emmanuel 1972). Emmanuel also makes a much bigger claim for the importance of UE. Although it does not explain all the differences between rich and poor countries, 'unequal exchange is the elementary transfer mechanism ... that sets in motion all the other mechanisms of exploitation and fully explains the way that wealth is distributed' (Emmanuel 1972: 265).

Table 5.2, depicting two countries or regions rather than industrial sectors, shows how the transfers might work. (The numbers are not those of Emmanuel, who also has a rather idiosyncratic understanding of constant capital and the presentation is instead conceptually close to Amin [1974, 1976].) In each country, the production process involves the same amount of capital and number of workers. The only difference is that the ratio of paid to unpaid labour, or of wages to surplus value, is higher in I than in II. By assumption, the rates of profit will be equal, and for this to occur, value is transferred from II to I (that is, from the lower to the higher wage location). The first scenario shows a value of 27 being transferred. Profits in I are now 67, but just 53 in II. The second scenario shows that the more wages rise in the core, the more value is transferred and that is it perfectly possible for no (or even negative) levels of surplus to be produced in the core but for equal rates of profits to be received once value is transferred to the higher-wage location.

Table 5.2   Unequal exchange in a narrow sense

	c	v	c + v	s	Total value	Total price	Profit	Value 'unequally exchanged'
Scenario 1								
I	120	80	200	40	240	267	67	+27
II	120	40	160	80	240	213	53	−27
					480			
Scenario 2								
I	120	120	240	0	240	288	48	+48
II	120	40	160	80	240	192	32	−48
					480			

This soon has repercussions for capital investment: 'Capital is not attracted by a low level, like the liquid in communicating vessels, but is, on the contrary, sucked up by a siphon effect, towards active markets and high levels of consumption' (Emmanuel, cited in Brolin 2006: 215). In the core, high wages become an incentive not a barrier to growth: '*No capitalist country has ever become poorer by having spent too much*' (Emmanuel 1972: 338). Therefore, once established, the 'superprofits from unequal exchange ensures a faster rate of growth' (Emmanuel 1972: 130). High wages encourage investment, increasing the organic composition of capital and expanding the market (Raffer 1987).

In poor countries, narrow and stagnant markets discourage capital 'which flees from it, so that despite the low organic composition of capital and low wages, a substantial proportion of the force is unable to find employment' (Emmanuel 1972: 136). Highly skilled labour, in particular, is displaced. The lack of attractive investment opportunities due to low wages also then means the social surplus is wasted on luxuries or invested abroad. If anything, the presence of foreign multinationals ameliorates the process, for example, oil company rents prevent the price of oil falling as far as it would if the industry were nationalized but in both core and periphery a self-sustaining logic predominates (Emmanuel 1972).

Emmanuel anticipates two lines of criticism. First, labour productivity can vary between countries so it is not absolute wages that matter but wages in relation to productivity. He acknowledges that 'the difference in productivity can for a certain time make up for the difference in wage levels' (Emmanuel 1972: 136). Emmanuel thinks this unusual and contrasts building workers in New York and Lebanon, doing similar work but with 30-fold wage differentials (Emmanuel 1972). It is a slightly unfortunate example because the products of building labour are not traded. The higher costs of non-traded goods also means that the relative nominal wage differences between the core and periphery are considerably less than those in real terms (Brewer 1990). However, for Emmanuel, the significance of relative productivity differences and the possibility of testing them is dismissed precisely because specialization means that country groups do not export the same products. It is certainly possible for productivity differentials to exceed wage differentials and it seems likely that in many cases they will do so by considerable margins. Indeed, for Emmanuel it is typically the poorer countries that have the greatest productivity advantages; for example, producing coffee, sugar, oil or exotic fruit, which would be very hard to produce in the temperate climates of most industrialized countries. In contrast, machinery, hardware and cars can relatively easily be transferred and productivity differences are quite small (Emmanuel 1972).

Second, not every rich country built empires or established extensive trading relations with poorer countries. However, 'the industrial countries that lacked colonies did not suffer from these. Either by direct trade in the margins left by these discriminatory measures or by the system of communicating vessels [between rich countries] each of them got its share in the world-wide unequal exchange' (Emmanuel 1972: 187). And if the association between levels of trade and rates of growth appears poor, the low levels measured in price terms are misleading, the point is precisely that the rich countries are getting something for nothing (Emmanuel 1972: 338).

Emmanuel's ambition is considerable. Suspicions of conceptual overreach are hard to avoid and some theoretical and empirical problems will be discussed below, while later chapters consider recent evidence. However, Emmanuel is surely right that wages cannot simply be assumed equal to value and that unequal exchange between countries on that basis is a real possibility.

WORLD-SYSTEMS THEORY AND THE BROADER DEPENDENCY TRADITION

Unequal exchange was accepted, with more or less modification, by many scholars working within a broader dependency tradition. This is a rich school of thought that cannot be reviewed in detail here and what follows is restricted to a few comments on Frank, Wallerstein and Amin. These writers each make telling criticisms of both mainstream trade and development theory and provide much richer depictions of history and geographical interdependence.

The key proposition is that poorer countries cannot be understood in themselves, in states of backwardness, experiencing progressive stages of growth, but only in relation to the historical processes of imperialism and the world-economy. Frank is probably the central figure, although several of his insights are anticipated by others, notably by Baran (1957). Frank was prolific and his intellectual trajectory evolved. His core claim is that mainstream development theory misunderstood the relation between the poorer countries and the industrial world. Countries and societies were not simply 'traditional' and undeveloped, awaiting modernization according to the model of the early industrializers. Their 'backwardness' was the result of their relations with the core. 'Underdevelopment' had been developed by imperialism. Frank's (1970) account describes how each metropolitan country was able to exploit its colonies, and could play them off against each other, while each colony had only one colonial master from which it had to buy manufactured goods. As for Baran (1957), it was capitalism that obstructed peripheral growth. Development was blocked, and in some formulations blocked absolutely, precisely by integration into networks of international trade. Poorer countries did somewhat better when the chains of monopoly were loosened and trade declined, during the wars and the slumps of the developed world (Frank 1970).

Dependency theory is primarily an explanation of persistent national poverty but Frank also provides an account of the social structures within poorer countries. What might look like 'backward' feudal relations within poorer countries, notably on the big landed estates, or *latifundia*, in Latin America were themselves products of a capitalist economy. Such 'backward' feudal relations had not existed in pre-Colombian America. Parasitic (*comprador*) ruling classes, like the *latifundia* owners, benefit from the sale of primary products to rich countries and have no interest in strategies of national development. They therefore safely manage exploitation within their country on behalf of the core (which no longer requires troops on the ground). These local elites also use their export earnings to buy luxury goods rather than invest locally. The chains of monopoly power then extend within the peripheral countries from capitals to regions and within the regions from local capitals to their hinterlands. Every class is then exploited by the one above it, from the peasant to the metropolitan capitalist (Roxburgh 1979).

A stream of wealth flows upwards. This analysis has similarities with, and could draw upon, the ideas of Prebisch and Singer discussed in the last chapter. However, it was usually much more sceptical about the prospects for any technical fix for countries within what remained an exploitative world-economy. Some later theorists from within the dependency tradition would suggest there was more room for manoeuvre and for local struggles than this suggested (Cardoso and Faletto 1979). In later work, Frank himself acknowledged that the position of the core and periphery could shift. Subsequent events would prove that at least some poorer countries could both trade and grow rapidly and some of Frank's bolder generalizations are clearly misplaced. However, Frank and others were surely correct to identify structural impediments to development. Patterns of international inequality did intensify for most of the twentieth century.

Much of the dependency tradition came from South America and wrote about that continent but one of the most powerful contributions is Rodney's book on Africa. He makes a compelling case for the devastating effect of slavery and colonization but also of on-going exploitative trade and investment relations. He also makes an important claim that 'Africa helped to develop Western Europe in the same proportion as Western Europe helped to underdevelop Africa' (1974: 75). For Frank too, at least occasionally, 'most development of one group ... comes at the expense of anti-development for others' (cited in Leys 1996: 33–4).

Wallerstein's WST develops this argument about the mutual constitution of core wealth and peripheral poverty. Wallerstein again stresses that particular countries cannot be understood separately: the methodological starting point, at least, should be the world-system and relations of production of the whole. World-systems theory incorporates ideas of UE into a broad and historically rich account of the development of an international division of labour, informed also by earlier Marxist writings, dependency theory and the French *Annales* School of historiography. Wallerstein's initial texts have been followed by extensive further studies and have produced a whole school of WST analysis. Adopting a grand historical sweep that goes back to the crisis of European feudalism, Wallerstein describes how an international division of labour was established.

The sheer ambition almost inevitably leaves gaps, accentuated in any brief precis. However, first, Wallerstein (1974) finds the source of European development in the 'long' sixteenth century, redefined as from about 1450 to 1620 or 1640. Already, Western Europe's advance is explained in relation to the apparent regression of the second serfdom in Eastern Europe. These were part of a unified process of surplus appropriation in 'a capitalist world-economy' (1974: 37); the East producing grains which helped to feed (what would eventually be) an industrializing West. There is nothing given about the particular factor endowments or country niches. For Wallerstein, world economy means self-contained rather than global in this context but the establishment of a genuinely global world-system would begin with the Portuguese and Spanish conquests. By the eighteenth century, the Dutch had displaced the Spanish and Portuguese and become the first hegemonic power. In turn they were displaced by the British in the next century (Wallerstein 1974). Political power thus established an international division of labour and UE between the core and periphery.

The causal relations between political power, the division of labour, UE and growth are not always consistent. Wallerstein initially posits the capitalist world-economy as having three essential ingredients: geographic expansion, variegated methods of labour control for different products and zones, and relatively strong state machineries. Here, the territorial expansion is key, with the second and third 'dependent in large part on the success of the first' (1974: 38). There is a debt to Luxemburg, with the ongoing need to engage in 'primitive accumulation', to exploit previously uncommodified surpluses from the periphery, with the demise of the capitalist world-system inevitable once these are exhausted. Once established, Wallerstein also sees the different regions involved in different production processes with different capital intensities and like Emmanuel, trade impoverishes the periphery and enriches the core. 'After all, the secret of the success of the core areas of a world economy is that they exchange their manufactures for the raw materials of peripheral areas' (1974: 219). Unlike Emmanuel, Wallerstein depicts a 'seesaw between "nationalism" and "internationalism"' (1974: 225). Rather than high wages straightforwardly producing growth, he posits 'medium wages' in the core (and peripheral low wages) as optimal. If wages are too high they can eat into profits, if too low they can undermine markets. Britain, in particular, was characterized by the not too hot or too cold 'Goldilocks' type wage relations, enabling its unique growth (Goldfrank 2000). Wallerstein also introduces a semi-periphery into his schema. 'Rather conveniently' suggests Brewer (1990: 177), this semi-periphery serves a political role, engaging in sub-imperialist practices and obscuring peripheral interests in a more fundamental challenge to the core. Economically, it is also intermediate in terms of capital intensity and wages. For Wallerstein, core workers do benefit from the exploitation of the periphery but this is more the consequence than cause of UE. It is, for the most part, the relative coherence of strong, absolutist European states that allowed them to conquer and impose a new international division of labour on the rest of the world.

Amin's account is similar in many ways. It synthesizes ideas found in Emmanuel, Frank and the 'monopoly capital' tradition of Baran and Sweezy. Again, 'the movement is always centripetal, the transfer of value is always effected from the periphery towards the center ... it is not the advanced countries that supply capital to the underdeveloped ones but vice versa' (1974: 91, 136). Amin's timing is close to Emmanuel's but shifts the beginning of UE a little later, to the 1880s. Before this there was 'equal exchange': cheap British textiles, for example, could benefit importers (Amin 1974: 87). This better fits the empirical story of monopoly capital and the rise of unions. However, as would seem evident from the economic advantages already achieved before the late nineteenth century, the core's greater wealth is now primarily internally generated, not reduced to exploitation of the periphery and 'the higher levels of rewards for labor at the center is due *not mainly* to the exploitation of the periphery' (1974: 23). There is only a reciprocal relation between the development of productive forces and the level of wages (Amin 1974; Raffer 1987). This softens the anti-worker implications of peripheral exploitation, putting more blame onto the structures of monopoly capital. Ultimately, however, there is a similar antagonism and the 'revolt of the masses [in the periphery], the main revolt, entails in turn a necessary aggravation of the conditions of exploitation at the centre' (Amin 1974: 26).

THE LIMITS OF THE TRADE-BASED CRITIQUE

All the perspectives discussed above have the singular merit of pointing out that trade is pervaded with questions of inequality and power. They go further than most of the arguments discussed in the last chapter in seeing this as systemic, not as something likely to be reformed away without fundamental structural changes. Predictably, they have also been subject to a number of criticisms. Liberals, of course, object to the Marxist prejudices; all this forgets the mutual gains from trade and fundamental harmony of interests inherent in capitalism. Probably more telling, there have also been substantial criticisms from other critical scholars including several Marxists.

Marx's schema quoted above about an 'obvious' method of political economy has been too often forgotten by subsequent Marxists, happy to jump from Marx's *Capital* to any number of conclusions about the world market and crises, without reflecting on what he saw as essential intermediate levels. These included that of the 'international relation of production. International division of labour. International exchange. Export and import. Rates of exchange' (Marx 1973: 108). It is surely justified to discuss the specifics of trade, without imagining them determined by some more fundamental economic imperative. However, without wanting to fetishize Marx's method, it provides a convenient way of thinking about different aspects of trade theory, some of the lacunae and perhaps how a more thoroughly socialized account might be developed.

Marx's fifth stage of the world market and crises, in all its concreteness, is probably best left to a later stage and Chapter 10 of this book. It is Marx's fourth stage that directly impinges on questions of trade and suggests two lines of criticism, the first is an 'internal critique' concentrating on what these theories do say about trade, and the second is about how this is, or is not, connected to a broader understanding of society.

It seems entirely reasonable to insist that international relations are unequal and that large rich countries and rich-country multinationals have power and use it to exploit the less powerful. They use such power particularly to exploit the workers 'of the periphery more violently and brutally' (Amin 1974: 600). More technical questions of exploitation as a transfer of value are often hard to evaluate empirically. This is particularly so of UE. The whole point of value in a Marxist sense is that under capitalism it is hidden; it does not present itself immediately. As indicated above, Emmanuel is equivocal about Marxist value categories and others have articulated versions of unequal exchange in more conventional or 'neo-Ricardian' terms, understood as occurring wherever wage differences exceed those in productivity. Amin (1974) begins with Emmanuel but also defines UE simply in these terms. However, if wage differences exceed those in productivity it would imply that profit rates were higher in the periphery, violating Emmanuel's assumption. A further problem identified by Janvry and Kramer (1979) becomes acute. Unequal exchange cannot apply to commodities that are 'non-specific', made in both the core and periphery, because value is determined by socially necessary labour time and there is one society and one price. However, for specific commodities it is impossible to compare productivities.

It is easier to examine some of the implications than to search for flows of value. Frank, for example, clearly posits that greater integration into the world economy reduces growth. Emmanuel often implies something similar but this is undermined by his own assumptions because he begins by saying, against Ricardo, that rates of profit are equalized across regions. They are as high in the periphery as in the core. Of course, Emmanuel introduces auxiliary hypotheses why profits in the periphery are not invested productively but it is only such additions, not UE itself, which would explain the slower growth of poorer countries. It may also be the case, as Singer (1950) and many subsequent writers in the dependency tradition have stressed, that foreign-owned capital repatriates the profits. Amin (1974) makes much of this, depicting an inexorable flow from the underdeveloped to the developed. However, Emmanuel characterizes such movements as both recent and counter-intuitive, describing 'the recent and current phenomenon of migration of capital "in the wrong direction," that is from the backward countries to the advanced ones' (1972: 44). There is no suggestion that these capital flows date back, with UE and widening inequality, to the nineteenth century.

The simple core–periphery distinction also reduces the complexity of international relations, hugely downplaying competition between 'core' states. As often, Amin is particularly forthright, taking accumulation on a world scale to refer only to centre–periphery relations and identifying in the centre 'a process not yet ended, to form one single market, one single integrated economy' (1974: 175). Frank's claims of chains of colonial monopolies, whereby each colonial power had several competing satellites, seems plausible. And again in the post-World War II world, at least within its separate capitalist and communist halves, international competition was attenuated.

Rivalry varies in intensity. However, for much of the history of the last 500 years, hopes or expectations of the civilized, rich countries co-operating in the exploitation of the barbarian peoples, as List (1885) would have it, have been dashed. Meanwhile, the logic of UE suggests that wage differentials should produce similar effects between relatively rich countries. Emmanuel's (1972: 47) own tables show wages in the US exceeding those in its nearest rival, Britain, by a factor of nearly four. Suppose, meanwhile, they were 12 to 1 between the US and Brazil, then if America only conducts three times as much trade with Britain, it siphons off a similar amount of surplus from both countries. Trade between rich and (some) poorer countries exploded in recent decades but for much of the twentieth century, and especially when Emmanuel was writing, the overwhelming majority of trade was conducted within the core (even allowing for an unfair lowering of the prices of peripheral

exporters). Meanwhile, some peripheral nations have sold huge proportions of their commodity exports to a single imperialist or core country
but most have several competing suppliers and markets. Poorer countries
are surely often in a relatively weak position but this is typically a
question of degree. A theory purporting to explain the decisive mechanism of exploitation captures only one dimension of multi-faceted issues
of competition, cooperation and international inequality.

Both unequal exchange and WST depict an essentially static system of
exploitation where global structures constrain the units, typically nation
states. Inequalities seem destined to beget bigger inequalities, with the
peripheral countries tending to be seen as 'passive victims', their
development 'but a reflux of the expansion of the centre' (Forbes 1984:
71; Raffer 1987: 10). Combined but uneven development intrudes into
the historical accounts, but it has to be explained away in an essentially
ad hoc fashion (Skocpol 1977; Brewer 1990). Emmanuel acknowledges
that both Britain and Japan were somehow transformed from low- to
high-wage economies and that many poorer countries did industrialize,
but quite how remains a mystery.

This seems to be related to the tendency, most conspicuous in
Emmanuel, to present trade as something above and independent of other
social relations however much it then becomes the motive force of
broader change. For others too, there is a repeated emphasis on trade as
the 'crucial axis' and 'unequal exchange … as the central point around
which the dynamics of this latest phase of imperialism reveals itself' (Sau
1978: 44, vii). As above, Wallerstein does describe different modes of
labour control as crucial but then reinstates powerful states as the
determining factor, imposing social relations 'from above' as it were,
according to the needs of the world market. There are important
differences. The state is crucial for Wallerstein and WST. In both
Wallerstein and Amin there are formulations of mutual construction but
broadly it is state power that produced and reproduces the international
division of labour (Evans 1984). As seen in Chapter 2, there is considerable truth to the story of powerful states transforming international trade
but it is far from the whole truth. From the start, the coherence of the
Dutch and British states in their ability to forge global empires was also
predicated on the prior economic development and social transformations. The Dutch and British states were not obviously 'strong' states in
Wallerstein's sense and they themselves emerged from the semi-
periphery to hegemonic status. Apparently strong, absolutist states
(notably France) did not play quite the role expected of them while
others, like Spain, did so but then disappear from the historical narrative
(Skocpol 1977). As Evans writes, the 'imperialist states of the centre tend

to appear on the stage with little analysis of their relationship to the interests of either workers or capitalists' (Evans 1984: 214). States matter, often decisively, but they take a 'motley diversity of form' (Marx 1974: 355) and it is necessary to investigate rather than assume the sources of their social power.

States seem less prominent in Emmanuel, for whom labour's power is the explanatory variable, and the simple dichotomy between industrialized and underdeveloped is pervasive (Sheppard 2012). Both core and periphery remain internally rather homogeneous. Nevertheless, a methodological nationalism, while never directly defended, lies not far from the surface. Emmanuel is explicit that his 'subject' is exploitation of nation by nation not man by man (*sic*) (1972: 330). Rather like his (neo-)classical counterparts, Emmanuel depicts a radical difference between internal and external exchanges, simply envisaging a perfect market for capital transfers where Ricardo thought it restricted. Where the possibility of peripheral resistance peeks through, it too is focused on state intervention. Emmanuel begins with comments on the inevitability of UE unless it is broken by autarky. Later this dissolves into more modest reform strategies, 'a tax on exports can be a very useful device', product diversification can also be 'a very effective weapon' and there should be cooperation between poorer countries (Emmanuel 1972: 233, 268). In most of this theorizing we are then left with the state as a fact of life. An important one it no doubt is but a pervasive emphasis on the wealth of nations remains unchallenged, with the putative critics engaging with orthodoxy on its own terrain rather than fundamentally challenging it (Skocpol 1977). Whether radical or reformist, states appear as remarkably singular and coherent bodies.

Marx pinned his putative analysis of the state on that of capital and class struggle, severely relegated in most of the perspectives discussed above. He saw social relations of production as determinant, if only 'in the last instance', an unsatisfactory formulation that has provoked much controversy, but at the very least, it pays to think about the changing dynamics of class and capital accumulation and how they might impinge upon trade.

In one sense Emmanuel does just this, finding the key explanatory variable in wage rates and in doing so he draws on Marx's discussion of value as socially constituted. The value of labour power is not condemned to a subsistence minimum. However, Emmanuel makes clear that what is involved in relation to Marx's analysis is more a 'setting aside' in the sense of rejection than as deferral. As seen above, he depicts 'unequal exchange [a]s the elementary transfer mechanism' (1972: 265). The power of labour in Emmanuel becomes extraordinary. He 'knows only one monopoly: the "monopoly of trade unions" in the centre that can force wages up' (Raffer 1987: 35). Indeed 'progress and industrialization do not precede the increase in wages, but follow it' (Emmanuel 1972: 124). The emphasis firmly put on trade and on wage differences, Emmanuel says little about the subsequent history or changing forms of capitalist accumulation. Later, Emmanuel states that the two processes of wage and productivity rises 'are not independent but interact dialectically' (1972: 336). Elsewhere, with more than a hint of explanatory circularity, Emmanuel writes of 'a regular rhythm of augmenting wages, which [...] in turn, has been made possible by external resources originating in the exploitation of the Third World' (cited in Brolin 2006: 230). In general, however, and rather implausibly, high wages and labour's power provide the independent variable and capitalism's motive force.

Emmanuel is bitterly hostile to workers in the industrialized countries. At times this seems to overcome his analytical judgement, and he describes how in 'former times dockers went on strike precisely in order to prevent imperialist intervention. Today they stop strikes they have begun for other reasons in order to avoid embarrassing these interventions in any way' (Emmanuel 1972: 181). The passage accurately depicts the conservatism of US unions in the post-World War II period but by identifying the earlier internationalist struggles, precisely at the time of rising domestic wages, it undermines Emmanuel's own argument that this conservatism is based on economic self-interest. Indeed, 'hardly thirty years ago the title of "social patriot" was regarded as a serious insult by any militant worker' (Emmanuel 1972: 181). Wallerstein too is ultimately quite complacent about the condition of workers in rich countries. Indeed, wage labour is no problem at all (1974: 127): 'Free labour is the form of labour control used for skilled work in core countries whereas coerced labour is used for less skilled work in peripheral areas. The combination thereof is the essence of capitalism. When labour is everywhere free, we shall have socialism.' The irony with which Marx used the term 'free' labour seems completely lost (Banarji 2011).

Since wages are lower in the periphery and capital can move, it is hard to fathom why, for Emmanuel or Amin, there is not a rush to produce there. (Today's reader might answer that there is such a rush but this is recent and both authors observed net capital flows in the opposite direction.) 'The capitalists, who cannot be accused of not knowing how to do their sums, are not deceived: they know that, generally speaking, it is more profitable to exploit the proletarians of the industrialized countries than their brothers in the poor countries' (Bettelheim 1972: 302). Workers won concessions in the US and many parts of Western Europe but often only after ferocious battles, which become hard to comprehend from capital's perspective if wages have no impact on profits. Raffer asks (1987: 131): 'Would it help peripheral workers if metropolitan workers were paid less, say equal exchange wages? Obviously there would be little reason for capital to pass this value added share to periphery workers.' Conversely, southern – or peripheral – elites might be expected to promote higher wages to counteract UE. Were high wages the driving mechanism by which rich countries become rich, it would be hard to fathom either capitalist resistance to wage increases in the core or why peripheral ruling classes are not more tolerant of them (Raffer 1987).

Accumulation on a world scale is dynamic and changeable, within which it is hard, pace Amin, to ignore the processes within core economies. By the 1960s, when Emmanuel was writing, there was something of a 'class compromise' in many leading countries, with real wages rising steadily and a reinforcing dynamic of capitalist investment and what Emmanuel saw as simultaneously rising organic compositions of capital and labour. But this hardly captures the turbulent history before (or since) or the substantial differences between core economies. If the power of labour seems exaggerated in these accounts, that of large corporations seems more plausible. It might then be possible for firms to pass on wage gains through monopoly pricing. That they should do so seems at least implicit in the claims of Lenin and Bukharin through to those of Emmanuel and those who adopt his interpretation of unequal exchange. Hilferding (1981) makes the opposite claim: that one might instead expect larger firms to be in a stronger position to deal with troublesome workers (Brewer 1990). Foster and McCheseney (2012), while they embrace unequal exchange, measure the power of monopoly precisely by the falling shares of labour income in rich countries. The emphasis on monopoly power, in trade or within national economies, seems to lose sight of class struggle and inter-capitalist competition and thus much of capitalism's dynamism and its temporal and geographical unevenness.

The most fundamental point is probably that trade cannot explain growth. The theory of UE is precisely that, an idea of redistribution or 'zero sum game'. In itself, exchange adds nothing to global wealth (Heller 2011: 160). Whether we date the process from the sixteenth or nineteenth century, global wealth did increase, and dramatically. This is the substance of Brenner's (1977) influential characterization of Wallerstein's approach as 'neo-Smithian Marxism', because it shifts the emphasis from production to exchange relations. For many poorer countries, while the story of trade disadvantage seems plausible, there was growth, sometimes very rapid growth. Emmanuel acknowledges (1972: 375):

> A wave of industrialization in the Third World between 1920 and 1960, with quite remarkable annual growth rates, ranging from 6 to 10 percent of gross industrial production and from 5 to 8 percent of net industrial production – percentages that were higher than those prevailing in the advanced countries.

Meanwhile, as Amin is clear, trade-based exploitation simply cannot explain the vast accumulation of wealth in the core. Even with Wallerstein's dating the advent of the modern world-system as far back as the sixteenth century, there are indications that Western Europe had something of an economic lead. This was emphatic by 1860. Many previously uncommodified resources were looted from the periphery and incorporated into the capitalist economies but the idea that rich countries simply live off a vast pit of peripheral wealth is profoundly unconvincing.

Finally, critical trade theory seldom ventures far into broader social issues or the realm of what Marx's schema sees as features common to all societies (Sheppard 2012). It is at this level that important criticisms of trade become clear, which remain invisible if attention stays focused on the capitalist, money economy. Perhaps most obviously, capitalism is quite capable of destroying its own bases, as recent Marxist ecologists have tried to articulate through ideas like a 'metabolic rift' and 'second contradiction of capitalism' (Foster 2000; O'Connor 1988). Trade contributes directly to this, for example through pollution and species invasion, and indirectly as trade competition encourages environmental degradation and resource depletion (Conca 2000; David and Gollasch 2008; Keller et al. 2011). Although resource depletion might also be expected to have negative long-term consequences for measures like gross domestic profit (Bunker 1984), claims of ecological unequal exchange identify how resources are inadequately accounted by price signals (Hornborg 1998). Much else too, such as the transformation of gender relations and moves from subsistence and informal economies, is missed by conventional measures.

CONCLUSIONS

The various perspectives discussed in this chapter identify systematic inequalities and pervasive power relations in international trade. They are right to do so. They recognize particularly the persistent spatial inequalities and the historical construction of trading relationships, which fundamentally challenge simple liberal visions of harmony. They go further than most of the perspectives discussed in the last chapter, not seeing the problems simply as distortions or imperfections in markets but as fundamental and systemic.

However, there are still substantial difficulties. Much of the criticism involves engagement on the same terrain as orthodoxy, producing a parallel set of problems. Where for the mainstream, trade was all harmony, all is now systemic inequality. Theory is again couched at the level of international relations, with little attempt to problematize the international or the nation state. In Emmanuel, class struggle is the original sin but it disappears from the account and rising wages have no impact on profit rates, which just as in neo-classical orthodoxy become simply 'proportionate to capital invested' (Emmanuel 1972: 163). As with much of the dependency and WST literature, any subsequent social conflict within countries is downplayed by the explanatory emphasis attached to international relations and international inequality. Where links are made with broader issues of social relations, rather than integrating trade into a more fully socialized account, trade tends to be seen as determining these. The idea of unequal exchanges remains an important one worth investigating and the subsequent chapters will look at some recent evidence – but there are reasons to be cautious about trade theory claiming too much.

6. Evaluating trade and growth

INTRODUCTION

This chapter discusses the relationship between trade and growth. Its main purpose is to evaluate big claims made in the previous chapters, that trade is good for growth or that it is bad, at least for poorer countries or those selling primary products. It also considers country size, the role of trade balances and the implications of trading with different types of country.

It begins with a brief review of some recent literature on trade, trade barriers and growth. The chapter then reports the results of some tests, conducted primarily drawing on data from the World Bank (WB 2014), available on an annual basis from 1960. The tests broadly confirm that there are weak, positive associations between trade openness, and trade opening, and growth. There is some evidence for this in aggregate, for rich and poor countries and for large and small ones. The chapter finds little evidence that a positive trade balance was conducive to growth, indeed one of the more remarkable findings is that a trade deficit appears to be positively associated with both present and subsequent growth. There is also some indication, particularly in the 1970s, that a positive balance in primary products had a negative impact, as various theories discussed in Chapter 4 anticipated, but this is not confirmed with any level of statistical confidence in subsequent decades. In the most recent decades, poorer countries, particularly in Asia, grew more quickly than rich ones. They did also trade extensively but there is little indication that this growth was itself based on trade. There is, however, some evidence that countries which traded more with poorer countries themselves grew faster.

ECONOMETRIC STUDIES LINK TRADE OPENNESS AND GROWTH

As seen in Chapter 3, there are powerful arguments why trade might foster growth. There are important counterclaims. Among other things, comparative advantage predicts rather small, one-off, gains. It would not account for any further growth after countries have specialized. The poorer-country perspectives discussed in Chapters 4 and 5 at least suggest distinguishing between countries and what is being traded.

Chapter 2 indicated that historically there is little correspondence between trade and growth. Perhaps most obviously, Germany and the US caught up and overtook Britain during the late nineteenth and early twentieth centuries, while heavily protectionist. Some authorities see this phenomenon as a more general one. Successful countries grow behind protectionist barriers and then try to kick away the ladder to prevent others using the same methods (Chang 2002; Jomo and Reinert 2005). Several countries that have had openness thrust upon them have performed poorly, from China in the nineteenth century to those suffering structural adjustment in the late twentieth century. Conversely, there are many success stories. In recent decades, several East Asian countries have opened to trade and grown very quickly. There is also a plausible claim that periods of relative openness, dominated by British and American 'hegemony' in the nineteenth and twentieth centuries, respectively, involved a freeing of trade, which was conducive to greater global prosperity. Between Britain's decline and America's assumption of this role after 1945, lay the dreadful interregnum of declining trade, the Great Depression and war (Kindleberger 1973; Gilpin 1987). It is, of course, treacherous to generalize from small samples or studies of individual countries but the American example is powerful. Winters writes that (2004: 6):

> Since the US growth rate has displayed no permanent changes over the period 1880–1987, one must conclude either that it cannot have been determined by factors that change substantially, such as trade policy or openness, or that changes in such factors have been just off-setting, which is not very credible.

Much recent research has involved larger-scale econometric tests. Most of the formal modelling reports a significant but usually small positive association between growth and greater trade openness, whether measured by trade ratios, tariff levels or other indicators of effective barriers like price distortions (Rodriguez and Rodrik 2000).

Levels of trade provide the most obvious indicator of a country's openness. There can seem to be something close to a consensus. Winters acknowledges some of the difficulties in definitely establishing any relation but maintains that the 'weight of evidence is quite clearly in that direction' (2004: 9). Many critics agree. Rodrik (2001), for example, broadly accepts that there is a positive association between growth and trade openness and thence also between growth and poverty reduction in poorer countries. Despite coming from a dependency perspective, the empirical work of Hall and Bass (2012) confirms that hypothesis.

A close reading can qualify some of the optimism. First, Rodrik (2001) sees the line of causation lying in the opposite direction. Richer countries tend to trade more. Some studies address this by looking at the timings of openness and growth and are still able to conclude that trade produces growth. However, the amount of extra growth is typically small. Rodrik reports some (predictably optimistic) World Bank forecasts of the gains from trade. These suggest that over a ten-year period to 2015 'developing countries stand to reap gains on the order of 1 percent of GDP (gross domestic profit), while developed country gains were substantially smaller' (Rodrik 2007: 16). Yanikkaya puts the figure a little higher, suggesting that 'a 10% increase in trade shares would increase the average growth rate of per capita GDP by 0.18% annually' (2003: 69). Such gains might be welcome but are small compared with established GDP growth rates. The stronger evidence is also of temporary rather than enduring impacts on growth (Winters 2004).

Some studies report much more substantial effects. Frankel and Romer (1999) again address the problems of causality, find no evidence that the positive association arises because countries that are richer engage in more trade and continue that 'increasing the trade to GDP ratio by one percentage point raises income per person by between one-half and two percent' (1999: 380-1). Unfortunately, they acknowledge that their results are 'only moderately statistically significant' (1999: 379). Dollar and Kraay (2004) also report strong effects. Importantly, their study controls for country population. Vast countries like China and India and their populations are more economically and socially significant than the numerous microstates often included in the samples, and it seems reasonable that the statistics should reflect this. However, this weighting means that a very small number of countries become responsible for the results. China and India undoubtedly both grew and became more open to trade but again the causal link becomes muddied. Rodrik (2001) emphasizes that in both countries trade followed reform and domestic growth. Such results therefore have to be interpreted very cautiously.

A parallel set of claims links the lowering of barriers to trade with greater growth. Here there are both conceptual and empirical problems. If, say, a country has few obvious barriers but actually trades little, it is hard to say whether it is really more open than one with more obvious obstacles but more trade. There are many barriers to trade, of which formal tariff duties are only one, while measuring anything else can be difficult. Sachs and Warner's (1995b) influential study categorizes countries as open or closed according to the level of formal tariffs but also non-tariff barriers and other indications of trade restrictiveness including state monopolies in export markets and black market premia. It finds the open countries grow much more quickly. Edwards (1998) surveys different methods and meanings of openness including subjective evaluations provided by the Heritage Foundation and the World Bank. Dollar (1992) uses indices of exchange rate distortion and variability. Both papers again clearly associate openness and growth. Wacziarg and Horn Welch (2008) revise and update Sachs and Warner's data and country classifications but support the original conclusions; finding that between 1970 and 1989 open countries grew by a remarkable 1.98 per cent a year more quickly than closed ones, although they also find that by the 1990s the relation no longer held.

Rodriguez and Rodrik's (2000) much-cited criticism of this literature unpicks some of the measures of openness being used. In trying to model the different dimensions in which trade is restricted, the focus shifts away from trade to other indicators only more or less related, including things like exchange rate policy but also geographical factors including location in sub-Saharan Africa (Rodrik 2001). Rodriguez and Rodrik argue that more straightforward indicators of tariff levels 'do a decent job of rank-ordering countries according to the restrictiveness of their trade regimes' (2000: 53). Looking just at tariff levels fails to show any relation with growth.

Yanikkaya goes further, arguing that although trade *volumes* had positive effects on growth, so too did trade barriers. Countries, particularly poorer countries, with higher tariffs and other barriers did better: 'a 10% increase in tariffs would increase the average growth rate of per capita GDP by 0.7% annually' (Yanikkaya 2003: 74). As discussed in Chapter 4, 'openness' and 'free trade' are not synonymous. Openness is 'managed', in Weiss's (1999) phrase. Countries might, for example, achieve high volumes of trade on the basis of industrial protection and export promotion rather than laissez-faire. Yanikkaya understands regional variation in this way. East Asian tariffs were higher than those among poor countries in the Americas and three times those in the OECD (Organisation for Economic Co-operation and Development), but trade volumes were higher. He concludes that 'while trade barriers have adverse effects on growth through reducing trade, they positively affect growth through superior resource allocation and/or positive externalities' (2003: 79). For example, revenue raised through tariffs can be used in redistribution or investment. Other studies produce more mixed results but there is 'at best a very complex and ambiguous relationship between trade restrictions and growth' (Yanikkaya 2003: 59). In this sense 'there is no convincing evidence that trade liberalization is predictably associated with subsequent economic growth' (Rodrik 2001: 6).

The rather inconclusive findings of the more thorough empirical studies do not necessarily temper what often remains an extraordinarily polarized debate. For that reason alone, it is worth repeating some simple tests. There are also several dimensions of trade, stressed by opponents, in terms of who is trading and what is traded, which are overlooked in much of the existing literature. Rodriguez and Rodrik end by suggesting the usefulness of looking at country differences, 'low- versus high-income', 'small versus large', with a comparative advantage in primary products versus those with comparative advantage in manufactured goods' (2000: 54). These issues are addressed below.

TESTING THE ASSOCIATION OF TRADE AND GROWTH

This section involves several simple econometric tests. The emphasis is on achieved levels of trade and in each case the dependent variable is the annual average growth rate, measured in terms of GDP, using constant 2005 $US. The discussions in Chapters 1 and 5 point to serious limitations of GDP as a measure of wealth and wellbeing but it is a readily available and useful economic indicator in terms of which of the existing debate continues to be conducted. The tests simply investigate whether different aspects of trade influence economic growth.

A few further words on the data are probably needed. The results are presented with statistical significance indicated throughout in the conventional way; three asterisks (***) marking 99 per cent confidence, two (**) 95 per cent and one (*) 90 per cent. It should be remembered that one series in ten would achieve the 90 per cent level quite randomly, which is therefore a very low threshold. For statistical purposes, natural logarithms of the values for trade to GDP ratios, population and GDP per capita are used throughout because the distributions of the simple numerical values (lower bound at zero) are highly skewed. Taking logged values substantially reduces or eliminates this. Unfortunately, logging makes the numerical results harder to read. For example, because the natural log of 2.72 is one, the value of 0.61 for the 1960s in Table 6.1 implies that annual GDP growth was 0.61 per cent greater for each 2.72-fold increase in trade openness. For example, countries with a trade to GDP ratio of 10, on average grew 0.61 per cent a year more slowly than those with a trade to GDP ratio of 27.2, which in turn grew 0.61 per cent a year more slowly than ones whose openness was 73.9. It will be seen that there is some indication of a positive association between trade and growth but it is weak and the effects of trade on growth are low. The vast majority of the R^2 (measuring the overall association or how much of the growth is 'explained' by these variables) in most of the series is produced by the variables controlling for specific country characteristics rather than by trade.

The first set of tests (M6.1) involves simple evaluations of the relationship between trade openness and growth. Trade is measured as the sum of exports plus imports to GDP. Growth is then measured as an annual average over the subsequent decade. (Other growth periods were considered but did not produce stronger results.) The tests control for country population and relative wealth measured as GDP per capita. These controls are needed particularly because larger countries tend to have lower levels of international trade and might be thought less reliant upon it, with more domestic resources or higher levels of 'internal trade'. As stressed by the New Trade Theories discussed in Chapter 4, size can also afford advantages particularly through economies of scale. Dummy variables are also included for the poorer-country regions of Africa, the Americas and Asia and, for the decade 2000–10, Eastern Europe and the former USSR (that is to say each country is coded as 1 or 0 according to whether or not they are in the region). Previous studies have shown that regional characteristics are very different and potentially influence such tests substantially. Only countries with a population greater than one million are included in the sample. This is done for consistency with what follows. The effects of country population and of trade on these small countries are also explicitly considered below. Here, the presence of the microstates does not greatly alter the results but it does when considering trade balances. The availability of data increases over the decades, so this is not a constant sample and it becomes less heavily biased towards richer countries over time. The first rows of Table 6.1 summarize the results.

In the 1960s and 1970s there are positive associations between trade openness and growth, although they achieve statistical significance only at the weakest 90 per cent confidence level. Subsequently, there is no evidence of a statistically significant relation and the signs are negative in the 1980s and 2000s, implying that, if anything, countries which were more open grew more slowly in those decades.

The tests also show that since the 1970s, Asian countries were consistently growing faster than other regions, and particularly faster in relation to the rich countries. Particularly towards the end of this period, Asian economies were typically trading more than those in other regions

Table 6.1 Trade and growth; regression analysis, dependent variable is annual average growth over the decade

	Number	R^2	Trade	$\Delta Trade_t$	$\Delta Trade_{t-1}$	Bal_t	Bal_{t-1}	Wealth	Pop.	Africa	Americas	Asia	EEurope	Constant
M6.1														
1960s	70	0.24	0.61*					-0.16	0.05	-2.15*	-0.73	0.02		4.25
1970s	86	0.23	1.03*					0.18	0.31	0.91	2.08**	3.20**		-6.87
1980s	96	0.26	-0.30					-0.12	0.27	-0.82	1.28	1.90*		0.38
1990s	113	0.24	0.21					0.09	0.11	0.64	1.55**	2.91***		-1.23
2000s	141	0.30	-0.17					-0.53***	0.12	0.98	0.85	2.09**	2.50***	5.87
M6.2														
1970s	83	0.29	1.47**	0.02				0.11	0.52*	0.83	2.33**	2.98**		-11.64*
1980s	88	0.43	0.08	0.05***				-0.19	0.15	-0.06	-1.05	1.67*		1.37
1990s	109	0.24	0.53	0.01				0.07	0.16	0.58	1.51**	2.60***		-3.13
2000s	140	0.31	-0.27	0.02				-0.53***	0.11	1.01	0.83	2.05**	2.48***	6.29
M6.3														
1970s	77	0.01			-0.03									-0.56
1980s	89	0.10			0.07***									-1.97***
1990s	99	0.04			0.04**									0.12
2000s	131	0.00			-0.00									2.17***

M6.4

1960s	70	0.27	0.65*	−0.23*		−0.04	0.16	−1.67	−0.38	0.11		0.93
1970s	81	0.34	1.51***	−0.25***		−0.05	0.84***	0.40	2.21**	1.65		−15.36**
	81	0.33	1.55***		−0.51***	−0.04	0.84***	0.44	2.24**	1.59		−15.60**
	81	0.35	1.56***	−0.24	−0.17	−0.04	0.88***	0.49	2.29**	1.61		−16.41***
1980s	88	0.34	0.19	−0.05		−0.13	0.29	−0.58	−1.24	1.88**		−3.21
	88	0.38	0.11		−0.16***	−0.03	0.33*	−0.15	−0.98	2.23**		−1.69
	88	0.40	0.09	0.10	−0.28***	−0.14	0.32	−0.34	−1.16	2.06**		−1.83
1990s	104	0.33	0.08	−0.09***		0.38*	0.15	1.31	1.85**	3.57***		−4.56
	104	0.33	0.00		−0.10***	0.38*	0.13	1.27	2.13***	3.52***		−3.87
	104	0.34	0.04	−0.06	−0.05	0.42*	0.16	1.38	2.03***	3.60***		−4.81
2000s	136	0.42	−0.48	0.05***		−0.87***	−0.03	−0.19	0.48	1.60**	2.16***	13.01***
	136	0.35	−0.30		0.04*	−0.66***	0.04	0.63	0.95	2.23***	2.40***	9.00***
	136	0.44	−0.40	0.08***	−0.06**	−0.89***	0.04	−0.38	0.37	1.30*	2.11***	11.65***

but these results would imply that this growth has little to do with openness as such. Africa in the 1960s fared worse than other regions while the Americas in the 1970s and again in the 1990s appeared to grow strongly. So did the countries of Eastern Europe and the former USSR in the 2000s. In this last case there is presumably a strong rebound from what for many countries was a disastrous previous decade, although insufficient data go back to 1990 to test this systematically. In the 2000s, growth was additionally negatively associated with initial GDP per capita; poorer countries in general grew more quickly than the rich, many of which suffered badly in the global financial and economic crisis after 2007.

The only associations between trade and growth that approach statistical significance are positive. However, the level of statistical confidence is low and the numerical values are modest. There is little indication from these simple models that trade made much difference to growth rates. These tests are a (simplified) version of much-cited econometric studies that claim to show a link between openness and growth. It is quite possible that controlling more fully for enough within-country differences might produce more convincingly positive relations. Yanikkaya's (2003) model does so by including, among other things, measures for the number of telephone lines, life expectancy, the nature of the political regime, the numbers of war deaths, tropical climate and access to international waters. Therefore, it should be stressed, the absence of convincing statistically significant results should not be taken to mean that no such relations exist. However, if the gains from trade were as great as is sometimes imagined, they might perhaps be expected to peak through the statistical noise a little more convincingly.

Conventional tests, like those repeated above, miss several dimensions of the arguments discussed in earlier chapters. There are many claims about how trade should work its magic, or alternatively why it should bring disadvantage. Of course, comparative advantage involves an argument that countries gain from specialization and opening. It does not claim that countries that trade more, that are more open at one given time, subsequently grow more quickly. This implies that attention should focus on changes in countries' levels of openness and its effect on growth rates.

First, therefore, similar tests are run but measuring the impact of the change in trade openness over the relevant decade rather than just the level at the beginning. Strictly it would be preferable to measure trends in openness rather than simply taking levels at the beginning and end of each decade but in practice the two are very closely correlated. (Liberia experienced extreme fluctuations in growth and trade and is omitted from the sample throughout. Including it substantially increases the strength of the apparently already highly significant result in the 1980s.) The results are reported as M6.2 in Table 6.1.

These tests show an apparently highly significant association between trade opening and growth in the 1980s. In the other decades, the signs are again positive but the results do not approach statistical significance. A similar positive association, not included in the results presented here, between opening and growth in the 1980s is also found at the 95 per cent confidence level within the poorer country regions of the Americas and Asia, considered as separate groups. The association is not found among African or rich countries.

These tests measure growth and opening simultaneously, so do not remove the problem of causation. It is still entirely possible that countries that were growing more quickly also then traded more. Therefore, changes in trade openness in the previous decade are instead taken as an independent variable to examine if these had any effect on levels of growth in the subsequent decade. The comparison between decades reduces the need to control for country characteristics, which changed relatively little. The results of what are therefore simple regression analyses are summarized as M6.3 in Table 6.1.

In the 1980s and to a lesser extent in the 1990s, there is clear evidence that those countries which opened more in the previous decade grew more strongly. However, this is not found in either the 1970s or 2000s. It is also notable that the numerical values are low and that trade opening, at most, accounts for a very small proportion of growth. The highest levels of R^2 were only 0.1. However, there is relatively clear evidence of a positive association in two of the four decades.

DIFFERENTIATING THE EFFECTS OF EXPORTS AND IMPORTS

The Ricardian and neo-classical traditions assume economic equilibrium, or rapid moves towards it. Accordingly, it is also often assumed that there is a balance of trade, that exports and imports are equal. It is clear that in practice, exports and imports are seldom identical. Nor are these simply momentary fluctuations competed away as the market returns to equilibrium. Countries can run substantial surpluses or deficits over extended periods. The incorporation of the possibilities of trade imbalances and thence debt and its implications for interest rates suggest a much more complex picture in terms of the consequences of trade (Hicks 1953; Metcalfe and Steedman 1974; Shaikh 2007).

Exports and imports are not simple reciprocals and it is both necessary and possible to distinguish their economic implications. The old mercantilist tradition (at least according to the liberal caricature) but also the 'Washington Consensus' reform strategy has concentrated on boosting exports and limiting imports. Most theorists stressing the benefits of trade emphasize exports, which allow cost-reducing, production efficiencies like low wages, while reducing any accompanying negative impacts from restricted final demand. In the formal accounting sense, exports are an addition to GDP, imports a subtraction. Radical critics can reach similar conclusions that trade surpluses are good and deficits damaging. Deficits bring debts which can undermine creditworthiness and the ability to service them. Shaikh's (1979) argument saw a permanent disadvantage developing for countries that incurred apparently temporary deficits.

However, imports can potentially bring substantial benefits. Yanikkaya (2003: 61) argues that:

> According to [the] theory of comparative advantage, international trade leads to a more efficient use of a country's resources through the import of goods and services that are otherwise too costly to produce within the country ... [In particular] trade plays an important role in growth by providing access to new products and inputs.

As seen in Chapter 4, Smith stressed that value consists in useful goods, and an excess of imports over exports implies a net gain in this sense. Importing, even moderate net imports, might not be such a bad thing.

Empirically, it seems important to move beyond measures of openness as the sum of exports and imports. Similar tests to those reported in M6.1 are therefore repeated but also now including measures for the trade balance. Average levels of the trade balance to GDP (as a percentage) were calculated over the previous (B_{t-1}) and current (B_t) decades. (A minimum of five years' data was accepted to derive these average values.) These average levels of trade balance to GDP are then treated as independent variables, alongside the overall trade to GDP levels, wealth, population and regional dummy variables, as above. For each decade, where available, there are then three sets of results; including the trade balance simultaneous with the decade of economic growth under consideration, the trade balance over the previous decade and the two indicators together. The results are summarized in as M6.4 in Table 6.1.

The results are rather striking. From the 1960s through to the 1990s, the evidence points to a negative association between the trade balance and overall economic growth. A trade deficit tends to be associated with stronger current but also, and particularly, with subsequent growth. This relationship is reversed in the 2000s, when there was a positive, and highly statistically significant, relation between growth and a current positive trade balance. Considered separately, the trade balance in the 1990s also has a (marginally) significant positive association with growth in the 2000s, whereas this association becomes (more strongly significantly) negative in the presence of data for the balance in the 2000s. This is an inconsistent result suggesting caution but similar results can be reproduced for a smaller constant sample of countries.

In the presence of these measures of the trade balance, the overall level of trade openness becomes positively associated with growth, particularly during the 1970s, at higher levels of statistical confidence than reported in M6.1 and M6.2.

It is perhaps relatively unsurprising that current growth and trade deficits should be associated. Strongly growing economies might attract more imports and those contracting, fewer. Currency appreciation and depreciation might work to that end. However, the association with subsequent growth is harder to explain in conventional terms. It would appear that imports did provide an economic stimulus. Because the overall trade openness indicators also tend to be positive, this seems more likely than that exports are having a negative effect, possibly as a result of restrictive domestic policies designed to increase international competitiveness. The positive association in the 2000s might be interpreted in terms of debt and deficit chickens coming home to roost in the crash of 2007–09. Many countries, particularly rich ones including the US, UK, Spain, Greece and Iceland, which had large deficits were very badly hit. However, it should be stressed that the positive relation in the 2000s is weak and of only marginal statistical significance, in contrast to the earlier, negative associations. For whatever reason, in the earlier decades and overall, countries tended to grow more quickly the greater their trade deficit, or more slowly the larger their surplus. This contrasts strongly with persistent mercantilist prejudices, reproduced in the export (surplus) strategies encouraged by the IMF, at least until recently.

TRADE, GROWTH AND COUNTRIES OF DIFFERENT SIZE AND WEALTH

It is worth repeating that few, if any, critics suggest that trade is a universal bad. Chapters 4 and 5 discussed two distinct claims of difference; that poorer countries in general or that countries exporting primary products suffer from trade. Poorer countries tend to be net primary producers and exporters so the second phenomenon may cause the first but clearly this is not universally true. Some poorer countries do not export primary products. Some rich countries do. As seen in Chapter 5, the pre-eminent advocate of unequal exchange, Emmanuel (1972), is explicit in rejecting the association with primary exports. It is high wages in the core that give it the advantages of unequal exchange; for Swedish timber and Australian minerals exports as much as German manufactured goods. Therefore, it is necessary to investigate at least two distinct claims. Trade in primary and secondary commodities is discussed separately below but questions of country size and wealth can be addressed immediately.

The tests (M6.1) reported in Table 6.1 are repeated but now dividing the sample into groups according to initial GDP per capita and country population at the beginning of each decade. Again, only countries with populations greater than one million are included in the samples of countries divided by wealth. The per capita divisions are arbitrary, producing groups of high-income, upper-middle, lower-middle and low-income countries of roughly similar size by the 1990s. This is a finer-grained categorization than the core–periphery distinction identified by dependency theorists but it allows a rough tracking of the experiences of country groups over time. The role of country size has not been a major source of controversy but, for reasons mentioned above, it also seems worth investigating. The relation between trade openness and growth on the countries with populations below one million is also now explicitly tested. The results are shown in Table 6.2.

The majority of the series, and all but one of those that reach any level of statistical significance, again show a positive association between trade openness and subsequent growth. The regional dummy variables are omitted from these tests but those on all countries with populations greater than one million otherwise repeat those reported in Table 6.1 and broadly confirm those results. It is notable that from the 1980s, the apparent association between openness and growth becomes stronger in the absence of the dummy variables and this result should accordingly be read cautiously.

There are some apparently significant results, which warrant discussion. There is a strong and highly significant positive association between trade openness and growth for very poor countries in the 1970s. The association is also positive and marginally statistically significant for the third category of countries in the 1960s and for the richest countries in the 1980s. Conversely, there is an apparently strong and significant negative association between openness and growth for the lower-middle-income group in the 1980s. This last result is not very robust and is substantially the product of the extraordinary contraction of the Liberian economy. If that country is removed from the sample the result loses all statistical significance. There is no evidence of statistically significant relationships between trade openness and growth in any income category in the 1990s or 2000s, although all the signs are positive rather than negative and we might therefore also impute some significance on the basis of sign tests; the results are unlikely all to have been positive just by chance.

In terms of size, during the 1960s and again in the 1990s, those countries with populations between one and five million appeared to do better when they were more open. Otherwise there was little evidence of systematic variation according to population. Even the very small countries did not appear to do significantly better when they were more open, although after the 1960s the signs were always positive.

Similar tests on the countries within each of the poorer regions and among the rich countries, the results of which are not reported here, similarly show little evidence of a significant association between trade and growth. There is some indication (significant at the 90 per cent confidence level) of a positive association between growth and openness among African countries in the 1960s, and for Asian countries in both the 1980s and 1990s (but notably not in the 2000s). Conversely, there is a stronger negative relation, significant at the 95 per cent confidence level, between openness and growth in Africa in the 1980s. The number of countries in some of the regional samples, even now including the small countries excluded from the overall sample, was often quite small and such results should accordingly be treated cautiously. Tests conducted only on the poorer countries, following M6.2 and M6.3 show similar results for the poorer countries to the overall samples.

In summary, what evidence there is supports a weak, positive association between trade and growth and with little indication of variation according to country size or wealth. This would appear to undermine straightforward claims of systematic disadvantage.

Table 6.2   Trade openness and growth by country wealth and size: regression analysis, dependent variable is annual average growth over the subsequent decade, wealth is measured in 2005$US

	n	R²	Trade openness	Population	Wealth	Constant
1960s						
By wealth						
>5600	17	0.56	-0.53	-0.08	-3.03***	36.81***
1400–5600	16	0.05	0.56	0.23	0.38	-2.61
375–1400	26	0.31	1.21*	0.24	1.73	-14.94
<375	11	0.27	1.19	0.07	-0.20	0.97
By population						
>25m	15	0.13	-0.42	-0.73	0.03	19.71
5–25m	23	0.33	0.25	1.09	0.48**	-17.52
1–5m	32	0.26	1.22**	-0.64	0.07	9.49
All >1 m	70	0.10	0.65*	0.24	0.25	-2.79
<1m	14	0.31	-4.69	1.98	0.57	-3.41
1970s						
By wealth						
>6400	21	0.19	0.57	-0.23	-0.29	27.80
1600–6400	20	0.22	1.40	0.84	0.75	-19.33
400–1600	33	0.30	-0.73	0.72	3.70***	-28.70**
<400	12	0.68	3.68***	1.08**	-0.07	-23.47**
By population						
>25m	20	0.31	-0.16	-0.51	-0.64**	19.56
5–25m	36	0.14	1.17	-1.48	-0.01	24.38
1–5m	30	0.15	1.61	-0.18	0.14	-0.44
All >1 m	86	0.07	1.30**	0.55**	-0.19	-7.58
<1m	16	0.02	1.32	0.01	-0.17	1.14
1980s						
By wealth						
>8000	26	0.26	1.60*	0.76**	-0.67	-9.53
2000–8000	25	0.12	1.94	0.46	0.13	-13.18

By population	500–2000	24	0.35	-4.16**	0.71	0.29	5.51
	<500	21	0.41	-0.06	0.75**	-1.46	-0.75
	>25m	25	0.27	1.13	1.36**	-0.38	-21.76
	5–25m	44	0.09	1.12*	0.68	-0.16	-11.64
	1–5m	27	0.04	-0.36	0.94	0.29	-12.54
	All >1 m	96	0.11	0.49	0.70***	-0.12	-9.63*
	<1m	31	0.18	0.26	-0.16	-0.01**	12.93
1990s							
By wealth	>9600	25	0.38	0.77	-0.22	-0.82	11.90
	2400–9600	26	0.13	1.39	-0.03	0.11	-2.37
	600–2400	30	0.15	1.05	0.52*	0.75	-14.49
	<600	32	0.17	0.05	0.80**	-0.41	-7.77
By population	>25m	31	0.26	0.69	1.41***	0.13	-23.62
	5–25m	51	0.07	0.66	0.82	-0.34	-10.25
	1–5m	31	0.31	1.31**	0.30	0.54*	-10.64
	All >1 m	113	0.05	0.80**	0.34	-0.10	-4.51
	<1m	34	0.09	0.32	0.23	-0.70	5.42
2000s							
By wealth	>12000	29	0.40	0.68	-0.23	-1.59***	19.67**
	3000–12,000	29	0.13	0.03	-0.15	-0.97	14.61**
	750–3000	40	0.09	0.05	0.19	-1.86*	15.45
	<750	43	0.14	0.36	0.66**	-1.47	1.62
By population	>25m	35	0.73	0.28	0.71***	-1.09***	-0.94
	5–25m	64	0.16	0.55	-0.22	-0.76***	-7.97
	1–5m	42	0.11	0.39	0.76	-0.33*	-5.99
	All >1 m	141	0.22	0.47	0.18	-0.73**	5.12
	<1m	35	0.23	1.36	1.22**	0.05	-17.55**

TRADING PARTNERS

As ever, rival perspectives are available about the implications of having particular trading partners. The mainstream tradition stresses difference. As will be discussed in more detail in the next chapter, the advantages from specialization supposedly come precisely from trading with countries that have different factor endowments. Mainstream accounts emphasize, in particular, the potential advantages for poorer countries of trading with richer ones. As export markets, they are larger and more stable. As import markets, they provide a source of more technologically advanced products, often unavailable locally but that can also be a means through which the importing countries can begin to upgrade. The innovative dynamism of the US economy, in particular, has been found to produce positive growth effects among its trading partners (Yanikkaya 2003). This, of course, contrasts strongly with claims of dependency and unequal exchange, for which it is not trade in itself but trade with the core which produces systematic disadvantage. The theory of unequal exchange posits that the power of larger states, their corporations and particularly of their labour movements, means that richer countries pass on higher costs as higher prices. Poorer countries have to pay more for their imports while competitive (more effectively repressed) labour markets keep down the price of their export commodities. Poorer countries lose from trade with the rich and would be better off trading among themselves (Emmanuel 1972). Conversely, there is an advantage to core countries in as far as they trade with countries poorer than themselves.

The World Bank (WB 2014) data, for a somewhat reduced sample of countries, also distinguish between trade with 'developing' and 'developed' countries. This allows two separate trade-to-GDP ratios to be calculated for each country, labelled T(poor) and T(rich), respectively. Much as above, but now because of more limited data availability for the 15-year period from 1995 to 2010, analyses are conducted into whether these ratios are associated with subsequent growth. The tests are run on the whole sample and two poorer country sub-groups, defined in terms of GDP per capita levels below $10 000 and $2000. Data are available for the level of trade with the US and similar tests were run including these measures, now also alongside the overall level of trade openness.

For the whole sample there was a negative association, significant at the 95 per cent confidence level, between growth and trade with rich countries but this did not reach significance for the poorer-country groups. The values for trade with poor countries were positive but did not reach statistical significance. If anything, these associations would support a narrative of unequal exchange rather than one that emphasizes the gains from trading with more advanced countries. However, the negative association of trade with rich countries seems more likely to be a product of the fact that rich countries trade more with each other, and as a group grew only slowly during this period. As seen above, this was a period in which the poorer countries were growing more quickly than richer ones. It would not be surprising if trading partners experienced some pay-off from this. There was no evidence of a significant relation between growth and trading specifically with the US.

When the country sample was separated according to population, the negative association between trade with developed countries and growth could only be shown at any level of statistical confidence for a middle group with populations between one and ten million and (weakly) for small countries with a population of less than a million. Throughout the data presented here, two countries, Liberia and Equatorial Guinea, are omitted from the sample. They are extreme outliers in terms of their recorded levels of trade to GDP (986 per cent) and growth (822 per cent), respectively. If these two countries are added to the sample, the statistical significance of the negative association of trade with rich countries disappears, while the positive association of trade with poorer countries is considerably strengthened. Tests specifically on trade with the US were unable to show any significant associations. Finally, unlike the tests in the previous sections, there is no attempt to control for regional variation, which was seen to play such a significant part in accounting for growth rate variation. This was avoided because the regional variables cross-correlate strongly with trading partners but in its absence there is a danger of misinterpreting the results.

PRIMARY AND SECONDARY COMMODITIES' TRADE AND GROWTH

Many arguments about the experiences of trade and growth have revolved around the particular character of primary products and how both their supply and demand is different from that of manufactured goods (Singer 1950; Robinson 1979). These ideas were discussed in Chapter 4, which also reported evidence that the terms of trade for primary products, in aggregate, declined over the twentieth century. There was, however, a reversal of this trend in the late 1990s and 2000s. This will be taken up in more detail in the next chapter but some provisional tests are possible.

As with the overall trade balance, it cannot be assumed that the balances of primary and secondary trade are simple reciprocals of each other. Indeed, in 2010, there was a weak but *positive* correlation between the level of net manufacturing and primary exports (r = 0.16). Among other things, therefore, if primary commodities constitute a certain proportion of exports this says nothing about the country's net position, either of primary products or manufactured goods. In each case it is necessary to calculate separately the net position in primary and secondary commodities and to treat these as independent. As above, these are then calculated relative to country GDP and their association with growth investigated. It is again also conjectured that the results might vary according to country wealth, size and region. The results are presented in Table 6.3.

In the 1970s, there did appear to be a strong and highly statistically significant negative association between net primary exports and growth. At the same time, although it was only significant at lower levels of confidence, net secondary exports also appeared to be negatively associated with growth. This confirms the results M6.4 in Table 6.1; that net exporters, whatever they exported, tended to do badly. There is little evidence that subsequently there was any systematic difference according to the character of the goods being traded. The results remain substantially negative but that this should be so in the 1990s and 2000s, despite a remarkable commodities boom, might temper any enthusiasm for primary exports.

Finally, fuel prices have historically behaved differently to those of other primary products and, by the 1970s, several oil-exporting countries became conspicuous exceptions to claims of poorer-country trade disadvantage. Therefore, for the slightly more restricted sample of countries for which data were available, the tests reported in Table 6.3 were repeated but also now differentiating between fuel and non-fuel primary exports. The results are very similar to those shown in Table 6.3, with little specific difference for fuel imports or exports. The sample does include some major oil-exporting countries – Algeria, Indonesia, Iran, Nigeria and Venezuela – although it is notable that most West Asian countries are not in this sample. By the 1980s (when oil prices turned down) the sample also includes Oman and Saudi Arabia. Again, however, after the 1970s, there remains little evidence of particular advantage or disadvantage according to the character of commodities being traded. It should be acknowledged that some important claims of the negative effects of resource extraction explicitly reject testing the impacts over such short periods (Bunker 1984) and data limitations preclude testing over anything more than 40 years. However, tests on the effects of fuel exports over the four decades from 1970 (not reported here) still fail to produce significant results one way or another.

Table 6.3   Economic growth and trade in primary and secondary commodities: regression analysis, dependent variable is growth over the subsequent decade

	1970s			1980s†			1990s			2000s		
	All	<$6400	<$1600	All	<$8000	<$2000	All	<$9600	<$2400	All	<$12,000	<$2400
Number in sample	72	52	34	75	50	29	74	50	30	127	98	71
R²	0.39	0.38	0.43	0.42	0.25	0.40	0.40	0.14	0.38	0.42	0.13	0.12
Net Primary exports to GDP	-0.10***	-0.10***	-0.17***	-0.01	0.03	0.01	-0.02	-0.00	-0.01	0.02	0.01	0.01
Net Secondary exports to GDP	-0.09**	-0.08*	-0.18	0.05	0.11*	0.10	-0.04	-0.01	0.05	-0.01	-0.02	-0.04
Trade to GDP ratio	1.41**	1.47**	2.25	0.85	2.21**	1.45	0.49	1.25*	1.58	-0.45	0.05	-0.10
Population	0.75**	0.95***	1.18***	0.16	0.57*	0.86**	0.23	0.51**	0.65**	0.09	0.33	0.60**
Wealth	-0.07	0.48	1.64*	-0.05	-0.64*	-0.17	0.11	-0.11	-0.14	-0.52***	-0.44	0.26
Africa	0.82			0.92			0.53			0.67		
Americas	2.43***			-0.28			1.54**			0.75		
Asia	2.03***			2.91***			2.51***			1.98***		
Eastern Europe and the former USSR										2.63***		
Constant	-13.48**	-19.15***	-33.10***	-2.85	-8.90	-13.85*	-4.38	-8.58	-11.29	7.29*	2.05	-3.09

† Samples exclude Liberia.

117

CONCLUSION

There is little evidence to support either the enthusiasm with which trade opening is pushed or the vehemence of blanket opposition. The balance of evidence, here as in most of the literature, shows some positive association between trade openness and trade opening and economic growth but this is still somewhat equivocal and any effects are rather small. At this aggregate level, there is little evidence to support claims of systematic disadvantage of countries of particular size or wealth or according to the character of their exports or imports. The most remarkable finding, which challenges claims made by both orthodox and heterodox authorities, is that trade deficits appeared to be good for growth, at least until the 2000s. These preliminary investigations will be extended in the chapters that follow. It should also be borne in mind that there is always much that escapes orthodox accounting but there are already reasons to be cautious about some of the bolder claims of straightforward links between trade and growth.

7. Factor endowments, trade and growth

INTRODUCTION

This chapter considers a key proposition of neo-classical trade theory, considering whether countries trade on the basis of 'factor endowments', and goes on to ask whether they grow faster when they do so.

This addresses what appears to be a gap in the existing literature. As discussed in the last chapter, mainstream approaches support trade, maintaining in particular that it fosters faster national growth. Such links between trade and growth have been extensively debated and while there is still argument, the balance of evidence supports some positive association. As will be explained below, following Heckscher and Ohlin (H–O), mainstream trade theory goes on to suggest that trade should be based on 'factor endowments'. Here again there is a considerable literature, debating whether or to what extent countries do, in fact, trade on the basis of their endowments as Heckscher and Ohlin conceived them. Most studies stop at this point. They assume rather than investigate the link between the two ideas. The fact that the connections between trade and growth and between factor endowments and trade are at most statistical tendencies invites the crucial supplementary question of whether or to what extent trading based on factor endowments is good for growth.

Some authors explicitly assume that trading on the basis of factor endowments is particularly beneficial. For example, Wood and Mayer write that for land-rich countries in Africa 'the highest priority is to raise the absolute levels of exports in all sectors, and particularly in sectors based on natural resources' (2001: 369). Meanwhile, even those working within an apparently similar conceptual framework can provide almost diametrically opposite advice. Leamer staunchly defends H–O but concludes that the best advice to countries reliant on land-based production is 'pray for favourable terms of trade' (2012: 106). Naude and Gries (2009) attribute Africa's lack of development not to weak primary exports but to insufficient manufactured ones. This appears to converge with an ostensibly alternative tradition, discussed in Chapter 4, which identifies the dangers of dependence on primary exports. Despite confident assertions on both sides, the issue remains open and under-investigated.

The next section introduces H–O theory, originally articulated by the Swedish economists Heckscher (1950) and Ohlin (1991) in the inter-war period. Readers familiar with these ideas can probably safely skip this section, although the presentation here follows Heckscher (1950) and Leamer's (2012) triangulation rather than the highly mathematical formulations of modern textbooks. The following section introduces and discusses some of the controversies the theory has stirred. While acknowledging the validity of some of the criticisms, it is argued that H–O theory at least represents an interesting claim worth investigating. It argues that the role of land has been relatively under-investigated and in particular that the focus on land provides a useful, simple basis for testing some important propositions about primary and secondary exports. The chapter then describes a few tests, examining whether and to what extent countries do trade on the basis of factor endowments, conceived on the simplest basis of labour, land and capital, with these proxied, respectively, simply by population density, its reciprocal and gross domestic profit (GDP) per capita. It considers data at ten-year intervals from 1980 to 2010. Among other things, it finds quite strong and highly statistically significant associations between land endowments and the propensity to export primary products, but only weaker associations between labour endowments (or land-scarcity) and manufactured exports. The final section develops a slightly more complex model to examine the supplementary question of whether countries do better when they trade according to the prescriptions of H–O theory. The condition, when trading in the ways predicted by theory, seems crucial in moving beyond simple arguments for or against trade openness to consider whether there are conditions under which trade is more or less successful. Here the results are much less conclusive.

FACTOR ENDOWMENTS AND INTERNATIONAL TRADE: THE HECKSCHER–OHLIN THEOREM

As discussed in Chapter 3, the theory of comparative advantage claims to establish that countries can gain from specialization and trade, even in situations where they have only relative rather than absolute productivity advantages (Ricardo 1951). It does not establish why countries' relative productivities in different branches of production should vary, or, therefore, in what they should specialize.

Heckscher (1950) and Ohlin (1991) provide an answer in terms of 'factor endowments'. Countries should specialize in the production and export of goods that require the intense use of the factors of production that they have in relative abundance. Samuelson, Vanek and Jones extend and formalize these ideas and various combinations of their names are sometimes appended. In what follows, the H–O terminology and simplest distinction of factors of production and categories of exports and imports are retained. One other preliminary disclaimer is needed. Heckscher's declared interest is in 'the distribution of income between land, capital, and labor' (1950: 276). However, questions of inequality and redistribution within countries are deferred until the next chapter and considered under the rubric of what is known as the Stolper–Samuelson (S–S) theorem. This chapter stops at the more limited questions of country characteristics, trade and growth.

Heckscher and Ohlin were liberal, neo-classical economists, employing a general equilibrium analysis, with all its limitations. With some qualifications, they accepted the benefits from free trade. Heckscher maintains that 'it follows from the nature of barter that trade will create the maximum satisfaction of wants or the maximum national income' (1950: 274). The familiar three-way distinction of land, labour and capital keeps a foot in the camp of classical political economy but from the start, Heckscher makes clear that the broad categories were just simplifying assumptions and could each be sub-divided: 'The number of factors of production is practically unlimited' (1950: 279). Some studies have differentiated more finely, such as between skilled and unskilled workers and according to land types. Even the three-way distinction challenges Ricardo, whose presentation sees labour as the only factor of production, ignoring (or abstracting from) differences in labour productivity and in countries' resources (Krugman and Obstfeld 2003).

Production always requires each of these three basic factors. All production occurs in some particular location, requires work and at least some tools. However, the intensity with which the factors are used varies enormously both within countries and in different production processes.

In a closed economy, the costs of production depend on local factor prices. It is assumed that where land is scarce its price will be relatively high, where labour is scarce, wages will be high. It is easy to find examples of densely populated countries where land is at a premium; modern Hong Kong and Singapore perhaps stand out. The US and Australia in the nineteenth century are often cited examples where the availability of cheap land to white settlers drove up the wages that employers had to pay to retain workers. As ever, this is far from universally true. Both land prices and wages are social achievements, seldom based on free markets. They are classic examples of Polanyi's (2001) 'fictitious commodities'; not produced by firms nor consumed, and only behaving like commodities through social power relations rather than strictly economic imperatives. Any association between wages and population density seems likely to be weak. We could contrast Sweden and Bangladesh but equally the Netherlands and Zambia. Of course, these countries all now trade and H–O theory tells us that this will change the levels of factor prices across countries. Heckscher maintains that it will equalize them. Conversely, countries that had identical factor endowments to begin with would have no incentive to trade. However, left as a plausible hypothesis, differences in relative scarcity were likely to mean different relative prices of the factors of production and different production costs. By trading, countries can then reduce their effective costs and bring the prices of the various factors towards internationally determined rates (Heckscher 1950).

The argument normally goes something like the following. Before trading, in a land-rich country with few (but well-paid) workers, the price of land-based goods like food will be low but that of manufactured products high. In a land-poor country, the prices of land-based products will be high but manufactures cheap. Heckscher (1950) makes the point through a simple example of two countries, Home and Foreign, producing meat and machinery. In Home, the price of 'a unit' of land (l) is equal to that of a unit of capital (c) and a unit of labour (w), or

$$l = c = w = 1p$$

In Foreign, land is relatively dear, and here one unit costs three units of capital or four of labour:

$$l = 3c = 4w = 3q$$

The letters p and q denote national money prices. Without trade, we do not know how much p is worth in terms of q. Heckscher further assumes that meat production requires the application of equal quantities of land, capital and labour (l + c + w) but machinery production uses relatively more capital and labour (l + 4c + 5w). Table 7.1 shows that in Foreign the relative costs of producing meat relative to machinery will be higher (4.75:10.75) than in Home (3:10). This creates a situation of comparative advantage and exchange will be worthwhile. Home exports meat, Foreign machinery. Heckscher goes on to argue this will reduce the costs of land, and increase those of capital and labour in Home, with the opposite effects in Foreign. By importing products, the factors of production of which were scarce, that scarcity is effectively reduced.

Table 7.1   Heckscher–Ohlin theorem, based on different methods of production and factor endowments

		Meat production	Machinery production
		$= 1 + c + w$	$= 1 + 4c + 5w$
Home prices	$1 = c = w = 1p$	$= 1p + 1p + 1p = 3p$	$= 1p + 4p + 5p = 10p$
Foreign prices	$1 = 3c = 4w = 3q$	$= 3q + 1q + 0.75q = 4.75q$	$= 3q + 4q + 3.75q = 10.75q$

The argument is therefore that countries should employ the appropriate mix of factors of production. Countries that are land-rich should specialize in primary production; those with abundant labour, in labour-intensive manufacturing; and those with abundant capital, in capital-intensive industry. For the H–O model, trade is then substantially driven by differences in countries' resources and the concomitant different intensities with which they use them. The H–O framework became and remains a cornerstone of textbook trade theory (for example, Bhagwati 1987; Husted and Melvin 1990; Markussen et al. 1995; Krugman and Obstfeld 2003).

Leamer's (2012) triangular diagrams provide a neat summary. If we posit the three factors of production at the corners of a triangle, then each country and each activity lies somewhere within this space. (Leamer's own presentation has some activities on the borders, implicitly using no land, labour or capital and so is adapted slightly here to put every activity somewhere within the perimeter.) The internal triangles shown by the dotted lines on Figure 7.1 then indicate how each country 'fits' a particular activity more or less closely. Countries, A, B, C, etc. have factor endowments lying in one of the 'cones'. They substantially compete with those in the same areas and would not be expected to trade with them. They would gain from trade with countries in opposite cones. So, for example, country A is capital-poor and would gain from exporting handicrafts, wood and logs to C, which could sell it textiles, machinery and paper. There might be more complex processes between countries in bordering zones; A and B compete to export handicrafts and wood but might trade logs for apparel to their mutual benefit.

Figure 7.2 plots data for 140 countries for 2010 onto a more conventional two-dimensional space using the simplest proxies of GDP per

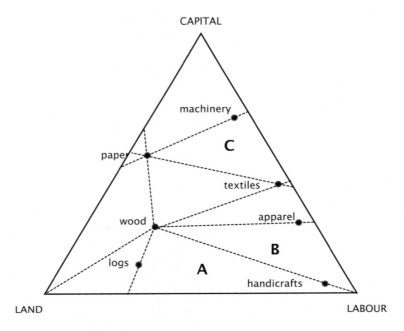

Source: Adapted from Leamer (2012: 90).

*Figure 7.1   A 'Leamer triangle' showing factor endowments and intensities
for different countries and activities*

capita, for capital endowments, and population density and its reciprocal
as measures of the relative abundance of labour and land. The circles
represent country size, giving some idea of the global distribution of
country endowments. As discussed in the next chapter, a similar mapping
has been used to evaluate different domestic interests in trade opening
(Rogowski 1989). It makes clear that even at this simple level, countries
have very different characteristics. There are substantial problems with
the H–O model, some of which will be considered in the next section.
The use of just three factors and these measures as proxies for them is a
huge simplification. Nevertheless, its parsimony is also a part of the
attraction of H–O and the idea that countries' differences provide the
basis for trade retains a considerable intuitive plausibility.

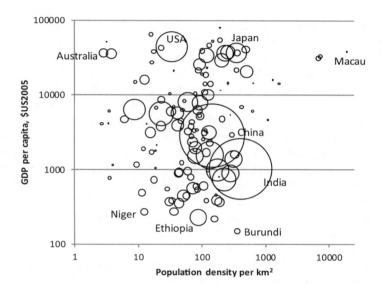

Source: WB (2014).

Figure 7.2   Factor endowments of 140 countries in 2010

ASSUMPTIONS AND OBJECTIONS

There have been many objections to the H–O approach. The original authors were usually cautious in what they were claiming and made clear where they were making simplifying approximations. Much of that caution and qualification was neglected in subsequent applications, giving 'the Heckscher–Ohlin paradigm a bad press' (Flam and Flanders 1991: 26). A few of the problems warrant at least a brief commentary.

As with the theory of comparative advantage, the models are usually static (but see Ohlin 1991). The very language of 'endowments' implies something given, where the factors are really social and historical constructions. Countries (or more accurately specifically institutions or actors within them, states, corporations, class organizations) do things to change their characteristics. Worse for the theory, the very act of trade specialization changes the 'endowments'. Where capital is invested, in vineyards or textile mills, what sort of labour skills are developed and how the land is cultivated (by the application of capital and labour) means that whatever was previously the basis of specialization is itself transformed. Specialization brings dynamic changes to any particular country, most obviously through returns to scale. Both Heckscher and Ohlin were aware of this and discussed some of the important consequences but it has significant implications for the standard presentation. As discussed in Chapter 3, in the context of Graham's paradox, doubling cloth production probably cost less than twice as much, while growing twice as many grapes is probably more than twice as costly, the most suitable fields being already cultivated. Dynamic models suggest changes in productivity can more than cancel out any comparative advantage gains and, as New Trade Theory (NTT) discussed in Chapter 4 makes clear, economies of scale can make trade between countries with identical factor endowments perfectly rational. Ohlin (1991) is clear that the very act of specialization changes the demand for the different factors of production and therefore the combinations in which they will be used.

Presentations like Heckscher's meat and machinery example and the Leamer triangle posit each activity as requiring a specific mix of factors of production. As Smith made clear, this is not the case. Even wine can be produced in Scotland using capital-intensive techniques. In practice, many goods are produced efficiently but in different ways using different combinations of factors and in different ways in different countries (Horvat 1999). This might seem rather obvious but without identical techniques the direction of trade becomes indeterminate (Heckscher 1950; Jones 2006). Flam and Flanders argue that 'factor intensity reversals were rediscovered in the literature on "switching" years after they became household terms to trade theorists' (1991: 30). However that may be, the substitution of different factors of production emphasized in the later debates around capital and labour 'reversals' present some stark problems. Any idea of 'aggregate capital' becomes hard to sustain (Pasinetti and Scazzieri 1987). Technical progress and economic growth do not imply the application of ever more 'capital' in the sense of higher levels of wealth (for example, in dollar terms) being spent on means of production rather than labour. There is no guarantee that richer countries, or higher wages, imply the use of more capital-intensive techniques (Steedman and Metcalfe 1977). Rather than there being any neat progress, factor intensity reversals are eminently possible. Therefore, the effects of factor endowments on patterns of trade become uncertain (Baldwin 2008). Samuelson was a central protagonist in these debates, hostile to the ideas of factor intensity reversals, but he eventually conceded the theoretical point (Samuelson 1966).

Another important sense in which factors are not simply given is that they move. Here again, Heckscher and, in particular, Ohlin (1991: 122–58) are aware that the Ricardian assumptions were approximate, that mobility was always a question of degree. There are real movements across borders and limited mobility within them. Heckscher (1950) openly acknowledges and discusses factor mobility from the outset and finishes with a discussion of how this means that national economies can be expanded through protection that creates premiums on mobile factors. However, in the standard versions, H–O theory assumes complete factor mobility within countries and none across national boundaries. In practice, within countries, land, labour and capital are always specific and can be shifted from one line of business to another only more or less easily. Some of the land-based examples are so extreme they can make the theory look ridiculous. Apple orchards cannot be converted into gold mines at will. Nor can capital and labour simply switch from making shoes to making microprocessors. Workers within a country may have little choice but to try to find employment, but they do not necessarily succeed, now undermining the models' assumptions of full employment. Land and capital too can both lie idle or sit in unproductive activities, for a considerable time. Meanwhile, capital and labour can and do cross borders. Capital has always been mobile but in recent years foreign direct investment has grown much faster even than trade. Workers are more constrained but they too can and do migrate in large numbers.

Capital's mobility and the different uses to which it can be put make the use of GDP per capita as a proxy for capital particularly problematic. The use of population density and its reciprocal as proxies for labour and land also become profoundly questionable, necessarily missing much of each factor's heterogeneity. Many studies incorporate more subtle distinctions (Krugman and Obstfeld 2003). Labour's differentiation is the focus of important theses regarding the recent performance of national economies and of income polarization discussed in later chapters here (Reich 1991; Wood 1994; Wood and Berge 1997; Babones 2010). A few studies also consider land of different types (Peterson and Vallaru 2000). However, with enough diversity and each factor of production sufficiently differentiated, it becomes hard to determine whether data confirms or contradicts H–O and there is sometimes more than a hint of reading back that trade must be based on factor endowments, with apparent contradictions accounted for by the almost infinite practical variety of factors and products.

Moreover, because of its comparative or relative nature, changes in any one country bring changes to all the others, even if they do nothing. For example, in the centre of Figure 7.2 the largest circle representing China has been moving rapidly 'northwards', not accepting its endowments of, say, 30 years ago. In the process, other countries' relative positions have become one of relatively greater labour wealth and capital poverty. What might seem obviously true of two countries producing two commodities becomes much more complicated and contestable when something closer to the complex realities of trade relations are considered (Ohlin 1991). The simple two-by-two presentation that students learn 'is fragile, even if the algebra extends effortlessly to high-dimensional even models' (Leamer 2012: 4).

Finally, as mentioned in Chapter 3, countries not only produce but also consume a vast range of products, in different ways. Unfortunately, 'the model assumes that consumers in two different regions of the world are essentially alike' (Shaikh 1979: 291). Even without specific prejudices in favour of locally made goods (which Smith among others takes for granted) countries seem likely to have different 'preferences', particularly given the (necessary) differences in levels of wealth, which the theory assumes. Most obviously, a richer country seems likely to consume a high proportion of luxury goods and relatively fewer basic necessities, more fine wine and relatively less cloth. This implies that the relative prices of these goods will be different and the idea of factor price equalization on which the theory depends, collapses. At the very least, measurement becomes (almost impossibly) complicated because trade is characterized by a variety of tastes and profusion of product types (Caves et al. 1993; Leamer 2012).

Thus, H–O remains controversial (Trefler 1993; Leamer and Levinson 1994; Peterson and Valluru 2000). Despite the difficulties, it continues to be widely used and discussed but the criticisms mean that it should be interpreted as at best a plausible empirical hypothesis rather than an established axiom.

TESTING THE HECKSCHER–OHLIN THEOREM

The relation between factor endowments and trade patterns remains sufficiently unclear that it still provokes considerable controversy, even among neo-classical economists. Leontief's (1953) early accounting established that the US had a higher proportion of capital-intensive products in its imports than exports. This runs counter to theory because as the richest country, by assumption, it was the richest in capital and would be expected to be a net exporter of capital-intensive manufactures. There are various explanations for the apparent anomaly. A focus on the labour–capital distinction neglects land and the relatively land-rich character of the US compared with European trading partners, or alternatively the capital-intensive character of resource-intensive imports (Caves et al. 1993). Leontief's 'paradox' can perhaps be explained away but it continues to provoke controversy. More broadly, H–O suggests that trade will be greater between any pair of countries, the more they differ but it quickly becomes obvious that this does not happen. The Netherlands' major trading partner is Germany, New Zealand's is Australia. Neighbouring countries may fairly obviously tend to have similar factor endowments but this is not the whole story. Japan and rich European countries also conduct enormous volumes of trade. At one level, 'gravity models' also make perfect sense. Countries trade more with others that are larger as well as closer. But the importance of distance complicates any dependence on factor endowments (and refutes sillier exaggerations of globalization) while persistently high levels of intra-industry trade among rich countries appear to contradict the factor-endowment-based models. Even 'sign tests' asking merely whether trade flows in the predicted direction provide only scant support (Baldwin 2008).

Any new testing needs to be approached through a few further careful steps. With neo-classical theory in general, the models typically assume trade balances, that exports equal imports (but see Ohlin 1991). If one country has a surplus of wine, this will be balanced by its deficits in cloth. Of course, this need not apply directly between any two countries but will be achieved through a harmonious flow and automatic adjustments between countries. As shown in Chapter 6, this need not happen in practice. More simply, for the purposes here as before, primary and manufacturing trade balances cannot be assumed to mirror each other and need to be evaluated separately.

Before moving to some tests, it also seems worth noting that the H–O literature on land and trade in primary products has been remarkably sparse; remarkably particularly given the importance attached to primary trade by numerous critics. Some of the early work had a land/labour focus (Samuelson 1948) but this has seldom been developed. Perhaps this is simply because the theory appears most successful in relation to land. Keesing and Sherk's early study, posing manufactured and primary exports as simple alternatives, confirms that 'per capita exports of manufactures are positively and strongly related to population density as well as per-capita GDP' (1971: 959). Other studies, although relatively small in number, broadly concur. The empirical relationship between trade in primary products and land endowments, even conceived at a very general level, appears to hold. There seems to be a clear tendency for countries to trade primary products according to whether or not they have abundant land (Wood and Berge 1997; Peterson and Valluru 2000; Wood and Mayer 2001).

However, the issue is worth revisiting for several reasons. The existing literature leaves some conceptual and empirical problems unresolved. Most of the studies simply measure primary products as a proportion of countries' total exports (but see Peterson and Valluru 2000). This seems unsatisfactory. The fundamental point of a trading relationship, and of these theories of trade, is precisely the difference between exports and imports. In effect, the tendency is to assume that countries will export and import different goods. This is what the theories anticipate but any tests should avoid assuming what needs to be shown. Some studies acknowledge the distinction but do not pursue it because it is found to be empirically unimportant (Wood and Berge 1997). However, this hardly establishes the legitimacy of a general approach to trade, which ignores imports. It was also precisely the 'net' position, which led to the Leontief paradox and the enduring objections in relation to capital-intensive production. Some studies also measure specialization simply by the proportions of the different components within a county's trade, rather than in relation to its wealth. A land-rich country with an almost closed economy and exporting nothing but a few surplus strawberries would offer weaker support to the theory than one with a very high level of trade, albeit that perhaps only 90 per cent of its exports were of primary products. In gross terms, the data produce some stark anomalies. For example, Singapore's primary goods' exports in 2010 amounted to a quarter of the total and a value amounting to 80 per cent of GDP. The net figure of minus 6 per cent of GDP, seems more plausible.

The global economy also changes rapidly. Trade levels increase and patterns alter between countries and regions. Most obviously, there was a rapid expansion of industry within, and of manufactured exports from, many formerly poorer countries. Despite this, primary products continued to account for between a quarter and a third of total merchandise trade and were the majority of exports for 84 of 152 countries for which data were available in 2010 (WB 2014). The prices of many primary products also rose, potentially increasing the incentives to utilize land resources. Again, it seems worth investigating whether, or to what extent, recent changes altered any association between the content of trade and factor endowments.

Finally, a focus on land avoids some of the problems of substitution between labour and capital and of capital movement and fungibility. Land is substantially different to labour and capital in its immobility and, while there can be substitution and more or less intensive land use, primary production at least requires substantial space, while manufacturing activities need relatively little. Land therefore seems to provide an obvious fulcrum for evaluating for H–O and it would appear to be worth revisiting the evidence.

DO FACTOR ENDOWMENTS PREDICT PATTERNS OF PRIMARY AND SECONDARY TRADE?

This section reports some tests evaluating whether or to what extent trade in manufactured and primary products is based on countries' factor endowments, understood in the sense of labour, land and capital, and proxied simply by population density, its reciprocal and GDP per capita.

It should be cautioned that trade and 'endowments' are measured at specific times, providing only 'snapshots'. These measures of endowments are inherently approximate and should not be expected to explain more than a small proportion of trade. In the spirit of comparative or relative advantage, land, labour and capital should in principle be conceived in relation to each other. So, for example, land-rich but wealthy countries like Australia and Canada might be reckoned relatively land-poor compared with low-income countries with nothing to sell but their resources. Similarly, countries further to the left or right of Figure 7.2, by virtue of their abundant land or labour, are in an important sense less capital-abundant than those of equal wealth, but towards the centre. However, calculations (not included here) based on modified measures show no statistical improvement, while including such measures of land, labour and capital simultaneously would reduce the models to circularity. The simplest proxies are therefore retained. There is also no attempt to differentiate types of products beyond the simple primary–manufacturing distinction. Manufactured goods are therefore envisaged simply as the products of labour and capital rather than land. Keeping the variables separate, while adding population as a control for country size and regional dummy variables, allows a straightforward, if necessarily crude, 'first-cut' investigation of the effect of countries' land and 'non-land' factor endowments.

As in Chapter 6, the distribution of the crude measures of population, population density and GDP per capita, in each case necessarily bound at zero, are highly skewed and for statistical purposes, logged values are used throughout to reduce this. Again, only countries with populations greater than one million are included in the tests. Some of the microstates have very high (and volatile) trade imbalances with the potential to unduly influence the results. The limited availability of data leaves a highly non-random sample, with rich countries relatively overrepresented, those from Africa, in particular, underrepresented, particularly in earlier series. As ever, the statistics should be approached cautiously.

Analyses are first performed on the whole sample of countries for which data available in 1980, 1990, 2000 and 2010. This sample is then divided into two, making an arbitrary divide between those with per capita GDP of $7000, $7500, $8000 and $10,000 in each of these years to provide rich-country and poor-country groups on a roughly consistent basis. The results are reported in Table 7.2.

There is a clear pattern throughout of an association between population density and primary trade. A low population density predisposes countries to net primary exports, a high population density to net imports. For the whole sample, the values are quite consistent over the different decades and the levels of statistical significance (except for rich countries in 2010) are also consistently high. The additional predisposition to export primary products as a result of 'African', 'American' or 'Asian-ness' was very strong, both numerically and statistically in 1980. This appeared to diminish somewhat for Africa and the Americas in the middle decades but become stronger again in 2010. The relation between primary trade and population density appears to hold for both rich and poor countries, at least until 2010. The relation is also evident within each of the poorer-country regions, when similar tests are run on the sub-samples (the results of which are not included here). The regional differences indicate there is more to the story but the evidence broadly supports H–O predictions.

However, emphasizing the point above that primary and secondary trade are not simple reciprocals, there is only much weaker evidence of land-rich countries also being importers of manufactured goods or of land-poor ones being exporters. The signs are usually in the 'right' direction but in the presence of the regional dummy variables, the results for the whole sample reach statistical significance only in 1990 (strongly) and (more marginally) in 2000. Among poorer countries, in particular, the results here provide no statistically significant evidence of a relation between population density and the net level of manufactured goods. For the intra-regional samples, there was evidence of such an association in the Americas and in Asia in 2000. In 1990 there was again evidence of such an association in Asia but in this year there was an apparently significant negative relation in the Americas. In short, labour abundance was a much poorer predictor of trade in manufactured goods than was land abundance of primary trade.

Table 7.2 Trade and factor endowments in 1980, 1990, 2000 and 2010. Regression results: dependent variable is the net level of exports to GDP, either primary of manufactured

		n	R²	Population density	GDP per capita	Population	Africa	Americas	Asia	Eastern Europe and the former USSR	Constant
1980											
Primary	all	76	0.41	-4.6***	4.64***	-1.2	21.5**	15.7***	23.5***		-10.3
	rich	25	0.32	-4.6**	-3.6	-3.4					111.7
	poor	51	0.21	-4.3**	1.3	-0.7					24.5
Secondary	all	76	0.56	0.6	0.9	3.5***	-7.3*	-5.6**	-8.9***		-70.7***
	rich	25	0.42	0.9	5.1	3.9***					-121.2***
	poor	51	0.39	-0.4	1.4	3.7***					-80.6***
1990											
Primary	all	72	0.40	-3.6***	1.6	-1.2	6.04	8.9**	10.6***		19.2
	rich	25	0.54	-3.8***	-4.7	-2.0					99.8**
	poor	47	0.18	-2.9**	1.2	-0.8					20.6
Secondary	all	72	0.56	1.6***	2.4***	2.7***	-0.8	-0.4	-0.8		-78.3***
	rich	25	0.62	2.1***	2.9	1.5**					-66.7***
	poor	47	0.46	0.9	2.8***	3.3***					-88.3***
2000											
Primary	all	129	0.23	-5.2***	2.2*	0.6	6.5	6.9	14.4***	6.7	-8.9
	rich	35	0.37	-3.7***	3.4	-4.6***					61.5
	poor	94	0.19	-5.9***	0.5	2.6**					-19.0

Table 7.2 continued

		n	R²	Population density	GDP per capita	Population	Africa	Americas	Asia	Eastern Europe and the former USSR	Constant
Secondary	all	129	0.33	1.1*	2.9***	2.5***	2.6	-1.7	1.6	0.8	-76.5***
	rich	35	0.18	1.9**	2.8	1.0					-54.4*
	poor	94	0.27	0.4	2.3***	3.0***					-76.7***
2010											
Primary	all	118	0.23	-3.8***	4.1***	-0.1	18.9***	16.4***	15.4***	5.4	-24.6
	rich	38	0.15	-1.8	4.1	-4.0**					34.3
	poor	80	0.22	-6.0***	0.5	1.7					-4.5
Secondary	all	118	0.40	1.2	4.0***	2.5***	0.9	-5.4	-0.3	2.8	-89.3***
	rich	38	0.06	1.1	1.2	1.6					-43.5
	poor	80	0.31	0.9	3.3***	2.9***					-88.7***

Conversely, from the 1990s onwards, the evidence suggests a stronger relation between per capita income and secondary trade than in relation to primary trade. However, wherever the results reached statistical significance the association is positive for both types of exports. In both 1980 and 2010 (and at a low level of statistical confidence in 1990) there is a positive association between country wealth and net primary exports for the whole sample. Not shown here, this relation is also found among Asian countries in 2000 and 2010 and, at a lower level of statistical confidence, in 1990. These included oil-rich countries in West Asia, which may be responsible for at least some of the result. This result is not found within the rich and poor country samples considered separately, so needs to be interpreted cautiously. For secondary trade, there is a strong positive association with GDP per capita among the poorer countries, consistently reaching high levels of statistical significance after 1980. This relation is not evident within the rich country sample. As no attempt has been made to differentiate manufactures according to their labour and/or capital intensity, this result is essentially neutral in relation to H–O, although it might reasonably be interpreted as evidence of successful export of goods made using capital-intensive manufacturing processes, at least that a certain level of wealth is conducive to manufacturing exports.

It may also be tempting to read the association between wealth and net exports in the 'opposite' direction, by inferring that net exports bring wealth. However, the previous chapter suggested this hypothesis can be rejected with reasonably high levels of confidence. If anything, it was countries with net imports that did better.

Population was introduced as a control, although the discussion of NTT in Chapter 4 anticipated that it might also be a predictor of net manufacturing exports (Keesing and Sherk 1971). This is quite strongly confirmed by the evidence here, although the relation does not achieve statistical significance for the rich countries in either 2000 or 2010. It is strongly confirmed for the poorer countries as a group and in each of the poorer-country regions. For rich countries, population appears to be negatively associated with net primary exports, significantly so in 2000 and 2010. There is no evidence of this among poorer countries and the opposite relation, of larger countries tending to export primary products, is seen in 2000.

The results appear to be robust. Some countries – Macao, Singapore and Hong Kong – are outliers in terms of population density, but removing them from the sample increases rather than diminishes the power of the results. The tests were also repeated on a consistent sample of 70 countries, for which data was available across the decades, and this broadly confirmed the results. In this sample, for the 39 poorer countries, the (negative) association between net primary exports and population density become progressively stronger both numerically and in its statistical significance over the decades. The message of orthodoxy appeared to be getting through. Meanwhile, for richer countries, although there was still a highly significant relationship, this level of statistical confidence weakened somewhat, suggesting a greater variety of trajectories.

This evidence broadly supports the basic H–O model. Countries do tend to trade on the basis of their factor endowments conceived even in the broadest terms. This tendency is stronger for primary products than manufactured commodities and stronger among poorer than richer countries. In particular, countries that are land-rich seem more likely to run surpluses of primary products, and those that are land-poor to have primary deficits. Among poorer countries, in particular, those that are relatively wealthy in GDP per capita terms were more likely to have surpluses in manufactured goods. This raises the important neglected question of whether following the prescriptions of H–O theory improves national wealth.

DOES TRADING ON THE BASIS OF FACTOR ENDOWMENTS LEAD TO FASTER GROWTH?

The task now becomes to investigate not simply whether trading, or trading particular goods, is beneficial in itself. It is whether countries benefit when they trade in accordance with (or alternatively in violation of) their factor endowments. To assess this, a slightly more complex model is developed, introducing an interaction term between the level of trade and countries' factor endowments. A focus on land, as the inverse of population density, is taken as an indicator of whether they 'should' export primary or manufactured goods. This interaction term is developed by simply multiplying the level of net exports, whether manufactured or primary, by the difference between each country's population density and world population density. The purpose of this simple manipulation is to produce a variable that has the same sign whenever countries conform to H–O prescriptions and the opposite sign whenever they contradict them. For primary goods the sign is negative when they follow H–O. Either population density is high (+) and there are net imports (–) or population density is low (–) and there are net primary exports (+). Multiplying these, the signs are then positive when countries' trade contradicts H–O (multiplying two positive or two negative values). The opposite is true for manufactured exports: countries conforming to H–O theory are those that are densely populated and with a trade surplus and those that are sparsely populated with a deficit. The interaction term would be negative in the opposite situations when countries trade counter to their factor endowment.

The interaction term is now incorporated alongside the levels of primary and secondary trade and the country characteristics as independent variables. The distinction between rich and poor countries, used above, is retained. Average annual growth over the subsequent decade is treated as the dependent variable. Calculations on growth over 20- and 30-year periods, not included here, showed no improvement on these results. For simplicity, the results are presented for tests without regional variables, which did not substantially alter the findings. The total level of trade relative to GDP was not found to have any significant effect on the models and the results of calculations including this are not reported here. The results are shown in Table 7.3.

The export of primary products, which appeared to have a significantly negative impact on growth in the 1980s, has a positive influence by the 2000s, at least for rich countries. Both results, in the presence of the other variables introduced here, are much stronger than those reported in the previous chapter.

In the 1980s, there is also an apparently strong indication that countries (both rich and poor) that traded primary products on the basis of their factor endowments grew more strongly than those that did not. This result should be treated very cautiously. It is not very robust, being produced by a few countries that had very low population densities, primary surpluses and strong growth, notably Saudi Arabia, Oman and Congo. Without these three countries in the sample there is no significant relationship. Nor was this relation seen in subsequent decades. In 2000, the signs were even positive, in the 'wrong' direction.

For manufactured commodities' trade, by contrast, the negative and weakly significant relation in the 1980s is in the 'wrong' direction, suggesting that land-rich countries also did better when they exported manufactured products. There did appear to be a positive association between the H–O variable and growth among rich countries in the 2000s, suggesting that rich countries did better when they traded manufactured goods according to their population density. The signs were also in the 'correct' direction for poorer countries and for the whole sample but here the results did not approach statistical significance. In short, the evidence offers little support to expectations that countries do better trading according to the prescriptions of H–O theory.

Table 7.3 *Does trading according to factor endowments foster growth? Regression results, dependent variable is GDP growth over the subsequent decade*

	1980			1990			2000		
	All countries	Rich countries	Poor countries	All countries	Rich countries	Poor countries	All countries	Rich countries	Poor countries
Number in sample	76	25	51	72	25	47	127	35	92
R^2	0.32	0.81	0.32	0.15	0.26	0.15	0.33	0.72	0.14
Primary exports	-0.07**	-0.12***	-0.08*	0.01	-0.07	0.01	0.03**	0.06***	0.02
Manufactured exports	0.03	-0.08	0.02	-0.05	-0.07	-0.06	0.00	0.04*	-0.02
Population density	0.01	-0.02	0.19	0.25	-0.00	0.44	0.22	0.21*	0.13
Primary exports × population density	-0.05***	-0.03***	-0.09***	-0.02	-0.05	0.01	0.00	0.01	0.00
Secondary exports × population density	-0.04*	-0.01	-0.04	-0.01	-0.02	0.01	0.01	0.04**	0.01
GDP per capita	-0.35	0.35	-0.13	-0.21	-0.20	0.08	-0.76***	-1.54***	-0.42*
Population	0.44	0.19	0.06	0.24	-0.03	0.43*	0.07	-0.24	0.33
Constant	-1.53	-4.52	-7.46	-0.38	4.88	-6.39	7.99***	20.78***	1.79

It is quite revealing to look a bit more closely at the sample for the 2000s. Of the 127 countries, 52 'got it right', as it were, trading both primary and manufactured goods according to H–O, with surpluses in one, deficits in the other, and these fitting their relative land abundance. These included rich and poor net manufacturing exporters like Japan, Germany, China and India and net primary exporters including Brazil, Russia, Canada, Australia and most of the oil-rich countries. The (unweighted) average growth of these countries was 4.14 per cent a year. It is 34 countries that get it right for primary exports and wrong for manufactured ones. Remarkably, all of these were relatively land-poor countries, which 'correctly' imported primary products but which also imported manufactures. This group included Bangladesh, Egypt, Britain, Spain and Poland. The average growth of these countries was a slightly higher 4.31 per cent a year. A smaller group of 17 countries got it wrong for primary but right for manufactured commodities' trade. Most of these were also net importers of both categories of goods – but as land-rich countries would now have been expected to export primary commodities. These include the US, Mexico and Mozambique. Just four countries (in the entire sample) were net exporters of both types of goods – Malaysia, Indonesia, Thailand and Ireland – and they also fall into this category. The average growth of this group was slightly lower at 3.99 per cent per year. Finally, a group of 24 countries traded both primary and manufactured goods in defiance of their factor endowments. These include densely populated countries like Vietnam, Nigeria, Ethiopia and the Netherlands exporting primary goods and importing manufactures and relatively sparsely populated countries like Sweden, Finland, Botswana and the Central African Republic exporting manufactures and importing primary products. The average growth rate of this group that got it wrong on both counts was highest of all, 4.58 per cent a year.

This is not to suppose that trading in the opposite direction to that predicted by Heckscher and Ohlin aids growth. As the previous chapter made clear, poorer countries in general and those in Asia in particular grew quickly and the figures may reflect this. However, these results caution against any simple adherence to the prescriptions.

CONCLUSION

This chapter addressed two related questions: whether countries trade according to their factor endowments and whether, in as far as they do, this is associated with stronger economic growth. A particular interest in primary products and endowments of land juxtaposed these to manufactured products and endowments of labour. Accordingly, the discussion substantially dodged debates concerning the changing character of manufacturing trade, the substitution of capital and labour or the respective role of skilled and unskilled workers.

The models are extremely simple, data availability is limited and any conclusions must, accordingly, be highly provisional. However, the results confirm significant relationships particularly between net primary product exports and countries' endowments of land. There is weaker evidence of an association between net manufactured exports and endowments of labour. Richer countries were more likely to export manufactured goods but also primary goods. The results for land and labour endowments would be anticipated by H–O theory, although factor endowments typically account for only a small part of the observed variation in patterns of trade.

The chapter then investigated whether trade as predicted by H–O theory influenced economic growth. This required a slightly more complex model to analyse the impact on economic growth of trade in particular commodities, factor endowments and the interaction between them. This interaction variable produced apparently significant results for primary trade in the 1980s. Land-rich countries that were net exporters and land-poor ones that were importers tended to grow faster. However, this result was neither strong nor robust and was not seen in subsequent decades. Thus, the conclusions are largely negative. It is not possible to show convincing evidence of systematic success or failure when trade is based on land endowments, either in relation to primary or manufactured products. Even in the decade from 2000, a period when many primary commodity prices rose and primary exporters in general did well, there was no obvious particular benefit for land-rich countries.

The evidence thus confirms the enduring relevance of factor endowments, even conceived at the simplest levels of land and labour, as the bases on which countries, particularly poorer countries, do in fact trade. Whether countries grow faster when they trade on such bases remains in doubt.

8. International trade and inequality within countries

INTRODUCTION

This chapter explores the relationship between trade and inequality within countries. Discussions about the pros and cons of trade too often stop at whether or not it is in the national interest. Questions about winners and losers within countries can be at least as important. Indeed, these distributional issues are often the crux of the matter. Countries are internally divided and the 'national interest' is illusive. Questions of who gains and who loses are critical.

The most influential proposition has been the Stolper–Samuelson theorem, a neo-classical theory which argues that there are likely to be winners and losers within countries from both protection and trade opening. As explained in the next section, according to this theorem, the owners of those factors of production in which a country is abundantly endowed are expected to reveal their efficiency on a world scale and increase their market and the prices received for their labour or for their products. Conversely, in a closed economy, the effective market remains limited and prices are kept down. Meanwhile, the owners of those factors of production that are relatively scarce within a country would be expected to be in the opposite situation. Having enjoyed protection, exposure to foreign competition would reveal their relative costliness and undermine their economic position.

The theory has been widely invoked to explain concomitant rises in trade and inequality in recent decades, particularly in rich countries. The picture in poorer ones is more mixed, raising interesting questions about these countries but also about the interpretation of the rich-country experience. If the theory works in some situations but not others, there may be problems. The subsequent section of this chapter explores these issues, drawing on material from an article published in the *Journal of Sociology* (Dunn 2014b) on the relation between trade and returns to education. Following this, the chapter then reports the results of some new tests of the relationships between trade and factor endowments; tests that specify the variables more carefully than has been the norm in the literature, separating trade in primary and manufactured commodities and considering class rather than just skill polarization. However, the results are not strong and it remains unobvious that the Stolper–Samuelson theorem can explain patterns of inequality. The final section considers how other processes might work alongside, or apart from, the effects towards which the Stolper–Samuelson framework has previously directed economists' attention. It considers the possible effects of skill-biased technological change, which might exacerbate inequality in rich countries and offset any egalitarian consequences in poorer ones. It ends by broadening the discussion to the social and political construction of inequality. The conclusions indicate there is much more to inequality than can be understood through the lens of conventional trade theory and that this should temper some of the rather strong, persistent and influential claims about trade's effects.

THE STOLPER–SAMUELSON THEOREM

Stolper and Samuelson (1941) argue that international trade generates a relatively complex pattern of winners and losers within countries on the basis of ownership of particular factors of production. Without repeating Chapters 3 and 7, a brief summary of their neo-classical underpinnings is in order. The roots of the theory can be traced to classical political economy, particularly Ricardian comparative advantage. This sees countries gaining from trade by specializing in goods in which they have comparative, that is relative, productivity advantages. Then, as seen in the last chapter, Heckscher (1950) and Ohlin (1991) suggest that countries should specialize in and export goods, the production of which predominantly utilizes factors of production that they hold in relative abundance. If, within a country, particular resources are plentiful, their costs will tend to be lower. Conversely, scarce resources will tend to be more expensive and using these would push up production costs. In the simplest models, the factors of production remain those of classical political economy: land, labour and capital. So, sparsely populated poorer countries are 'land-rich' and utilizing this resource, they should specialize in producing primary products like agricultural goods or minerals. They could then export some of their production and import capital-intensive and labour-intensive manufactured goods more cheaply than they could make them themselves. Conversely, a densely populated rich country is relatively abundant in labour and in capital, so it would do better specializing in, say, pharmaceuticals or microprocessor production than raising llamas. The last chapter's evidence provided some statistical support for these ideas.

Stolper and Samuelson argue that 'it is clear from the Heckscher–Ohlin theorem that the introduction of trade must lower the relative share in the real or money national income going to the scarce factors of production' (1941: 59). Writing from a US perspective, they contrast the experiences of capital and labour. As the most capital-rich country, the US has enjoyed a comparative advantage in the production of capital-intensive manufactures. American capital (although it was only slowly being persuaded of the benefits of trade after a long history of rather successful protection) would gain from openness. Workers, by contrast, relatively scarce within the US, could bid up their wages in a closed economy. Openness would undermine this. For such workers, a failure to support free trade reflected less an ignorance of Ricardo's elegant logic than their rational self-interest. Similar reasoning can be applied to the contrast between land and labour. Samuelson (1948) does this in another widely cited article. Looked at from this perspective, the US was relatively land-rich compared with labour-rich Europe. Again, US workers would be the losers from trade openness.

Stolper and Samuelson remain supporters of free trade. The national economy still gains and, as Heckscher (1950) anticipated, any losses experienced because of openness could be ameliorated through redistributive tax systems. As Rogowski writes, 'the gainers from trade can always compensate the losers and have something left over'. However, he continues: 'it remains unobvious that such compensation will in fact occur. Rather, the natural tendency is for gainers to husband their winnings and to stop their ears to the cries of the afflicted' (1989: 17). This is an important point because it draws attention to the fact that the relation between trade opening and inequality is socially and politically mediated. However, it is inconsistent for free trade supporters to identify trade's significant positive impacts on national economies but to dismiss as insignificant its redistributive economic logic (Rodrik 1997; Dreher and Gaston 2006).

Rogowski (1989) goes on to account for a series of historical struggles within countries on the basis of the Stolper–Samuelson theorem. He proposes a two-by-two matrix, classifying countries as capital-rich or capital-poor according to their GDP per capita and then either land-rich or labour-rich according to their population density (see Figure 8.1). This could be mapped onto the country plots presented in Figure 7.2 in the last chapter. For Rogowski, urban–rural struggles predominate where capital and labour are united against land. This occurs in the densely populated rich countries, like Ricardo's Britain of the nineteenth century. It also occurs, in the opposite direction, in poorer, land-rich countries where capital and labour's anti-trade interests coincide. Populism in twentieth-century Latin America provides a powerful example. Class struggles predominate where labour finds itself in opposition to both capital and landowners. This occurs in densely populated poorer countries, where only workers have an interest in openness, and in sparsely populated rich ones, where only workers oppose trade. This typology, and labour's changing interests as we move from top left to bottom right in Figure 8.1, will be revisited in what follows.

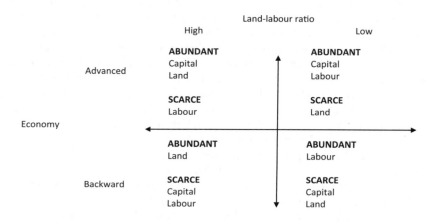

Source: Rogowski (1989).

Figure 8.1   Rogowski's four main types of factor endowments

For Heckscher and Ohlin and for Stolper and Samuelson, the three-factor model was only ever an analytical tool and each factor could in principle be sub-divided. In practice, of course, countries have different sorts of land and a variety of capital goods, based on varied technologies. The attributes of workers are variable too and, recognizing this, Stolper and Samuelson (1941) distinguish a highly skilled minority from the majority of unskilled or only moderately skilled workers. They posited that while the majority in the US would lose, experiencing real wage reductions as a result of increased trade openness, the skilled minority were relatively abundant and would be expected to gain.

There is a telling corollary to this. It is seldom clear who exactly qualifies as skilled and unskilled. In practice, of course, there is a continuum. However, it is hard to find any estimate that puts the figure for the proportion of high-skilled winners from trade in rich countries like the US higher than 30 per cent of the workforce, which is roughly the proportion who are university graduates. Even on the widest estimates, fully 70 per cent are therefore expected to lose from trade opening. So impeccably liberal theory indicates that trade liberalization is against the personal economic interests of the majority of the population in rich countries.

The reverse effects might reasonably be anticipated in countries with the opposite factor endowments. Other things being equal, poorer countries (or at least those poorer countries with which rich ones like the US trade) would be expected to sell the products of their relatively less-skilled labour on international markets. Therefore, despite some returns for greater skill and education in all countries, the gaps between the skilled and unskilled might be expected to diminish with trade opening in poorer countries.

CONTEMPORARY CONTROVERSIES ABOUT SKILLS, INCOME POLARIZATION AND TRADE

Rich-country income polarization has been the focus of much recent scholarship (Reich 1991; Wood 1994, 1998; Reuveny and Li 2003). There have been at least roughly concurrent increases in trade openness and inequality in the US and several other countries (Chusseau and Dumont 2013; Hellier 2013). Rich countries' abundance of high-skilled labour seems to have become the basis of their comparative advantage. Highly skilled workers are already relatively rich and now the heightened demand for the products of their labour increases their pay. Meanwhile, the unskilled in rich countries are outnumbered absolutely and relatively by those in poor countries and the demand for the products of their labour has declined. The high-skilled gain, the low-skilled lose, and the gaps in pay between them widen. At first sight, this experience fits with the Stolper–Samuelson theory, neatly associating 'North–South' trade with rising inequality.

Critics of these claims initially emphasized that for the US, on which much of the early literature focused, trade volumes with the South were small in relation to GDP. It seemed implausible that it was responsible for the substantial income polarization taking place (Krugman 1995; Lawrence 2008). However, by the 2000s, trade with poorer countries represented a much higher proportion of the US economy, and the main trading partners were now also considerably poorer (China and Mexico rather than Korea and Taiwan). The weighted average per capita income of America's trading partners was only 65 per cent of the US level in 2005, where it had been 81 per cent as recently as 1990 (Krugman 2008). Hellier therefore insists the objection that trade with poorer countries was insufficient to account for the observed inequality 'is no longer valid' (2013: 108). However, even if the theory fits the evidence better than before, this hardly removes the original objection. Inequality was growing before it could plausibly be attributed to trade openness, which surely casts doubt on trade's role. The suspect has a good alibi for the first of the crimes, which does not necessarily absolve them from suspicion of later offences but might reasonably shift the focus of the investigation. As Wood (1998) acknowledged, it was also only those at the very top of the income scale who were being rewarded and many apparently skilled workers did not experience the expected benefits. Lawrence reports that 'from 2000 to 2006, an astonishingly small fraction of workers – just 3.4% with doctorates and professional graduates ... fell in a category that on average sustained an increase in average inflation-adjusted take-home pay' (2008: 4).

It is worth reflecting briefly on the different meanings and measures of inequality. It can be conceived on a class basis, in terms of the 'functional distribution of income' between labour and capital. More often it is understood on an individual, or more problematically, on a 'household' basis (UN 2012). It can be assessed in terms of accumulated wealth or income in a given year. Useful but different measures compare the income of a certain percentage at the top with the median or bottom 10 per cent, while the Gini index attempts to provide an aggregate measure between 0 (complete equality) and 100 (where one person receives all the income). There are also recurring measurement problems and a common tendency in the literature to simply take changes in levels of inequality is itself evidence of the changing skill premiums (Chusseau and Dumont 2013; Hellier 2013). This is really assuming what needs to be shown, that changes in income reflect changes in the labour-market position.

International comparisons of the relations between trade and inequality remain underwhelming. A simple comparison of the trends of change in trade openness and the Gini co-efficient for 24 rich and 97 poor countries for which data were available (for a minimum of ten years) between 1990 and 2010 shows only a weak positive association for the rich countries and virtually no trend in poorer ones (calculated from Solt 2013 and WB 2014). Where for rich countries there is at least some case study and anecdotal evidence, empirical studies of poorer countries consistently struggle to find even that. Poorer countries' experiences are much more 'uneven' (Chusseau and Hellier 2013) or frankly 'at variance with the model predictions' (Hellier 2013). According to Dreher and Gaston, the available evidence leaves matters 'an almost complete mystery' (2006: ii).

One reason why Stolper–Samuelson effects may not be observable in poorer countries is that patterns of specialization between North and South change over time. The claim is that trade is based on exchanging goods based on different endowments. So it is possible for countries to change character as they grow and increase their levels of trade. The expanding effective size of the South, according to Chusseau and Hellier, means an increase in the 'world skill premium and thus inequality in both the North and the South' (2013: 59). As the South increases its total production, the demand for skilled workers within it increases (Hellier 2013). However, these models envisage a situation where the size of the South is such that the North now becomes completely specialized, only competing in high-skilled products. If both North and South were to export goods produced on the basis of both skilled and unskilled labour, this would contradict Heckscher–Ohlin and the theory of comparative advantage. However, were the North to become completely specialized, there would no longer seem to be any reason to anticipate further polarization in the North. Rescuing Stolper–Samuelson from the anomalous evidence from the South undermines the previously stronger evidence from the North.

The persistent difficulties make it pertinent to look at one study, which is an exception in showing a clear divergence between the experiences of rich and poor countries and their workers when exposed to trade. Babones (2010) does not interpret his results in terms of the Stolper–Samuelson theory, arguing instead that everywhere the knowledgeable reap a premium in an increasingly global economy but the dominance of 'education-as-credential' in poorer countries means its recipients suffer on exposure to foreign competition. However, the results might be interpreted as providing a rare example of rigorous contemporary support for the predictions of the Stolper–Samuelson theorem and a careful examination seems warranted.

Drawing on data from the World Values Survey, Babones (2010) shows that the returns to education are positive in all countries except one (Armenia), but to varying degrees. The level of this association is then plotted against trade openness (taken from the World Development Indicators database), measured as the logarithm of the trade to GDP ratio. Using a global sample of 81 countries, Babones (2010) finds no significant association between the levels of trade openness and the relation between education and income. However, splitting the sample into two groups, according to the World Bank definition of 'developed' and 'developing', a significant positive correlation is demonstrated in the former and a negative one in the latter. This is to say that in rich countries the premium for being more highly educated increases the more the country is exposed to foreign trade. The converse is true in poorer countries where the association between education and income declines the more open the economy.

These results can be verified. Here, Babones' data for the returns for education as the dependent variable are retained but slightly different data sets are substituted for the trade to GDP ratio and GDP per capita from the United Nations Human Development Report (UNHDR) (UN 2007). The United Nations Organization for Education, Science and Culture (UNESCO) (2011) database is revisited to provide data for secondary school enrolments. In several cases, the original sample reverted to alternative sources or made estimates of one or more variable. Here, where complete data are not available from these sources, the country is simply omitted from the sample, leaving a reduced but still respectable 73-country panel. Following Babones, Table 8.1 shows the results of regression analyses, for the whole sample and for developed and developing country sub-samples. The results in the first three columns of the table show similar numerical values to those produced by Babones and confirm the positive and negative associations between the returns to education and trade openness in developed and developing countries, respectively. The fourth column in Table 8.1, again following Babones, introduces a dummy variable for countries' development status (1 or 0) and an interaction term between this and the level of openness. Again the results confirm the positive association between trade openness and widening returns to education in rich countries, while for the sample as a whole the relation between trade opening and returns to education now becomes negative. While the R-squared in the overall models and the numerical values for the particular relations are not large, they are highly statistically significant; at least as convincingly with this data as in the original sample. It would appear that returns to education increase as rich countries become more open to the international economy, while in poorer countries they diminish.

Babones interprets this result in terms of the different content and contribution of education in developed and developing countries. In the former, 'education-as-knowledge' predominates. The educated acquire the skills with which they compete successfully in an open global economy. In the latter, 'education-as-credential' gives the better-qualified

Table 8.1   Returns to education and trade in developed and developing countries: education-as-knowledge or credential models. Regression results – dependent variable is the correlation between education and income

All countries	All countries	Developing countries	Developed countries	All countries	All countries
Number in sample	73	47	26	73	73
R²	0.16	0.36	0.21	0.28	0.35
Trade openness	–0.06	–0.21**	0.17**	–0.24***	–0.92*
log GDP/cap	0.16**	0.33***	–0.04	0.22***	–0.19
Secondary enrolment ratio	–0.00***	–0.00***	–0.00	–0.00***	0.00*
Developed status (1 or 0)				–0.70***	
Interaction of openness × development status				0.41***	
Interaction of openness × GDP / capita					0.23*
Africa					0.12
Americas					0.20***
Asia					0.04
E.Europe and former USSR					0.02
Constant	0.03	–0.26	0.31	0.06	1.18

advantages with which they can prosper in a closed economy but these advantages are undermined once exposed to foreign competition. The argument is stated cautiously, with acknowledgement that it represents only a 'package explanation of a set of interesting empirical facts' (Babones 2010: 58). The results could also be read as confirmation of Stolper–Samuelson. On that reasoning, skilled workers gain from trade where they are relatively abundant but lose where they are relatively scarce. Indeed, Babones' results could be seen as a slightly different version of the same thing. Both interpretations agree that there is, in effect, a 'surfeit of education' in poorer countries where the privileges of the educated are competed away in an open economy (Babones 2010: 58).

However, there are reasons to be cautious. Babones' interpretation, in terms of 'credentialism' produces some significant problems. Levels of education in poorer countries undoubtedly tend to be lower than in the more economically advanced. However, counterposing 'education-as-knowledge' and 'education-as-credential' suggests more than this. As I understand it, the argument requires that credentialism in poorer countries increases the more education one has. If the proportion of education-as-knowledge and education-as-credential were constant, then there seems little reason to anticipate a changing distribution of national income with foreign trade. It is specifically those at the top, those with most formal education, whose privileges are apparently eroded by foreign competition and this seems to imply that credentialism is relative in two senses. First, in poorer countries, universities are relatively worse in terms of providing merely credentials than are the high schools, which in turn are relatively worse than the primary schools. Second, it is not the absolute levels alone that are greater in rich countries but also that this phenomenon of increasing credentialism is (at least) relatively less pronounced.

Both propositions can be challenged. Spending per student increases faster at higher levels in poorer countries than in rich ones (UNESCO 2011; Dunn 2014b). A substantial literature also describes how education in rich countries often involves large elements of credentialism. Education can often be about maintaining 'cultural capital' and a mechanism for elite perpetuation (Bourdieu 1984; Brown 1995). There is evidence that in at least some rich countries, over-education relative to the jobs being performed was increasing steeply at exactly the time being considered around the turn of the century (Green and Zhu 2010). As will be discussed below, inequality and educational attainment might rise together, without this involving a meritocratic reward for increased skills. Meanwhile, elites in many poorer countries increasingly obtain foreign qualifications, studying in private 'international' schools within the home country and attending metropolitan universities (Lowe 2000). Of course, none of this proves that credentialism is not greater in poorer countries. It remains possible that the knowledge content of education decreases as public funding increases. In some countries, particularly at higher levels, education does not rely on state funding but reaches high standards for those who can afford it. Other factors may also be significant, the quality of teaching, for example, is no doubt highly varied. The prevalence of 'education-as-credential' in poorer countries should nevertheless be treated cautiously.

The evidence also seems to remain contestable. Two themes seem worth investigating. First, there is a high level of inter-regional variation of inequality. Babones' study showed that on average the level of association between education and income was broadly similar for developed and developing countries. Behind these averages lay the apparently divergent relations between trade openness and returns from education described above. However, his data also revealed substantial differences in terms of the average correlation between education and inequality on a regional basis. Second, rather than there being a simple two-way distinction between countries, their relative income lies along a continuum. Levels of national GDP per capita were included in Babones' models as a control for the demand for education but might also be used to develop an interaction term between trade and wealth on a more nuanced basis than is possible using the simple developed–developing binary.

Taking these two points into account, the final column in Table 8.1 reports the results of a slightly modified regression analysis with a simple four-way regional categorization for the poorer countries, and an interaction between GDP per capita and trade openness. In the presence of these variables, the statistical confidence with which the overall relations hold is much reduced. The strong and highly statistically significant association between returns to education and the regional variable for the Americas indicates that this might be responsible for a substantial part of the overall earlier result.

It is also notable that Reuveny and Li (2003) anticipated similar results to those of Babones but could not find them empirically. The tests above are also performed only on a cross-sectional panel. Unfortunately, time-series data for returns to education are not readily available but other studies suggest there may be substantial differences between changes over time and the pattern of international characteristics at any moment. Babones' own earlier research had shown 'profoundly inconsistent' variation between longitudinal and cross-sectional samples (Babones and Vonanda 2009: 21). So Babones' later results are highly suggestive but there are reasons to doubt the generality of any connection between education, inequality and trade.

REAPPLYING AND RE-TESTING THE STOLPER–SAMUELSON THEOREM

There are further reasons to question existing work on the Stolper–Samuelson theorem. This section considers two important but overlooked dimensions. First, it is implicit in the Stolper–Samuelson argument about winners and losers that countries trade according to their factor endowments. Many studies of the impacts of trade openness simply consider the total level of trade (usually the sum of exports and imports) as a proportion of GDP. This can be a useful measure of openness both of particular countries and of the global economy. However, for these purposes it is insufficient. As discussed in the previous chapter, there are statistically significant associations along the lines Heckscher and Ohlin anticipate but also many exceptions. It is entirely possible for a country to trade in violation of what theory deems appropriate. There would then be no reason to expect the Stolper–Samuelson theorem to hold, no reason why the owners of abundantly endowed factors should benefit from trade. For example, increased trade by a land-rich country might enrich landowners and weaken labour (Samuelson 1948) but only if the country was actually a net exporter of primary products and importer of labour-intensive manufactured ones. It is quite possible for such a country to instead increase its labour-intensive manufactured exports. In this situation workers would be expected to gain. This also underlines the importance of evaluating the net position. Theories of trade are precisely that, about trade, about exporting some goods and importing others. The import and re-export (perhaps after a minimal working-up) of goods with similar factor content would hardly be expected to impact dramatically on income distribution. Further, and again as discussed in previous chapters, we should not assume that the balances of manufactured and primary goods are simple reciprocals of each other. It is therefore more appropriate to study the trade balances in particular types of commodity considered separately than to rely on aggregate measures.

Second, the Heckscher–Ohlin and Stolper–Samuelson theorems were originally conceived on the basis of land, labour and capital. As neo-classical economists, they generally avoided explicit use of the term 'class' but they were looking at the relative incomes of these groups as a whole. Both theories went beyond Ricardo by introducing land and capital as factors of production alongside labour. This has almost completely dropped out of the picture in the recent debates on skill polarization, which instead focus on the divide among workers. While, differences of skills (or credentials) may be important dimensions of contemporary income polarization, there is little reason to assume they are the only one or even the most important. The simple skill dichotomy is also rather convenient politically. Rather than seeing inequality in class terms, it becomes a matter of within-class polarization. As in the original formulations, we might reasonably also expect the owners of land and capital to have an interest in or against trade openness (Meschi and Vivarelli 2009).

Any attempt to broaden the analysis undoubtedly complicates the mathematics and the difficulties of empirical testing but the spirit of

Stolper–Samuelson requires at least a provisional attempt. The expected implications of trade for patterns of overall national inequality seem most clear in Rogowski's 'class struggle' scenarios. Labour's gains would be expected to increase equality. In terms of simple aggregates, these would be achieved, according to the Stolper–Samuelson theory, by increased manufactured exports from labour-rich countries and manufactured imports into labour-poor countries. Effective labour endowments can then be calculated on the basis of population density divided by GDP per capita, so they run from bottom right to top left in Figure 8.1. A simple interaction term can also be developed by multiplying the level of exports by the labour endowment considered relative to the average. The purpose of this is that the term becomes positive in situations where labour gains (net exports and labour abundance, and net imports and labour scarcity) and negative where labour loses (net exports and labour scarcity, and net imports and labour abundance). The effects of primary trade on inequality are less clear-cut but a similar variable multiplying labour endowments by the level of net primary exports can be developed on an experimental basis.

The year 2000 provides the best available statistical coverage, with data for 128 countries for the Gini coefficient (from Solt 2013), levels of trade, including the balance of primary and secondary trade, population, GDP per capita and population density (from WB 2014). It is therefore hypothesized that the level of inequality might be a function of: the level of trade; the trade balance in particular commodities; country factor endowments; and the interaction between these and the trade balance. As above, there are strong indications of regional variation in levels of inequality and regional dummy variables are included as controls. For a 112-country sample, somewhat more biased towards rich countries, data were also available for the changes in inequality and of trade for at least a ten-year period between 1990 and 2010. Similar tests can then be run on the changes in inequality and in trade.

The cross-sectional sample produces a weak, negative association (–0.68), significant at the 90 per cent confidence level, between the Gini coefficient and the interaction term. This is in the 'right' direction, confirming that inequality tended to be less where labour's gains were expected. However, this relation was not found among the regional groups when considered separately. There was a strong negative association between inequality and labour endowments (–10.55**), indicating labour-rich countries tended to be more equal, while the regional dummy variables for Africa, the Americas and Asia (but not Eastern Europe and the former USSR) were strongly and significantly positive, indicating countries in these regions tended to be more unequal than the rich countries in the sample. None of the other specifically trade-related variables produced significant results. In terms of the time-series data, there was no significant relation between the interaction term and changes in inequality. Increases in trade, and secondary trade in particular, were now positively associated (0.16***) with increased inequality but this occurred irrespective of countries' factor endowments.

It is difficult to predict the net impacts on national inequality of Rogowski's urban–rural struggles without knowing more about patterns of land ownership. However, similar tests can be run along other axes on an experimental basis, examining the implications for inequality of capital and land and their interaction with trade. Again in terms of the cross-sectional data there appeared to be a positive association (6.24), significant at the 95 per cent confidence level, between inequality and the interaction of land-wealth and secondary trade. It appeared that land-rich countries were more unequal the more they exported manufactured goods and land-poor ones the more they imported. Within regions, this result is only confirmed with any statistical confidence among Asian countries. It is not found in the time-series data. No significant association was found between inequality or changes in inequality and the interaction of the levels of GDP per capita with the levels of trade.

Further tests, not reproduced here, on a more limited sample of countries measuring changes in inequality in terms of the income at the top, bottom and middle of the distribution also fail to show any clear correspondence between the ways this was occurring and predictions based on the Stolper–Samuelson theorem (ILO 2008; OECD 2010; Dunn 2014b). Once again, the evidence in support of Stolper–Samuelson seems rather weak. Of course, few would believe that trade is the sole cause of inequality or changes in inequality but the thesis that it plays a major part has been very prominent in the literature. This seems hard to justify.

INEQUALITY AND CHANGING GLOBAL POLITICAL ECONOMY

The Stolper–Samuelson theorem does not exhaust the story of trade and inequality. As ever, there are alternative perspectives and some of these might also provide reasons why Stolper–Samuelson effects are hard to verify empirically. Exploring some of these alternative perspectives can provide the foundations for a more adequate understanding of the forces impacting on inequality.

First, it is pertinent to note that there are several reasons why trade might lessen inequality. Birdsall (1998) argues that imports increase price competition, lowering the costs of consumption goods and increasing real wages for the poor, while breaking the power of monopoly of the already privileged. Although Chapter 6 suggested the evidence is rather weak, trade might also be associated with less inequality because it promotes growth (Chakrabati 2000; Reuveny and Li 2003; Chusseau and Hellier 2013). Kuznets (1953) proposed an inverted U-shaped relationship between inequality and wealth, so for countries beyond the top of this curve, perhaps an increasing number as time goes by, growth-producing changes might also augur greater equality. As above, recent data confirm there is a significant negative association between country wealth in GDP per capita terms and inequality, although this now appears to have none of the curvilinear characteristics described by Kuznets (1953). Inequality seems more attributable to regional variation rather than to wealth as such.

Conversely, there are many theses attributing widening income polarization to increased trade openness, not only in rich countries and not simply because of Stolper–Samuelson effects. Many critical perspectives see trade inducing greater inequality in poorer countries. The 'dependency' literature typically focuses on international inequalities but it can also detail how chains of metropolitan control reach deep within the dependant countries and produce new patterns of land ownership, dispossession and inequality. There is thus an interdependence between inter- and intra-national relations (Frank 1970; Cardoso and Falletto 1979). It is possible to read several elements of Singer's (1950) analysis as suggesting that trade fosters inegalitarian pressures within poorer countries, notably through the development of dualist economies and the weakness of multiplier effects between export-oriented and domestic sectors. Prebisch (1950) and Emmanuel (1972) attribute considerable explanatory power to labour and to rising or high wages in the North. This probably also implies relatively low levels of Northern inequality but the effect is to create or perpetuate low wages and therefore higher levels of intra-national inequality in the periphery.

Much of the critical dependency literature also stresses the differences between primary and manufactured exports, and the declining terms of trade of the former (Singer 1950; Robinson 1979). Whether as cause or consequence, we might accordingly anticipate increased inequality in primary-goods-exporting countries, less inequality in manufacture-exporting countries. Primary imports, in particular, might tend to lower prices, including food prices, to the benefit of the poor, while exports would tend to raise them. Similar effects for manufacturing imports might be offset more strongly by their labour-displacing effects (Leamer 2012). While the relation is not straightforward and not evident in the tests reported above, again this would imply that trade tends to increase inequality in many poorer countries.

Bringing technology into the discussion can also be helpful in understanding the trade-inequality connections, although it also introduces some further conceptual and empirical difficulties. One influential argument sees increased trade as likely to foster skill-biased technological change. This in turn is thought likely to increase the demand and reward for higher skills and thence to increase income polarization. Trade openness is linked to increases in the opportunities for the talents of the highly skilled and already relatively privileged. Meanwhile, with capital replacing unskilled workers, greater competition for fewer jobs pushes down the conditions of the unskilled (Wood 1994; Acemoglu 2003). Thus, Babones maintains that 'economic models predict that trade globalization should increase returns to education in both developed and developing countries' (2010: 47). This is why he suggests that ideas that globalization might disproportionately benefit the less educated in poorer countries 'flies in the face of common sense' (2010: 58).

In rich countries, skill-biased technological change would add to the inequality-producing effects predicted by Stolper–Samuelson. In poorer countries it would be expected to counteract the anticipated equality-producing effects, accounting for the difficulties in verifying the expected relations (Acemoglu 2003; Chusseau and Hellier 2013). This is supported by studies that find the nature of the trading partners to be decisive. When poorer countries trade with high-income countries (both via imports and exports) this worsens their income distribution, whereas trade with other developing countries has the opposite effect (Anderson 2005; Meschi and Vivarelli 2009). These are important and influential ideas. However, both the claims of technological change and of skill-bias need to be treated very cautiously.

First, it is very hard to quantify skills. Neo-classical arguments assume that labour markets, like others, work perfectly. So rewards for each factor of production are assumed to reflect accurately their economic contribution. Wage differentials reflect skill differentials, by assumption. Time and again, the literature on skills and pay becomes completely circular, with no attempt to measure skills in any other way (Anderson 2005). There are honourable exceptions. As seen above, Babones looks at levels of education and other studies have similarly measured schooling at various levels (Wood 1994). Some authors survey occupations (Krugman 2008). The measurement of different forms of work, 'blue collar' against 'white collar', at least provides a relatively independent variable, even as it is fraught with conceptual problems (Meschi and Vivarelli 2009). Such classifications might have little to do with the actual amount of skill needed to do particular tasks. Qualifications, in the North as much as the South, can be credentials, perhaps useful to employers as indicators of particular social attributes but providing little indication of the skills needed to perform particular workplace tasks. Jobs can be seen as low skilled because those who do them are low status (Adler 2004), often women rather than men and ethnic minorities and migrants. Huge and persistent gaps between male and female earnings and between white and non-white workers (see, for example, Mishel et al. 1996) should qualify any simple association of pay and skill. For example, in the US, even as female graduates became the majority, pay gaps narrowed only slowly (Dunn 2009). Often those with high levels of work skills, gained through experience and apprenticeships will precisely be those who lack formal educational qualifications.

Second, skills are also specific and only imperfectly transferable. Galbraith and Hale's (2009) work on sectoral inequality in the US reveals some sharp differences between industries and over time. Sometimes the highly skilled gain. So 'students who studied information technology in the mid-1990s were lucky; those completing similar degrees in 2000 faced unemployment' (2009: 16). Meanwhile, in the latter period, construction workers did very well. Of course, many construction workers are highly skilled but they are hardly those envisaged as winners by the influential depictions of the new economy and increasing returns to education. Galbraith and Hale conclude that 'education and training have become a kind of lottery, whose winners and losers are determined, *ex post*, by the behaviour of the economy' (2009: 16). Calculations of intersectional inequality in the few countries for which statistics are available from 1991 to 2008 also suggest a very mixed pattern both in terms of the rise and fall of inequality and the sectors responsible (ILO, 1997, 2008, 2010; Dunn 2014b).

Third, technological innovation and its impacts are hard to quantify. Technological change has been continuous, endemic to capitalism. Levels of domestic inequality fell for much of the twentieth century in most of the dynamic capitalist economies. The question therefore becomes why it is only recently that technologies are supposedly having specifically skill-inducing and polarizing effects. Technologies may have deskilled many traditional blue-collar jobs but white-collar work can be susceptible to exactly the same pressures, the bank teller as much as the machine minder operating highly capital-intensive but skill-displacing technologies. This is not to envisage an inexorable process of deskilling, as some early Marxist interpretations insisted (Braverman 1974), but it is to question claims of any straightforward upgrading produced by the 'new economy' or new forms of work organization (Bell 1974; Womack et al.

1990; Reich 1991; Adler 2004). There is again a suspicion that these effects are simply being read backwards from increasing pay differentials. In fact, since the 1970s, levels of investment as a proportion of national income, which might be thought a crucial source of innovation, have fallen across rich-country economies. By this token, the argument might look stronger in relation to the South, where investment levels have risen in many countries and in aggregate across the developing world.

There are, of course, numerous other causes of inequality, related to characteristics of national political economies, which might work independently of trade or alternatively might interact with it. Other, concomitant aspects of openness, foreign direct investment (FDI), financial flows and migration might pull in different ways (Reuveny and Li 2003). Empirical studies of particular countries have maintained that foreign investment, in particular, has raised the demand and wages for skilled workers and increased inequality (Colen et al. 2008). Various studies report multinational corporation outsourcing as having a 'statistically significant negative influence [...] on the labour market position of low-skilled workers' (Chusseau and Dumont 2013: 28). Simple tests on data for levels of debt, FDI and capital formation, not included here, found no significant association. Anderson similarly finds 'there is almost no support for the [...] hypothesis that greater openness raises aggregate inequality in all countries' (2005: 1050). It remains possible that these processes contribute to changes in skill and income distribution in complex ways, and some of the data, particularly for levels of FDI is notoriously unreliable. However, the existing evidence remains weak. Chusseau and Hellier's (2013) econometric sampling selectively ignores countries in West Asia and Africa because political and social factors are felt likely to explain inequality better than economic ones. They are probably right, but these regions may not be so unusual.

Walker (1999) goes further to argue against dominant interpretations of labour's weakness as being the result of globalization and anonymous economic processes. Instead, he concludes that labour's problems were more the result of worldwide political defeats. The next chapter will engage at greater length with arguments about labour's decline but it is worth emphasizing the inextricably political character of inequality and the enduring relevance of national systems of political economy.

National institutions, from the level of democracy to minimum wage laws and industrial relations regimes, may mean that trade has very different impacts (Reuveny and Li 2003; Dreher and Gaston 2006). Effective systems of redistribution might lessen, or increase, the effects produced by any changes in trade. At least one study of trade and inequality also controls for inflation and finds a stronger correlation between inequality and this than any of the trade-related variables (Meschi and Vivarelli 2009). It is quite possible that we might find associations between trade openness and country characteristics without any causation. Many countries, particularly rich, English-speaking ones, have witnessed substantial economic liberalization, including both greater income polarization and greater trade opening (Babones and Vonada 2009). This need not imply a causal relation, in either direction, between trade and inequality. One of the more remarkable things about the gains of the political right has been the growth of anti-labour legislation, despite persistent claims that economic liberalization is providing a radically disciplining force. Economic power appeared to need political reinforcement. In many poorer countries, in particular, the liberalizing changes of which trade opening is a part can involve profound restructuring of subsistence and informal economic activities. As above, even the most sensitive measures of national inequality are likely to struggle to capture the impact of such changes. Trade openness can also impact profoundly on gender relations, for example as work in export-oriented industries brings women into the paid labour force. Again this might well be missed by aggregate measures of inequality.

One of the 'achievements' of recent restructuring has been persistently high levels of unemployment in most major economies. Meanwhile, unemployment is completely missing from the mainstream trade models, which assume efficient markets. It is quite possible to envisage the reality of unemployment exacerbating the effects identified by Stolper–Samuelson. For example, manufactured exports from a labour-abundant country might reduce unemployment, helping to lift wages. However, the effects of a reserve army of unemployed may keep wages low, effectively providing a buffer for capital against having to raise wages. Levels of unemployment vary hugely, as do their consequences in terms of protection for the unemployed and the impact on those with jobs. Once again, substantial national and regional variations in levels of unemployment had little obvious correspondence with countries' propensity to trade or their overall levels of inequality.

In a sense, these qualifications reinforce the most fundamental point of Stolper–Samuelson: that trade opening is likely to benefit some sections of society and to disadvantage others. At the same time it is useful to be aware of the limits of that model and the dangers of looking for a narrowly economic explanation of what are contested social and political processes.

CONCLUSION

Mainstream trade theory, and the Stolper–Samuelson theorem in particular, provide powerful grounds for anticipating considerable variation between countries in patterns of trade and inequality. The evidence, both in the wider literature and in the tests reported here, is not very compelling.

One of the few studies to show a systematic variation in the effects of trade on countries of different types (Babones 2010) looks less convincing once high levels of regional variation are incorporated into the model. The chapter also reported tests that more carefully separated primary and secondary trade than has been the norm and reconceived Stolper–Samuelson in class terms. These showed some evidence from the cross-sectional data of manufacturing trade interacting with country endowments to influence inequality in ways compatible with the theory. However, this was not found for primary trade nor confirmed with the time-series data. It was argued that it was necessary to look more closely at other economic factors that might contribute to inequality but also and particularly at the specifics of regional and national political economies.

This is not to discount the importance of trade but to emphasize that political economy is a contested process. Among other things, concomitant trade liberalization and (neo-)liberalization as anti-labour politics in many rich countries might be producing a non-causal association between the two. Right-wing governments could push anti-worker or 'free labour market' policies and trade openness at the same time and for that reason alone we should not be surprised at the coexistence of growing inequality and increased trade. Unions might themselves be weakened by trade, so there are potentially all sorts of feedback mechanisms and the next chapter will explicitly look at what impact trade has had on workers' organization.

9. Trade opening and the decline of industrial action

INTRODUCTION

This chapter investigates the relationship between trade opening and the situation of labour, focusing particularly on the decline of industrial action. A rich literature describes multidimensional processes of change but in both academic and popular accounts 'globalization' is typically blamed for many of labour's problems. The prospects of labour acting as an independent political or social agent have either dropped off the agenda or, where they are discussed, are overwhelmingly rejected. Much as with questions of rising inequality and trade discussed in the last chapter, there is at least coincidence. In recent decades, many countries have become more open and have seen falling levels of industrial action. However, this apparent association warrants careful critical investigation for several reasons.

As was stressed at the end of the last chapter, social practices are complex and contested, likely to be influenced by economic changes but not determined by them in any straightforward way. Claims of labour's structural weakness are intensely and inescapably political and labour's opponents have vested interests in overstating the case, insisting that there is no alternative and that economic change means that resistance is now futile. The idea of 'globalization' is extensively debated and contested. It means different things to different people, if it means anything at all. Therefore, if something called 'globalization' is taken to have weakened labour it is necessary to enquire more closely into exactly what mechanisms and what particular processes this is supposed to have involved.

In what follows, a series of arguments about how trade might weaken labour are discussed and investigated. The next section comments on the literature of labour's decline. It identifies some important claims but also reasons to anticipate differentiated impacts on workers in different countries and different economic sectors.

The following section accordingly looks at how changes in the level of trade openness impact on levels of industrial action in different countries.

It finds little evidence that increased trade openness per se weakened labour in any straightforward way. Revisiting the models discussed in the last chapter to evaluate the Stolper–Samuelson theorem and the possibilities of a more differentiated experience according to country type, it is shown with reasonable levels of statistical confidence that, in the presence of an interaction term between trade opening and country wealth, trade opening itself is negatively associated with levels of industrial action. However, the interaction term produces positive and clearly statistically significant results, which run in the opposite direction to that 'expected': the decline in industrial action is steeper in rich countries that open less and in poorer ones that open more.

The subsequent section compares cross-national rates of industrial action across different economic sectors, which it is suggested might face different degrees of exposure to international competition. It confirms that the fall in the levels of industrial action were significantly more severe in manufacturing than in the relatively less 'exposed' sectors of construction and transport and communications. The result broadly confirms 'conventional' readings of globalization and of the impact of capital mobility on labour but it is cautioned that a numerical decline in the number of manufacturing workers probably at least contributes to this and that further research is needed.

The last section combines the national and industrial to consider whether or to what extent there was a 'disembedding' of levels of industrial action in particular industries from those of wider national labour movements. This develops suggestions that sectoral rather than national strengths might have become more important (Dunn 2004a). Somewhat surprisingly, evidence for this appears to be stronger in construction than in either manufacturing or transport and communications. There is little evidence that this is associated with trade opening but, in manufacturing in particular, this disembedding is positively associated with country wealth – it is a rich country rather than a global phenomenon.

The results appear to confirm that economic structures and restructuring had significant impact on industrial action but this occurred in highly mediated ways, not adequately captured by influential accounts of globalization.

ARGUMENTS AROUND ECONOMIC RESTRUCTURING AND LABOUR'S DECLINE

The literature on labour's decline is huge and spans several academic disciplines. It is impossible to summarize all of this but it is worth identifying some key themes that will inform the more specific hypotheses and empirical work reported below.

An important argument interprets labour's decline as a consequence of state retreat. Labour is a victim of what the International Labour Organization (ILO) sees as 'an unquestionable decline in national policy autonomy' (1997: 69). A vast literature discusses claims that globalization reduces the power of nation states. For the purposes here it is sufficient to note two things. Firstly, it is often implicit, and in influential accounts including those of Strange (1996) and Castells (2000) explicit, that the weakening of the state has severely negative consequences for labour. Capital's mobility and movement steals a march on nation states, which are therefore no longer able to provide the social protection, including labour protection, they once did. As Frieden (1991) argues, the movement and mobility of capital not only squeezes the capacity of welfare states but shifts the burden of paying for them onto the less mobile, particularly workers. This can be associated with a general withdrawal of the 'left hand' of the state, in Bourdieu's (1998) phrase. The priorities of sound money mean higher unemployment and downward pressure on wages and workers' capacity for resistance. Striking to demand state protection therefore makes ever less sense (Scheuer 2006). Systems of industrial relations were established on an overwhelmingly national basis and these are now substantially undermined (Radice 2000). Political processes, such as European Union (EU) rules, can also override national bargaining regimes (Vandaale 2011).

Against this, an influential minority perspective contests claims of state retreat (Weiss 1998; Hirst and Thompson 1999; Garrett 2000). Less frequently, this sceptical literature also explicitly questions claims of labour's decline by such a mechanism (Navarro 2000). Some cruder popularizations aside, even the more forceful statements of the globalization thesis acknowledge that it is an uneven and ongoing process. International convergence may be the 'litmus test' (Strange 1998), 'deterritorialization' the direction (Scholte 2000) but for the time being considerable heterogeneity remains. At least some large states – the US, Japan, Germany, China and others – manifestly retain more than residual power. Even if some degree of decline is accepted, we might reasonably expect nation states to continue to play a substantial role and for some states to have more power than others.

Other arguments see labour as more directly undermined by capital's mobility and movement. Workers lose as capital's freedom increases. Firms can abandon their existing workers to employ others who are cheaper or more obedient. It is useful to distinguish capital's potential and actual movements. The actual movements were the core of the *New*

International Division of Labour thesis (Fröbel et al. 1980), which has informed much subsequent writing about global capital and the de-industrialization of rich countries (Barnet and Cavanagh 1994; Greider 1997). It provides a powerful reason for anticipating labour's retreat, particularly in manufacturing, a former bastion of militancy whose decline might then account for falling national levels of industrial action (Scheuer 2006). This is then specifically an argument about labour in richer countries and much of the literature focuses on these. However, as capital's movements take it from one definite place to another, the logical corollary here would seem to be that new possibilities and potential strengths were opened in poorer, still industrializing, countries (Moody 1997; Silver 2003). We see contrasting trends in the numbers of workers and perhaps also in the repertoires of industrial action. Silver character-izes changing forms of action '*within* any single industry along with shifts in the geographical location of production' (2003: 75). She describes this as a shift to 'Polanyi type' defensive action from more assertive 'Marx type' organization of previous periods, particularly in the North. The Marx-type action might remain pertinent in still industrializ-ing countries.

Of course, not all workers are likely to be victims of capital relocation, even in rich countries. As discussed in previous chapters, classical trade theory suggested mutual gains for countries engaging in trade based on the utilization of 'factor endowments', with the implication that, within any country, the owners of the abundantly endowed factors would benefit from trade while the owners of the factors in which the country was relatively poorly endowed would lose from opening (Stolper and Samuel-son, 1941). The losers could therefore be expected to rationally oppose increased trade and support protection. Stolper and Samuelson's original paper, concerned particularly with the US experience, emphasized the likelihood that 'certain sub-groups of the labouring class, e.g. highly skilled labourers, may benefit while others are harmed' (1941: 60). The last chapter discussed influential recent claims that all but the most highly skilled in rich countries now lose (Reich 1991; Wood 1994, 1998). There is a contrast with the situation in poorer countries where the 'average' worker would be expected to gain.

However, in rich and poor countries alike, workers might be vulnerable to ineluctable pressures wrought by heightened capital mobility, which can be effective even in the absence of any actual relocation (Thomas 1997). Workers face the threat to 'shape up or be replaced' even in firms which end up staying put. There are grounds for thinking that improved transport and communication technologies bring a new dimension to what has admittedly been a longstanding problem for workers. However, any discussion of mobility, distinct from actual movements, introduces both conceptual and empirical problems. In principle, it is easy enough to measure actual relocation. For example, we could count the number of garment workers laid off in the US and the number hired in Cambodia and record the level of trade between the countries. It is harder to measure potential. Capital has always been mobile and there must be a temptation for firms to exaggerate (Holloway 1995). Despite all the technical innovations, there are many hard-to-quantify social and political as well as economic restrictions on corporate mobility.

Heightened mobility might be expected to impact on workers in both rich countries and poor, and aggregate labour-market effects might work to their common disadvantage. However, it also becomes clear that workers in some sectors are more vulnerable than others (Kelly 1998). Manufacturing firms are typically mobile, although even here there are enormous differences according to what is made, how it is made and the final markets for which it is intended. Skilled labour markets, sunk capital, sensitive just-in-time production systems, relatively high transport costs and many other factors can more or less firmly fix even manufacturing capital in particular places (Harvey 1990; Fine 2004). Some sectors are much less mobile. A whole range of in-person services and public utilities are unlikely to go offshore. Construction provides a particularly interesting comparison with manufacturing because it involves some comparable physical production processes but necessarily takes place in situ, at the point of consumption. It may be possible to pre-fabricate, to transform some of the tasks previously performed on site into manufacturing industries, but construction itself necessarily takes place where the final market demands. Accordingly, construction workers do not face the same threats of relocation. At most, workers in less mobile sectors seem likely to experience any such pressures indirectly, in more highly mediated fashion and presumably over a longer period.

Further, some groups of workers might be expected to be positively advantaged by a logic of heightened capital mobility. Capital does not move itself; it is moved by workers. So the obvious example here is that of transport and communications. It is notable that Strange (1996), articulating one of the more highly globalized worldviews and depictions of labour's decline, makes an exception of groups like lorry drivers. Castells' (2000) vision of a network society and the demise of class and class politics also sees at least one axis of its reformation along that of the 'networkers, networked and "switched-off"'. Again, certain workers involved in the movement of capital appear to be (relatively) privileged and exempt from the general pattern of decline. In an earlier study (Dunn 2004a), no evidence is found of either such a strengthening or of a 'disembedding' of the experiences of transport and communications workers from wider national labour movements, measured as the level of correlation between the annual strike rates in that sector and those of other workers. This can be interpreted as a reason to be sceptical of broader claims of transformation.

In short, it seems plausible that changes in capital's spatial mobility and geographic reorganization have weakened labour but this is likely to be experienced unevenly. Any such processes are also usually understood to work in combination with other factors. Amongst other things, there is an enormous literature that discusses a range of transformations in the nature of the firm, the character of work and the workforce and their implications for labour organization. In the extreme, these see the working class disappearing as a political force. Amongst more nuanced suggestions, contemporary capitalism becomes more individualistic, the working class more heterogeneous, with skill polarization rewarding those at the top but on an individual basis without the need to resort to collective action while setting those at the bottom into fiercer competition with each other (Hyman 1999). Some of these changes have been directly related to international trade and globalization (Wood 1994; Castells 2000). Conceptually, however, the diverse 'new economy' or 'post-Fordist' processes are distinct from the spatial dimensions (Silver 2003; Dunn 2004b) and might counteract or reinforce their influence.

There are also empirical problems confronting any evaluation of capital's spatial transformations and any effects on labour. There are several useful if imperfect measures for many of the economic indicators, for trade openness and for foreign direct investment (FDI), which can provide proxies of countries' openness and capital's geographic reorganization. However, labour's power is notoriously hard to quantify. Two indicators are commonly used. For most developed countries, data for levels of unionization are available. Of course, the social content of trade unionism varies; it can be militant and assertive of workers' sectional or class interests, or 'responsible' and collaborative, prepared to prioritize company or national interests. Nevertheless, levels of union membership and union density have been widely studied and tell an important if partial story. The trend across Organisation for Economic Co-operation and Development (OECD) countries between 1981 and 2007 was clearly downward but at the same time the variation between countries rose, confirming that the picture is complex and uneven (calculated from OECD 2010). Unfortunately, reliable comparative statistics for union densities are not available for most poor countries.

Strike statistics provide a second commonly used indicator of labour's power. Three sets of data are available from the ILO (2010), for the number of strikes, strikers and of days 'lost'. These data are available for a substantial number of poorer countries as well as many rich ones and the empirical work that follows relies substantially on these statistics. Again, figures for industrial action provide only very limited measures of labour's strength. Strikes can be a last resort, a sign of weakness rather than assertiveness. Indeed, the ILO measures used here include both strikes and lockouts. Some writers suggest a 'curvilinear' relation in the incidence of strikes, where non-use could be a sign of effective bargaining power (Vandaale 2011). Work on rich countries has suggested an interaction between levels of unionization and levels of industrial action so that where unions are strong, openness does not undermine levels of action but it does where they are weaker (Piazza 2005). Strike rates have also been reported to rise where there is inter-union competition (Akkermans 2008). Practically, data is collected on different bases across countries and this creates problems for any cross-national comparison. This is partly, but only partly, reduced by considering trends rather than absolute values. The number of strikes, in particular, in any year can be very low and the imputation of trends becomes accordingly unreliable. Thus, strike data provide very imprecise measures. Nevertheless, the ability to organize and to take industrial action can reasonably be seen as at least a *sine qua non* of effective independent trade unionism. Few would dispute that the periods of heightened militancy were ones of union rejuvenation and strength. It also seems plausible that a decreasing efficacy of industrial action 'might have a "demonstration effect" and initiate a self-reinforcing process of diminishing resort to strikes' (Vandaale 2011: 30). In what follows, strike data will therefore be accepted as reasonable proxies but the results need to be interpreted cautiously.

Finally, it is worth repeating that in as far as it is possible to demonstrate clear connections between economic restructuring and labour's changing fortunes, claims that any perceived weakness is *just* politics are undermined. However, any discussion of labour remains inextricably political. Unionization and industrial action are never simply 'spontaneous' responses to economic pressures but involve real women and men making decisions about how to respond to difficult circumstances. Existing institutions, labour's own organizations but also things like systems of industrial relations bargaining at national or sectional level can make an enormous difference. It is well established that rates of unionization and industrial action vary hugely between countries at an aggregate level but also in terms of who is likely to be best organized and to strike, whether for example in manufacturing or in the public sector (Bordogna and Cella 2002). Any new potential, such as being opened in poorer countries or amongst strategically important groups, may not be realized or may only be realized after a considerable time. It often took many decades for labour organization to emerge in the original industrialized countries. The idea of 'Fordism' is now often invoked to depict a lost era in which unions were powerful bargaining parties alongside firms and states. It is worth remembering that it took 38 years of sometimes brutal struggle for workers to win a union at Ford Motor Company (Dunn 2009). Building unions is usually a difficult political task in which issues of rank-and-file leadership, political activism and links with non-workplace-based communities can be crucial (Darlington 2009).

These simple observations are made to emphasize that what follows can illuminate only some of a hugely complex set of social relations. There are other possible paths from economic restructuring to the decline of industrial action which are not investigated here. At most it might be possible to detect certain trends amongst a lot of statistical noise, noise that reflects the imperfection and variation of the data but also diverse social practices. However, once it is accepted that globalization is uneven and highly patterned, at least the beginnings of a reasonably systematic investigation of some important claims becomes possible.

EVALUATING TRADE OPENNESS, NATIONAL ECONOMIES AND INDUSTRIAL ACTION

This section examines whether, or to what extent, the decline in levels of industrial action vary with trade openness and across countries of different sizes and relative wealth. The reasons for looking at levels of trade openness are probably self-explanatory. Not all countries open to the same extent and if increased exposure to foreign competition is posited as the reason for labour's decline, this varies enormously between countries. The previous section suggested several reasons why it might be worth considering the different effects in countries with different characteristics, of different size and wealth. Firstly, if workers are being weakened via a process of enforced state retreat, we might expect this to be more severe in poorer and smaller countries than in larger, richer ones. Secondly, if a movement of capital from richer to poorer countries is being posited we might expect an opposite effect, whereby labour's decline in rich countries is compensated by a rise in poorer ones.

Trends of industrial action are calculated for the longest available series (of at least ten years duration) between 1980 and 2007 and the change in trade openness per year as a proportion of gross domestic profit (GDP) calculated for that same period for each country. (The 2007 end point is the product of data availability but does conveniently exclude any volatility associated with the subsequent economic slump.) Levels of GDP and GDP per capita are taken for 1995. Although these changed over the period, the relative ordering of countries did not alter much. As in previous chapters, values of GDP and GDP per capita (necessarily bound at 0) are highly skewed and are logged throughout for statistical purposes to reduce this. In addition to the qualifications above about the use of strike data, it should be re-emphasized that the cross-country sample is limited and biased towards rich countries.

A regression model is first developed taking the indices of the trend of industrial action as dependent variables and the data for country trade opening, wealth and size as independent variables. It is hypothesized that labour's experience might be a function of the change in trade openness, country GDP per capita and population. Further, as discussed in the last chapter, classical trade theory suggests a relatively complex interaction between trade openness, country characteristics and labour's situation. The discussion of the Stolper–Samuelson theorem suggested that in both rich and poor countries, the majority of workers are likely to be at least relatively unskilled and therefore to face opposite pressures. A simple interaction term is therefore developed by calculating each country's GDP per capita relative to an 'average', arbitrarily posited as $5000. For each country, this is then multiplied by the trend for change in trade openness. The purpose of this simple manipulation is to produce a variable that will be positive in rich countries that become more open and in poorer ones that become more closed, in both of which labour's situation is hypothesized as likely to deteriorate. Conversely, the sign of this term will be negative for rich countries that become more closed and poorer countries that became more open. These are the situations in which it is being hypothesized that the workers' situation becomes more positive. The results of the regression analyses are reported in Table 9.1.

The first three series show that there is no evidence of a statistically significant association between the number of strikes or days lost and any of the independent variables. In terms of the number of strikers there is again little evidence that labour's decline is associated with country wealth in any straightforward way. There is some indication, although significant only at the 90 per cent confident level, that the decline was steeper in larger countries. There is, however, a stronger indication that changes in the level of trade openness did have a negative impact on the total number of strikers, a result that appears robust to the removal of the most significant outliers.

Table 9.1   Industrial action and trade openness. Regression model with trends of industrial action as dependent variables, levels of country wealth, size, trade opening and the interaction of trade opening and wealth as independent variables

	n	R^2	Log GDP/ capita	Log population	Change in trade trend	Change in trade trend ×log GDP/ capita to average	Constant
Strikes	62	0.04	0.02	−0.00	−0.00		−0.14*
Strikers	67	0.10	−0.01	−0.02*	−0.01**		−0.01
Strike days	65	0.06	0.04	0.01	−0.00		−0.19*
Strikes	62	0.04	0.02	−0.01	−0.00	0.01	−0.10
Strikers	67	0.21	−0.05*	−0.02*	−0.02***	0.04***	0.21**
Strike days	65	0.15	−0.02	0.01	−0.01**	0.05**	0.06

The model including the interaction term does not produce statistically significant results for the number of strikes. However, for both strikers and strike days the analyses do produce statistically significant and apparently robust results. When considered alongside the (positive effects of the) interaction term, increased trade does appear to have the anticipated negative impact on both the number of strikers and strike days. For both measures, the interaction terms for the product of trade and GDP per capita also produces significant results. However, the positive signs imply that the relations run counter to the Stolper–Samuelson-based theoretical predictions. The trend in industrial action is more negative in richer economies that tend to become at least relatively more closed and in poorer countries the more they open. In richer countries, this would be compatible with Silver's (2003) reading of different types of action, with a turn to the defensive. The experience in poorer countries is harder to interpret. However, particularly with low levels of strikes, the relative weight of action by the relatively skilled rather than unskilled increases and it is possible that this is reflected in these results. The results also indicate, although only at the 90 per cent confidence level, that with the interaction term introduced, the numbers involved in industrial action fell more sharply in larger and richer countries. This is not confirmed in terms of the number of strike days.

THE UNEVEN MOBILITY OF CAPITAL AND LABOUR'S DECLINE

This section distinguishes between capital's movement and mobility. As discussed above, increases in capital mobility would appear to have much more clearly and generally negative effects on labour across countries. There is believed to be a relentless pressure on workers wherever they are and not simply a shift from industrialized to industrializing countries. This is inherently hard to quantify. It is difficult to know how mobile firms might be in the absence of actual relocation. However, as above, it seems reasonable to hypothesize that firms in some sectors are more mobile than others and their workers accordingly more vulnerable. In particular, there is a contrast between manufacturing, in which firms are likely to be mobile, albeit to different degrees, and other industries. The contrast between manufacturing and construction and transport and communications seems particularly worth further investigation. Firms are not similarly mobile in construction and where they do move this is a market-seeking rather than cost-reducing activity. In transport and communications, it is possible to imagine scenarios where workers are positively strengthened by capital's mobility.

Trends are calculated for the levels of strike activity on an aggregate national basis and in the different sectors: manufacturing, construction, and transport and communications. Data were available for 39 countries for the number of strikes, for 44 countries for the number of people involved and 47 countries for the number of strike days. It is then possible to evaluate whether there is a systematic difference between what happened nationally and what happened in each sector by performing t-tests on the cross-country samples of the paired two-sample means between the total and sector specific trends. The totals include the sector-specific data, so a test for difference is in each case conservative.

The averages show that trends of industrial action in manufacturing fell more rapidly than overall national average rates by each indicator and this difference was highly statistically significant. The results of the two-tailed t-tests of the probability of zero difference with the total were, respectively: for strikes 0.0061; strikers 0.0002: and strike days 0.0009. In construction the average decline was even more precipitous than in manufacturing in terms of the number of strikes but there is more sample variation and the difference is significant only with a probability of zero difference of 0.019. The decline in construction appears somewhat less sharp in terms of the number of strikers and strike days and the differences cannot be asserted with statistical confidence. The trends for transport and communications were on average slightly less negative than those of national labour movements and with no evidence of a statistically significant difference.

Manufacturing workers do appear to be more vulnerable than those in other sectors. However, this result has to be interpreted extremely cautiously. The data are simple numerical values and manufacturing employment fell in rich countries, while the number of transport and communications workers, if anything, tended to increase. Manufacturing typically either rose or declined less steeply in poorer countries. However, simple calculations, not reproduced here but easily verified, show little evidence that the sectoral trends varied systematically according to country wealth, size or changing openness to trade, which implies that the indications of sharper decline in manufacturing might be a real consequence of its specific characteristics. Figures for the rate of strike activity per worker, currently available for only a small number of mostly rich countries, would be particularly useful here.

GLOBAL CAPITAL AND THE NATIONAL EMBEDDEDNESS OF LABOUR

The sections above show an interaction between levels of industrial action, trade and country wealth, and that there is variation by sector. The decline seems more substantial in manufacturing than other sectors. This section investigates the relation between these processes by asking whether there has been a 'disembedding' of rates of industrial action in particular sectors from those of wider, national labour movements.

Previously (Dunn 2004a), no evidence was found between 1980 and 2000 for a limited number of large economies. As here, it was hypothesized that transport and communications workers' experiences might diverge from those of wider national labour movements as a consequence of their strategic location within an increasingly globalized economy. The absence of evidence of any systematic disembedding was interpreted as a reason for labour to retain the strategic importance of the national level. What follows updates that study, increases the sample size and, while still using simple techniques, applies a more systematic statistical procedure.

By 'disembedding', a process is hypothesized whereby the strike rates of workers in one industrial sector correlate decreasingly closely with those in the rest of the national economy. To test this, a two-step analysis is developed. Firstly, strike levels in manufacturing, construction, and transport and communications are compared with those of wider, national labour movements (now calculated in each case as the total levels minus those in the sector under consideration). Data for as many countries as possible from 1980 to 2007, or for the greatest continuous period available between these years, is split into two equal periods, comparing the later with the earlier. (The mid-point is accepted in both series if the total number of available years is odd. One exception is Pakistan, for which there is no data for 1993 but for which the ten years before this date are compared with the ten subsequent years.) From this, separate correlation coefficients are derived for the earlier and later periods between the strike rates for each sector and for the 'rest', for each of the periods. There are, of course, numerous spurious correlations including many negative results. However, simple regression analyses can provide an indication of the statistical significance of each association and, perhaps surprisingly for such short series, there are several highly significant associations. By each measure, there is then a clear decline in the number of significant associations and again for each series, except for the number of strike days by transport and communication workers, the cross-country average value of this correlation clearly declines, indicative of disembedding. This dissociation was most marked, and on a cross-country basis most clearly statistically significant in construction, at the 99 per cent confidence level by each measure. For manufacturing workers, the cross-country variation between the two periods was only weakly statistically significant in terms of strikes and not according to the other indicators. For transport and communications workers the difference was strongly significant in terms of strikes and weakly significant in relation to strike days. The apparently stronger effect in construction is immediately hard to square with narratives which attribute labour's decline to heightened capital mobility.

The second analytical step involves calculating measures of disembedding as the difference in the correlation coefficients between the two periods for each sector, in each country and by each measure, and treating these as the dependent variables in tests against the country characteristics as outlined above in the discussion of trade openness. This second step is therefore asking whether there is a greater or lesser tendency for the dissociation of industrial action in particular sectors from the national rate in countries with different characteristics, different levels of openness and of different sizes. It might reasonably be expected that disembedding is more pronounced in countries that were more exposed to trade, in smaller and perhaps in poorer countries. The results of the relevant regression analyses are shown in Table 9.2.

Table 9.2 Trade and the disembedding of industrial action: regression model with disembedding of levels of industrial action as dependent variables, wealth, size and change in trade openness as independent variables

		n	R²	Log GDP/capita	Log population	Change in trade trend	Constant
Strikes	Manufacturing	41	0.13	-0.41**	-0.00	-0.02	1.46*
	Construction	39	0.14	-0.45**	0.03	-0.05	1.48*
	Transport and communications	40	0.01	-0.00	0.04	-0.01	-0.22
Strikers	Manufacturing	45	0.20	-0.55**	-0.14	0.09*	2.04
	Construction	42	0.06	0.11	0.09	0.06	-0.86
	Transport and communications	44	0.04	0.05	-0.07	0.04	-0.28
Strike days	Manufacturing	48	0.25	-0.49***	-0.23**	-0.02	2.12***
	Construction	44	0.05	-0.04	-0.14	0.04	0.04
	Transport and communications	47	0.04	-0.08	-0.03	-0.04	0.35

There do appear to be consistently significant relationships for the disembedding of industrial action by manufacturing workers, results that appear robust and applicable to each of the indicators. In particular, the process of disembedding appears to have tended to be greater in countries that were richer in GDP per capita terms. In terms of the number of strike days this disembedding also appears to be stronger in larger countries. In terms of the number of workers involved there is some suggestion that disembedding was less pronounced, the more countries opened to trade. In construction, in terms of the total number of strikes there is again evidence, significant at the 95 per cent confidence level, that disembedding was stronger in richer countries than poorer ones. This is not found in terms of the other indicators. Perhaps surprisingly, there is little evidence of disembedding having systematic national or trade-based elements in transport and communications. At the very least, these results should caution against seeing states in larger and wealthier countries as more likely to protect their national labour movements. Beliefs in powerful states as natural allies of labour contrasts, of course, with those of Marxists and other critical social scientists.

CONCLUSION

This chapter considered several arguments why economic restructuring might impact on rates of industrial action and reported some simple tests set up to evaluate them.

It should be re-emphasized that this is a limited objective. Although it seeks to contribute to broader debates, the chapter has not investigated other indicators of labour's power or weakness and, in keeping with the themes of this book, has looked at trade openness rather than other indicators of economic globalization. Some preliminary analyses using measures of FDI either instead of or alongside trade, and not reproduced here, suggested these added little if any explanatory power.

The three empirical sections each show apparently systematic and statistically significant relationships between levels of industrial action, trade openness, and country and industry characteristics. These seldom occurred in straightforward ways. First, an anticipated negative impact of trade openness on levels of industrial action became stronger in the presence of an interaction term between the level of trade openness and countries' relative wealth. This interaction term indicated that the decline in industrial action tended to be stronger in richer countries that opened less and poorer countries that opened more. The richer-country experiences might be interpreted in terms of relatively greater defensive resistance to the pressures from openness. The poorer-country experience remains harder to explain.

The second empirical section considered the different experiences of workers in different sectors and confirmed the markedly steeper downward trend of industrial action in manufacturing. This would be compatible with the greater pressure on manufacturing workers associated with that sector's greater spatial mobility. It might potentially be associated with the numerical decline in manufacturing in many countries, although the evidence does not suggest that the decline in industrial action is greater in richer countries where such numerical decline is more severe.

The third section showed significant processes of disembedding of the incidences of industrial action in particular sectors from national contexts. This disembedding was observed in each of the sectors but it was most clear in construction. The processes of disembedding could not be shown with much statistical confidence to be linked to countries' relative exposure to trade. In manufacturing, in particular, there was evidence of a negative association between this disembedding and country wealth in GDP per capita terms. That is to say that in richer countries, manufacturing workers formerly tended to strike alongside other workers but this diminished. In as far as they continued to strike, manufacturing workers in rich countries were more likely to do so alone.

These results provide evidence that international economic forces influence national variations in strike rates but indicate that this happened in highly mediated and contingent ways. They challenge narratives that see labour's situation as worse where state retreat might be thought to be more severe. Nor is there convincing evidence of a shift of the locus of action from North to South. The findings should qualify assumptions of a straightforward relationship between economic globalization and labour's decline and, it is hoped, might stimulate further research into what remain important but poorly understood social processes.

10. Global restructuring, trade and the crisis of 2007–09

INTRODUCTION

The chapter takes up the story of trade, where it left off in Chapter 2, discussing how and why trade and trade imbalances grew from the 1970s to the crisis of the late 2000s. These imbalances have been widely recognized, from different perspectives, as contributing to the crisis (Wade 2009; IMF 2011). It is argued here that they were not simply maladjustment, susceptible to a little light re-engineering, but reflected deep-seated changes in the organization of the global economy. The experience of these changes also confirms the themes of this book that trade in itself is neither good nor bad. It benefits some and harms others in particular circumstances. Trade relations are about power and need to be understood in relation to other political economic processes.

The chapter is organized into four sections. The first describes the crisis of the 1970s and how that crisis provoked key reorientations in the global economy. The second section looks specifically at rich countries and changing relations between the 'Triad' of the US, Japan and Europe. The third section concentrates on the changing situation and increasingly outward orientation of many poorer countries. Finally, the chapter comments briefly on how trade imbalances fed the financial fragility that was revealed in the crash of the late 2000s.

THE CRISIS OF THE 1970s

Trade increased enormously in the late twentieth century. The story has been widely told. The level of trade, measured as the ratio of total exports plus imports to gross domestic profit (GDP), jumped from 28 per cent in 1970 to 40 per cent in 1980, held steady for a decade then jumped again to 51 per cent in 2000 and 58 per cent in 2010 (WB 2014). This was not an anonymous economic process, let alone the automatic triumph of the market. It was driven by powerful corporate and state interests as part of a strategic response to the crisis of the 1970s. There was not simply a general increase in trade but an increase in particular forms of trade: trade organized within or by multinational corporations (MNCs), trade in particular goods and trade between particular locations. It was argued in Chapter 2 that trade imbalances became a significant contributor to the demise of the Bretton Woods currency system and to the crisis of the 1970s but trade and also trade imbalances would now soar to new heights.

This is not a book about economic crises (see Dunn 2014a) but it is worth stressing three aspects of the downturn of the 1970s, each of which produced pressures to reorganize the international trade regime. First, the crisis of the 1970s was one of falling profit rates. This was predicated fundamentally on high and rising levels of capital investment throughout the preceding period. At a world level, gross fixed capital formation accounted for 21.2 per cent of GDP in 1960, rising to 24.1 per cent in 1973 (WB 2014). Rising investment, even as it meant rapid growth, ate into corporate returns. Second, from the late 1960s, wage rises also exceeded productivity gains and worked to the same end. Third, the uneven pattern of accumulation in the previous period produced dislocations. There were geographical dislocations between leading countries, which substantially caused the collapse of the Bretton Woods currency regime (as discussed in Chapter 2). There were also dislocations between economic sectors, with a relative lack of investment in primary industries over preceding years producing tight markets, which, among other things, made possible the Organization of the Petroleum Exporting Countries (OPEC) price rises of 1973 (Armstrong et al. 1984; Webber and Rigby 1996; Dunn 2014a).

The subsequent trajectory can be seen as a response to these problems. This does not mean that the particular responses and forms of crisis resolution were in some sense inevitable. The crisis involved a period of intense social and ideological contest and it is quite possible to imagine alternatives and how these might have 'worked' better even for capital, never mind from some imagined perspective of abstractly 'objective' economic theory. However, the consequences intended or otherwise, of the crisis were to send the global economy in new directions. Initially the shifts were modest and might even be thought of as 'experimental'. What has been called a 'neo-liberal' re-orientation was never linear and applied much less to some places than others. However, after 40 years, the overall direction of change and the role of trade in this seem fairly clear. The geographical dimensions and how these produced trade imbalances are discussed further in the next two sections but it is first worth noting the declining levels of investment and labour shares of income within rich countries.

Investment fell within leading economies: gross fixed capital formation went from a 1973 high point of 24.8 per cent of GDP, to 21.2 per cent in 2008, before collapsing to just 17.7 per cent in 2010 (WB 2014). This decline was especially steep in Japan and German, albeit from very high levels. In the US it was less precipitous with a significant revival in the 1990s boom, but was very pronounced in manufacturing. In the immediate crisis period of the 1970s, firms had little incentive to invest in new capital when demand for the products of existing capacity was hard to sustain. Better and safer returns could be achieved in financial markets. Corporate borrowing fell and savings increased. This meant that many 'real economy' corporations, which had previously been relatively sanguine about inflation wiping out their debts, also prioritized protecting their financial assets (Krippner 2011). As will be seen below, there were international dimensions to the US policy turn but the 'Volcker Shock' of 1979, radically raising interest rates, protected domestic finance. Inflation fell from 13.5 per cent in 1980 to 3.2 per cent in 1983 (IMF 2014). High interest rates exacerbated the unwillingness to borrow and invest. There were tensions and conflicts within US capital, as high interest rates pushed the economy into deep recession but the point here is to caution against reading the policy shift simply in terms of state capture by narrowly financial interests. Similarly, another key aspect of financialization was that it allowed real-economy corporations to switch more easily both to other lines of business and, in the liberalization of international flows, to move to other geographical locations (Helleiner 1994; Krippner 2011). As US Treasury Undersecretary Taylor would put it in 2003, 'the free transfer of capital in and out of a country without delay is a "fundamental right"' (cited in Wade 2003: 633). The greater facility with which corporations could move to other markets and to lower-cost production locations further entrenched the lack of domestic investment within rich country economies.

The crisis of the 1970s also provoked an uneven but clear trend towards more strongly anti-labour policies in leading economies. This was most marked in the US, where wages fell from 53 to 46 per cent of GDP between 1970 and 2005 (Foster and McChesney 2012). There were falls in real income for many workers. Income distribution became more polarized, with the wages of the highest paid increasing sharply. Corporate profits increased. Elsewhere labour's relative decline was often less dramatic but across the Organisation for Economic Co-operation and Development (OECD) by the mid-1970s the trend was clearly downwards (Glyn 2008). By the 2000s, real wages were stagnant at best in Germany and falling progressively in Japan (OECD 2014). Particularly in the US, these changes fed financialization. On the supply side, increased profits and elite incomes put money into the financial system. On the demand side, increased borrowing filled the gap left by falling wages. As discussed in the previous chapter, labour's situation was also conditioned by international changes and trade in complex ways. Offshoring could hit employment and put downward pressure on wages while it also reduced the costs of many consumer goods, lessening the impact of falling labour shares of national income.

The decline of investment rates within rich countries was partially, but only partially, offset by a rise elsewhere. The vast literature on globalization produces some extraordinary overstatement. Forty years on from the crisis, capital investment was renewed, sometimes many times over, but still about 75 per cent of total and 50 per cent of foreign investment was made within established rich countries. As of 2010 only 31.1 per cent of foreign direct investment (FDI) stocks were in developing countries, a relatively modest increase from 25.2 per cent in 1990 even with a significant spike in the last few of these years (WIR 2011). When investment went to poorer countries it was seldom to those at the bottom and it was only some poorer regions, particularly in Asia, where investment now soared. Notably, countries in sub-Saharan Africa continued to be substantially ignored, receiving less than 2 per cent of all FDI (WIR 2011). The character of investment as well as its location changed. The switch to poorer locations in aggregate also reflected and reinforced less capital-intensive forms of production. While the rise in investment in many poorer countries involved rapid economic growth, it also often still depended on final markets within rich countries.

Trade increased, more quickly than levels of growth and investment, but reflected their unevenness. Figure 10.1 indicates that as late as 2000, exports from and between rich countries took comparable shares of the total to those of 1980 and even 1948. There was, however, a substantial change in the 2000s, which will be discussed in more detail below. Asian exports, particularly Chinese exports, increased very rapidly. Outside Asia, the growth of trade was real but much less steep. Huge unevenness remained but the point here is simply that in the aftermath of the crisis of the 1970s, geographies of production, consumption and trade shifted substantially.

COOPERATION AND COMPETITION BETWEEN THE 'TRIAD'

The story of cooperation and competition between the leading economies, particularly the US, Japan and Germany, has been told in detail,

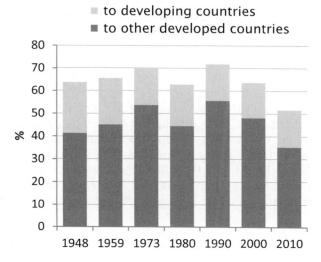

Source: Calculated from UN (1962, 1993, 2011).

*Figure 10.1   Developed country exports as share of world total,
1948–2010*

notably by Brenner (2003). What follows summarizes some key developments, particularly in terms of how these impinged on trade relations.

As above, the crisis of the 1970s increased US corporate interests in protecting finance and preserving openness. Over the subsequent decades, capital became less 'national' in terms of the basis of its production and sources of its profits (Milberg and Winkler 2010). The phenomenon was not confined to the US but the process underscored persistent dilemmas from the perspective of the US national economy and the US state in terms of securing the role of the dollar and the balance-of-payments position.

The international use of the dollar affords the US privileges of seigniorage, the ability to use its own currency in international trade, including the ability to buy key commodities like oil. Competitors had already complained in the 1960s that paper dollars were being held rather than redeemed for gold or US goods. With the ending of the gold link the willingness of foreigners to accept dollars looked more precarious. There were potential alternatives, notably with the development of European monetary coordination. To maintain faith in the dollar its value had to be at least relatively high and stable. High currency values imply good terms of trade, among other things, and low US import prices reduce domestic inflationary pressures. However, a high dollar simultaneously reduces US competitiveness and potentially undermines the balance-of-payments position. Conversely, a fall in dollar values increases competitiveness and effectively defaults on US dollar-denominated debt but makes imports more expensive and potentially threatens faith in the currency.

The end of the gold–dollar link would precipitate a series of turns. Despite the enthusiasm of people like Friedman for a market-based system in preference to Bretton Woods, leading state powers were never likely to simply abandon their national economies or currencies to the vicissitudes of the market. The US got its devaluation and by 1979 the dollar had fallen from Japanese yen ¥360 and German deutschmark DM4.2 to ¥219 and DM1.8 (IMF 2014). This increased US competitiveness and trade returned to near balance. However, the fall in the dollar threatened to undermine dollar pre-eminence and American seigniorage privileges.

The Volcker shock, coming the same year that Europeans began moving towards monetary coordination, raised the value of the dollar (to ¥239 and DM2.9 by 1985) but this undermined American trade competitiveness and (with the Reagan boom in full swing) the deficit blew out to unprecedented heights. Agreements at the Plaza (the New York hotel) and the Louvre (in Paris) in 1985 and 1987 then raised the value of other currencies, the dollar falling to ¥94 and DM1.4 by 1995, stabilizing the trade position (IMF 2014). This in turn was reversed in 1995 – under pressure from the Japanese struggling in the aftermath of the bursting of their bubble economy while the US was enjoying the dotcom boom. When that boom burst in the US, and Greenspan and the Treasury responded with radical cuts in interest rates, the dollar started another prolonged slide.

What was particularly interesting in this last turn was that falling dollar values in the 2000s had little (positive) impact on the trade position and US deficits continued to grow. The prolonged fall in investment in manufacturing within the US economy meant that there was now little industry left in key sectors to benefit from any increased competitiveness afforded by falling dollar values. Instead, the falling dollar largely just meant that the terms of trade deteriorated and the US paid more for its imports, at least until the crash of 2007–09. This remained possible as long as foreigners were willing to accumulate dollar reserves.

Meanwhile, in Japan, the initial revaluation of the yen after the ending of Bretton Woods reduced competitiveness and improved the terms of trade. This had the particular compensation of reducing the cost of oil imports for a heavily fuel-dependent country. After 1979 the situation changed with competitiveness again improved. The American boom of the early 1980s particularly attracted high levels of Japanese imports. It provoked 'voluntary' export restraints, notably with restrictions on the number of Japanese car imports, to which the Japanese were able to respond with larger, more expensive cars – for which demand conveniently rose as fuel prices now dropped. The yen revaluation after 1985 prompted, among other things, a wave of overseas investments by Japanese companies. There were moves into other rich country economies including the US and a shift of production to cheaper locations elsewhere in Asia. The revaluation made Japan considerably richer in dollar terms and fuelled the stock market and real estate bubble, which would burst in 1991. There was subsequently a prolonged downturn with consumption slow to recover and investment now on a long-term downward trajectory. Japanese firms tended to adopt lower-cost, lower-wage strategies. The yen was down to 120 to the dollar in 1997. It nevertheless became increasingly difficult for Japan to retain its export surplus strategy and that it did so was testament to suppressed domestic demand more than successful export growth. The Japanese share of global exports peaked at 10 per cent in 1986 and fell to just 4.3 per cent by 2012 (WB 2014).

With the ending of Bretton Woods, Germany was in many ways in a similar situation to Japan. One crucial difference was that rich European countries conducted a high proportion of their trade with each other. The revaluation of the deutschmark after 1971 increased the cost of German goods and improved the terms of trade, but did little to undermine markets given the extent to which Germany's trading partners had become reliant particularly on German capital goods. Importers paid their German suppliers more, while Germans paid less for their imports. By 1979, German exports had jumped to $172 billion and trade surpluses to $12 billion.

Other European countries experienced different pressures. The Italian lira devalued, even against the dollar, significantly improving Italian competitiveness within Europe. The French economy stood between the German and Italian, and its trade experiences fell between two stools. France had a relatively strong financial sector and continued to pursue a relatively strong franc policy. The franc fell nearly 50 per cent in relation to the DM but rose about 20 per cent relative to the US dollar and therefore still further against the lira. However, French exports competed more closely with the Italian than the German (conspicuously in consumer goods like wine and small cars). The trade deficit blew out. The French, in particular, had an obvious incentive to push for a restoration of currency stability, while for the Germans and Italians, fixing currency values might lock-in recent gains.

The initial European Monetary System (EMS) involved currency coordination such that values were supposed to stay within a specified 4.5 per cent band of each other. This band or 'tunnel' would itself move in relation to other international currencies and the individual European currencies could 'snake' up or down within its limits. If currency values approached the top or bottom of the allowed band, the relevant government would be obliged to intervene. They could raise or lower interest rates or buy and sell currencies in 'open market' operations to adjust their values. By 1992 the rare aberration of expansionary money in Germany following reunification was being reversed and interest rates rose. This lifted the value of the DM but, given Germany's weight within the EMS, also meant that the tunnel as a whole turned upwards. This made it increasingly difficult for the currencies of weaker economies like Britain (which had joined in 1990 at a relatively elevated rate of DM2.9 to the pound) and Italy to stay within the specified limits. It prompted speculation that they would drop out, and this speculation itself made it increasingly likely that they would do so. Speculation was rational, with the losses at most the 4.5 per cent that the currencies might rise within the EMS, and this was always very unlikely. It was almost inconceivable that the British or Italians would leave the EMS on the 'up-side', exceeding their prior values. The real problems of competitiveness and the structural features all pointed in the opposite direction. Should the currencies drop out of the system and be devalued, speculators stood to make huge gains. After futile government reactions, spending huge quantities to defend the currencies and raising interest rates to levels that were clearly economically and politically unsustainable, the lira and pound fell out of the EMS, the latter never to return. The speculators could cash in their winnings.

There is some irony in that the prospect of a single currency was an element in provoking the crisis, forcing the recognition that the currency levels were unsustainable. However, the crisis then became an incentive to move towards a single currency, which would prevent such speculation.

A great deal has been written about the project of European unification in general and the eurozone in particular as a triumph of 'neo-liberalism'. The rules were able to lock in anti-Keynesian monetary policy, limiting the scope of elected governments to adopt more expansionary or pro-labour policies. In practice, powerful states like France and Germany were able to violate their own rules, with deficits going beyond the allowed 60 per cent of GDP. However, the disciplining effects were real and other European states now adopted policies close to those of the German model of the earlier period, which had combined restrictive policy at home with export-led growth. This has been read as a fallacy of composition. What worked for Germany, able to export into other expanding economies, could not work simultaneously for all the European economies, which had each other as their main trading partners. However, this coordination still made sense for German firms also competing with the US and Japan and increasingly with other low-cost locations. The eurozone as a whole remained in rough trade balance as the currency rose or fell in international exchanges, in principle reflecting changes in productivity, and particularly German productivity, in relation to the rest of the world. Within the eurozone, Germany only had to outperform its neighbours to increase its surpluses. Germany and a few other 'core' countries like the Netherlands ran systematic surpluses, German ones rising from $55 billion in 2000 to $266 billion by 2007 (WB 2014). 'Peripheral' economies, like Greece but also Spain and increasingly Italy and even France, ran deficits. With no mechanism of currency adjustment and few internal transfers between what remained independent states in terms of their ability to raise and spend taxes, the experiences tended to diverge. Weaker European economies were importing from the European 'core' but also from poorer countries.

THE CHANGING GLOBAL ECONOMIC RELATIONS OF POORER COUNTRIES

The North American, European and Japanese 'Triad' had dominated economic and trade relations until the 1970s, but then this began to change. As Figure 10.1 makes clear, poorer countries still accounted for a minority of world trade until the 2000s. However, processes of liberalization and increased openness meant they contributed substantially and increasingly to the total and to the growing imbalances. Global trade volumes increased but so did the surpluses and deficits of important countries and country groups. Most importantly, the US ran huge deficits, reaching $892 billion by 2006, while China, several other poorer countries in Asia and the oil-exporting countries ran growing surpluses. This section identifies five aspects of changed trade relations of poorer countries: the debt crisis of the 1980s; the Asian currency of 1997; the role of the World Trade Organization (WTO); the rise of China; and finally a renewed rise of oil-exporting countries.

The details of the debt crisis of the 1980s are well known. The crisis is sometimes seen as one of the import substitution industrialization model, even a crisis brought on by misguided attempts to construct closed national economies. It is true that most of the affected countries had high trade barriers. Many countries had attempted to build locally oriented consumer goods industries, but among other things this meant importing capital goods. Latin America's import substitution did not stop trade, as Table 10.1 demonstrates. The strategy had also involved borrowing, principally from Western commercial banks. This avoided the conditionalities imposed by the International Financial Institutions. By the mid-1970s, borrowing costs were low. Here again, (unfree) trading becomes at least a part of the story because high oil prices had meant that oil-exporting countries ran surpluses and accumulated dollars which were saved rather than immediately spent or re-invested. These 'petrodollars' were themselves deposited in Western banks. With hindsight, both borrowers and lenders have been criticized as irresponsible (Cohn 2005) but lending dollar reserves, at low and even negative real interest rates, made better sense than sitting on the deposits. In a competitive world-system it could equally be seen as irresponsible not to borrow and achieve at least some return given the opportunity and to undertake the growth strategies that borrowing made possible. As Table 10.1 shows, many of what would be the worst hit countries grew very quickly, and this at a time when many rich-country economies experienced a severe downturn. For most of the 1970s, growth far outstripped real interest rates and repayments could be made quite easily.

The situation changed rapidly with the Volcker shock and its raising of US interest rates. The Federal Reserve rate set a floor on international interest rates, with other, riskier borrowers paying more. Costs jumped for Latin American and other poorer-country debtors. The Volcker shock induced a recession in the US (and other countries), which in turn limited the export markets of many poorer countries including oil exporters like Mexico and Venezuela and thence the dollar earnings with which debts might be serviced. By 1982, the crisis came to a head with Mexico announcing that it could no longer pay its debts. Mexico's default was followed by fears of contagion, even of a 'debtors' cartel', whereby other countries would similarly stop paying. This threatened US banks and potentially the Western banking system.

Various emergency measures and different strategies were attempted before a deal was finally reached, with banks accepting some debt write-off in response for US guarantees of the remainder, but with 17 debtor countries agreeing to economic restructuring to ensure the remaining debts would be serviced. This was the beginning of the shift to what would later be called the 'Washington Consensus', a standard prescription for indebted countries seeking assistance from the International Monetary Fund (IMF), which Williamson (1990) summarized in terms of ten liberalizing policies.

Table 10.1 The debt crisis: growth, debt, trade and inequality, 1982–2007, selected countries

	Average annual GDP growth			Debt as a percentage of Gross National Income			Trade Openness (Exports + Imports as a percentage of National Income)			Inequality, gini coefficient		
	1970s	1980s	1990–2007	1982	2007	change	1982	2007	change	1982	2007	change
Argentina	3.0	-1.5	4.0*	55.0	45.6	-9.4	16	45	29	38.6	42.3	3.7
Bolivia	3.9	0.1	3.7	63.9	39.5	-24.4	58	76	18	n.a.	50.0	n.a.
Brazil	8.5	1.5	2.9	35.2	17.6	-17.6	16	25	9	51.8	48.0	-3.8
Chile	2.9	3.8	5.6	77.6	38.7	-38.9	41	80	39	49.6	47.6	-2.0
Colombia	5.5	3.6	3.4	27.3	21.8	-5.5	26	37	11	52.7	52.3	-0.4
Costa Rica	5.6	2.5	5.3	165.0	33.0	-132	87	102	15	46.7	44.6	-2.1
Cote D'Ivoire	5.3	0.7	1.5	128.0	73.3	-54.7	76	90	14	49.0	40.4	-8.6
Ecuador	6.9	2.6	3.0	62.1	40.7	-21.4	49	70	21	n.a.	47.0	n.a.
Jamaica	n.a.	n.a.	n.a.	92.2	86.9	-5.3	87	106	19	65.6	n.a.	n.a.
Mexico	6.7	1.8	3.1	53.3	19.1	-34.2	26	57	31	45.1	46.0	0.9
Morocco	5.2	3.9	3.5	81.9	27.7	-54.2	51	81	30	48.7	39.1	-9.5
Nigeria	4.7	-0.9	5.0	24.6	5.6	-19	39	67	28	41.3	42.5	1.2
Peru	3.6	-0.8	4.5	45.0	28.7	-16.3	36	51	15	58.8	49.7	-9.1
Philippines	5.9	1.7	3.7	67.0	46.0	-21	46	87	41	47.5	50.9	3.4
Uruguay	3.0	0.0	2.7	29.4	49.2	19.8	32	47	15	43.0	44.5	1.4
Venezuela	2.7	0.8	3.1	42.8	20.0	-22.8	47	57	10	43.0	38.8	-4.2

* to 2006.

Source: Calculated from World Bank (2014).

Three of Williamson's (1990) ten points explicitly refer to trade or export promotion. There is a discussion of trade policy itself, of the exchange rate and FDI. Many of the other policy prescriptions (privatization, cutting public spending, limiting taxation and deregulation) work in the same direction, reducing costs and making exports competitive. The policies have been widely criticized. The social consequences were often appalling and even in narrow economic terms, growth stagnated, certainly in the early years after their adoption and compared with previous growth rates. Table 10.1 shows the changes in growth, debt and trade over the next 25 years for 16 of the 'Baker-17 countries', targeted in the early plans of US Treasury Secretary Baker (data are not available for the seventeenth, the former Yugoslavia). The figures show total GDP growth, so with rising populations even modest increases represented a fall in average real incomes. In several countries, restructuring also substantially increased inequality. In the 1990s, even as growth returned, inequality increased in all of these countries except Brazil and Nigeria. It is surely also legitimate to criticize the way these policies were often dressed up as development strategies where their primary purpose was to ensure debt repayment. In every case here, trade openness increased and in all the countries except Uruguay, the debts fell, at least relative to national income. Higher levels of trade meant that there were more foreign currency earnings and the ratio of debt to export earnings fell still more steeply. In most cases, debts remained huge in absolute terms but they were being repaid and in that sense the crisis was averted. It is also apparent that by the 1990s, most of these countries were again growing strongly and by the 2000s in several of them inequality was falling, notably in Bolivia, Brazil and Ecuador and more modestly in Argentina, Chile, Cote D'Ivoire, Peru, Mexico, Nigeria and Venezuela. This is not to minimize the hardships faced by many at the bottom of society as these countries underwent structural adjustment, or the difficulties they still face, but it is also apparent that changes in inequality were neither universal nor linear.

Debt and liberalizing responses to it were not confined to the Baker-17 countries. The median debt to GDP ratio for 83 poorer countries for which data are available between 1982 and 2007 fell from 40.8 to 32.3 per cent (calculated from WB 2014). Most countries became open to international trade and (again) therefore more able to pay their debts. Most of the exceptions were in Africa. In sub-Saharan Africa, few countries incurred comparable commercial debts because lenders had largely avoided them and they were already dependent on the international agencies and conditional loans. There is only a weak association between cross-country levels of initial indebtedness and the extent of subsequent opening but there is little doubt that indebtedness in general helped foster 'liberalizing' changes over the next few decades.

If the debt crisis helped to lever open poorer countries so too would a series of currency crises, the most dramatic of which occurred in Asia in 1997. Chapter 2 described how the currency stability of Bretton Woods helped to foster international trade and particularly enabled Japan and Germany to adopt a successful export orientation, overcoming potential domestic demand problems by selling abroad. Particularly for poorer and smaller countries there has subsequently been a considerable temptation to try to recreate similar relations by pegging their currencies to the dollar or to the currencies of other leading economies or trading partners. However, there are important asymmetries. It is relatively easy, and both economically and politically painless, for states to set low interest rates and to sell local currencies, while high interest rates can be harder to sustain and the supply of foreign currency is limited. As happened on a grand scale with the collapse of Bretton Woods in 1971, the apparent stability can be revealed as brittleness. Currency pegs have encouraged a suppression of domestic demand and export-oriented success and as such have been supported by the IMF (for all that they involve government interference in the supposedly free market). But pegs are also vulnerable to speculation. Both the relative ease of keeping currencies low and the need to accumulate reserves as a bulwark against speculators have encouraged an orientation towards trade surpluses.

Some similar stories were played out in other countries, including Mexico, Argentina, Brazil, Turkey and Russia but it is worth briefly recalling the Asian experience. The yen revaluation after 1985 meant that other Asian economies that pegged their currencies to the dollar, or to trade weighted indices in which the dollar was prominent, could capture increasing export markets in the US. They also attracted FDI, as Japanese corporations in particular established regional production networks utilizing what had become lower costs in these countries (Burkett and Hart-Landsberg 2000). The 1995 reversal of Plaza, involving dollar appreciation and yen devaluation, had huge repercussions for several East Asian countries. Added to a Chinese devaluation of the year before, it made several currencies pegged to the dollar relatively dearer, making it hard to sustain export growth and to attract investment. With the Japanese recession in the early 1990s, corporate investment to other Asian economies was already in decline and slumped further with the heightened costs brought by the fall of the yen. Borrowing rose to sustain domestic investment. Fortunately, or so it appeared, borrowing was itself facilitated by low interest rates and booming stock markets in America and Europe, while the fast-growing economies still attracted short-term, portfolio investment. However, speculation developed that the growth levels and the currency pegs were unsustainable. Thailand was first in line, with the Thai government spending $54 billion trying to defend its currency peg (Higgot 1998). Once the battle was lost and the baht fell, assets within Thailand, including those of speculative portfolio investors, were devalued. Those who had exchanged baht for dollars before the fall could cash them in at huge profits. This experience encouraged similar attacks on other currencies in the region, notably the Malaysian ringgit, Indonesian rupiah and Korean won.

The subsequent slumps were severe, in Indonesia provoking the revolutionary situation that finally overthrew the Suharto dictatorship. However, the crisis was contained. In Malaysia the government organized its own restructuring (Burkett and Hart-Landsberg 2000). Elsewhere, IMF-sponsored packages rescued the lenders and pushed substantial liberalization onto the affected countries. Large sections of Korean capital, in particular, became available for sale to foreign MNCs in a way not previously possible. Foreign ownership tripled to 41 per cent of GDP from 1996 and 2004 (Kho et al. 2006). Devaluation and domestic recession put downward pressure on wages, limiting imports and reviving the export performance. Economic growth soon resumed but on a more liberal basis, with Thailand in particular becoming considerably more open to trade. As in Latin America after 1982, trade surpluses could pay increased debts but they also enabled the accumulation of dollar reserves.

The establishment of the WTO represented an important third driver of poorer-country trade liberalization. Under its auspices trade continued to increase and the WTO was widely welcomed by mainstream commentators. However, it has been the focus of intense debates and even more consistent liberals acknowledge inconsistencies in its practices (Bhagwati 2005; Wolf 2005). The WTO was formally instituted in 1995, the outcome of protracted negotiations within the General Agreement on Tariffs and Trade (GATT), which dates back to 1947. To understand the motivation for the WTO, it is again worth going back to the crisis of the 1970s. There were fears of a repeat of the 1930s in terms of a retreat from trade and into rival blocs. By the 1980s, the US in particular saw both a need and opportunity to extend the formal institutionalization of global trade rules and structures. As discussed above, for many poorer countries, by this time increased openness became a necessity rather than a choice (Narlikar 2006). Perhaps tellingly, the last of four fundamental tasks that the WTO set itself from the beginning was 'to cooperate as needed with the IMF and the World Bank' (cited in Matsushita et al. 2006: 9).

The WTO institutionalized an asymmetric system. Critics argue that poorer countries were in a relatively weak position and assertive developed-country governments and corporations were able to shape the international regime to their advantage. The WTO's structures were skewed in terms of the processes, rules and disciplinary measures (Narlikar 2006; Bown 2011). Unlike the GATT, the WTO had real power to arbitrate and to impose sanctions, for example around enforcing patents, and it was only the sanctions of rich countries that could really hurt. New countries joining had it particularly tough, often being obliged to sign up to a whole set of existing rules (Wade 2003). Rich countries could also more readily ignore or subvert agreements, most obviously in agriculture. Other areas of subsidy were permitted, like export finance, infrastructure provision, and government science and technology and innovation and investment support, and these were much more pertinent to rich countries. National security was allowed as an exception and was used, particularly by the US, to protect a wide range of goods (Weiss 2005).

There were also substantial asymmetries in the way the WTO extended its remit. Rich countries pushed for rules on new issues in what became the General Agreement of Trade in Services (GATS), Trade-Related Intellectual Property Rights (TRIPs) and Trade-Related Investment Measures (TRIMs) legislation. GATS and TRIMs stretched the concept of 'trade' beyond any reasonable linguistic breaking point, while increased patent protection restricted rather than freed trade. There was intense corporate lobbying, most successfully with regard to TRIPs, mainly by 'pharmaceutical companies, software and Hollywood' (Wade 2003: 639). The TRIPs legislation epitomized the economic unevenness; it was pushed by rich countries and companies with advanced technologies. Not only was there less technological development in poorer countries but often only a small share of patent applications within them were made by domestic residents. 'Trade-related' investment measures had no necessary connection with trade as it would normally be understood and could simply protect corporate operations in foreign countries, for example disallowing various requirements in terms of local content or procurement from local suppliers of the sort that had previously been imposed (Wade 2003). Corporate takeovers now had to be treated the same as new, 'greenfield' investment (Buckman 2005).

The WTO clearly produced extra layers of constraint, particularly on poorer countries, but it soon became obvious that these were far from absolute. There was what Narlikar (2003) calls an 'evolving' balance of power and poorer countries could and did block reforms. In 2001 India and Brazil prevented TRIMs legislation from banning all performance requirements (Wade 2003). Many Special and Differential Treatment provisions remained in place, either mandating action by developed countries or permitting exceptions among the developing. Different 'boxes' – red, amber and green – were distinguished whereby activities deemed non-trade-distorting were placed in the green box and allowed to continue (Wolfe 2004). Particularly in GATS, the agreement was quite weak with large exemption provisions that many countries exercised (Sell 2000; Wade 2003). The TRIPs legislation went further and was the focus of much popular and official protest but here regulation was modified, for example to improve developing countries' access to anti-retroviral drugs. Brazil notably retained laws allowing the production or import of drugs defying TRIPs in case of national health emergencies and used these to bargain better deals with pharmaceutical companies (Wade 2003). This was still a complex and ambiguous bargaining process. The self-imposed deadlines of the Doha round, the negotiations following the 2001 meeting in Qatar, were missed and reform proceeded slowly (Cottier and Elsig 2011).

One example of the dealing concerned the 'ACP waiver'. This dated back to agreements between European countries and their former colonies in Africa, the Caribbean and Pacific (ACP) at the 1975 Lome Convention, granting non-reciprocal access to European markets and eventually affecting 79 countries. This, of course, broke rules of equal treatment and was contested by other poorer countries, especially in Latin America, and by US multinationals that operated within them. Famously, European Union (EU) regulations on banana imports were overruled and the US imposed sanctions. However, most of the EU restrictions remained, even after the waiver formally expired in 2007 (Wolfe 2004; Erasmus 2010). Among other things, the ACP counties would reciprocate by supporting the EU at Doha (Buckman 2005).

Wolfe (2004) characterizes the development of policy a process of 'crossing the river by feeling the stones'. So although the WTO helped to sustain a liberalizing agenda it did not produce the deepening and freeing of markets as quickly as had been hoped or feared. The WTO (2014) itself eventually called only for 'freer trade gradually, through negotiation'.

The concessions and disappointments meant that the agenda of leading states and corporations were increasingly pushed in other directions. Regional and other preferential agreements proliferated. These were not necessarily opposed to WTO deepening and they typically met WTO rules. The process also worked the other way, with China being required to negotiate bilateral deals with the US and EU before its WTO accession was accepted (Matsushita et al. 2006). However, these deals, violating principles of universality and non-discrimination, probably played the bigger role in trade proliferation (Bhagwati 2005). The US alone had made 20 such deals by 2014 (USTR 2014). Smaller and poorer countries were again in a weaker bargaining position, as many became more open.

Trade openness clearly 'worked' for several poorer countries, it was not the inexorable recipe for national impoverishment identified by stronger versions of dependency theory. However, once again there is an apparent fallacy of composition in seeing what worked for Japan and Germany, and later for the Asian Tigers, as a general model (WB 1993). It is, of course, impossible for every country to run a trade surplus. Wolf's (2010) account of the crisis of the 2000s puts much emphasis on what he calls a 'global savings glut' but by definition this cannot be global. American deficits allowed many countries to run surpluses but competition also drove down prices and export earnings. By 2007 more countries were in deficit than surplus; 118 against 73, according to the IMF (2012). Just three countries accounted for almost half the combined surpluses; Japan, Germany and China.

China's remarkable rise makes the potential problems of export orientation particularly clear. An enormous amount has been written about China but three things are particularly worth noting. First, China's dramatic increase in openness does not amount to free trade. Although levels of direct state ownership of production in China fell, the economy in general and its trading relations in particular continued to be managed. In this it was like the earlier Asian export-oriented industrializers. China was also able to manage its currency values so that from 1994 until 2007 it maintained large and growing trade surpluses. Its exports rose almost exactly ten-fold from $121 billion to $1.22 trillion and its surpluses fifty-fold from $5.4 to $264 billion (WB 2014).

Second, rapid rates of investment sustained growth but were themselves sustained by increasing investment shares and falling consumption shares of national income. This implied the trade surpluses were vital as an outlet for final demand.

Third, China's size has potentially serious implications for the rest of the world economy. One vital assumption of the theory of comparative advantage, small country terms of trade, discussed in Chapter 3, manifestly does not hold. There are several dimensions of this. Most obviously, China's exports challenge those of other countries. The rest of East Asia's share of world exports fell in the 2000s, as China rose so fast. China's output drove down prices to such an extent that Samuelson (2004) warns of the effects of 'self-immiseration' (that China's own output could eventually under-cut its own prices). China's terms of trade fell by 22 per cent between 1980 and 2004 (UN 2006). Its growing surpluses were only one side of the story and China was also a vast importer. It bought capital goods, so a country like Korea, could run substantial surpluses with China, more than compensating for its loss of consumer goods markets in developed countries. However, as China continued to industrialize and rise up the technological ladder these imports too might be threatened. China seemed more likely to continue to rely on imported fuel and raw materials. Its success was based in substantial part on being able to provide competitive labour-intensive rather than capital-intensive ways of producing. This probably also involved the greater relative use of raw materials and fuels.

This leads to a final comment in this section on the volatile history of oil prices and fate of oil-exporting countries since the 1970s. The initial price rises associated with the OPEC restrictions of 1973 have been widely debated. Ostensibly a reaction to the Yom Kippur War and the revenge on Israel's Western supporters in that war, loyal US allies like Saudi Arabia now supported the price rise, which hit more fuel-dependent competitors like Japan much harder than the US (Gowan 1999). As above, oil-exporting countries accumulated huge surpluses, whose recycling contributed to the debts and debt crisis of the 1980s. Subsequently, OPEC was weakened and its members accounted for a smaller share of world oil output than they did in the 1970s. Oil prices peaked in 1980, after the Iranian revolution, then fell rapidly in real terms to the mid-1980s and then more slowly and unevenly until 1998. From then they escalated more than five-fold to 2008 (InflationData 2014). This rise was part of a wider commodities boom that was fuelled by speculation and by legislative change, which for example encouraged institutional investors like pension funds to buy commodity futures, which in turn drove up the current price in an apparently self-fulfilling spiral (Wray 2008). However, the rises were underpinned by the more extensive strategies of accumulation that increased demand for raw materials and particularly for fuels both in production and in transport. Oil-exporting countries again accumulated huge surpluses.

THE CRISIS

The story of the sub-prime crisis in the US and its rapid spread is now familiar. The proximate causes lie in financial practices that allowed firms to sell sub-prime (that is high-cost) mortgages to people who ultimately could not afford them. The mortgages were repackaged as complex derivatives and sold on, so it was not only the original lenders who were at risk but also those holding these new financial products. The boom had been sustained by rising property prices, so the security looked good even if borrowers' incomes failed to match the repayments, while low Federal interest rates allowed the easy borrowing. Critics, from both left and right, pointed out the role of changes in housing legislation that encouraged home ownership but also outlawed racial discrimination, which would previously have excluded many non-white borrowers from these markets. It is quite possible to argue that tougher financial regulation might have prevented the bubble.

However, the underlying structural transformations also encouraged the processes that led to the crisis. As above, financialization was part of a broader process of change. On the demand side, falling wages encouraged rising household debt. Meanwhile, rising corporate profits and falling corporate investment within the US fed financial supply. Even as production went overseas, the profits returned and US corporations' share prices jumped (Milberg and Winkler 2010). Domestic financialization and trade deficits rose together. In a real sense Europe experienced the crisis as a backwash from the US. Germany, for example, did not have any domestic housing bubble but several of its banks got caught in the US speculation. However, there were similar underlying processes whereby stagnant wages and falling levels of investment left a surplus which could be speculated in the open, deregulated US markets.

It is also easy, with hindsight, to criticize lax US monetary policy, but low interest rates were only possible because of the enduring willingness of foreigners to buy US treasuries, itself a function of the accumulation of foreign exchange reserves. These substantially reflected enduring dollar seigniorage and the development of trade surplus strategies. The previous period had seen a remarkable transformation. Total foreign dollar reserves jumped from $610 billion in 1995 to $2723 billion by 2008 with the majority held by developing countries (Cofer 2012). The dollars were not 'held' but lent back to the US, at interest but low interest, befitting the dollar's global role and the security provided by US Treasury bills. These dollars then circulated within the US economy, feeding low interest rates, domestic borrowing and the speculation. Laibson and Mollerstrom (2010) put the line of causations the other way round, from domestic asset bubbles to trade deficits, but confirm a clear correlation between trade and debt.

As mentioned at the beginning of the chapter, both mainstream and more radical commentators attribute considerable responsibility for the crisis to trade imbalances with the IMF maintaining that while the imbalances remain any recovery 'stands on increasingly hollow legs' (2011: 26). In the immediate aftermath of the crisis, reflationary measures and talk of financial regulation dominated. The IMF even called for a two-way rebalancing in which both deficit and surplus countries would make adjustments. There was evidence of more domestically oriented growth in China and its surpluses fell. Several other poorer countries' levels of domestic investment also grew quickly. However, in rich countries, austerity soon put the onus back onto those with deficits to cut imports rather than surplus countries to increase domestic consumption. Austerity did reduce or even reverse the deficits in the US and badly hit countries of the European periphery, including Iceland, Greece and Spain. However, overall, the trade imbalances soon began to grow again, suggesting that the crisis may prove not to have been a real turning point, instead deepening rather than challenging many trends of the earlier period. This rebound of trade imbalances suggests that recovery might be fragile.

CONCLUSION

It is now fairly widely accepted that global imbalances constituted significantly to the crisis of the 2000s. Once again this does not mean that trade in general is bad. Trade relations were transformed in particular interests and in response to the particular characteristics of the crisis of the 1970s and this sent economic relations in general and trade relations in particular along ultimately unsustainable trajectories. Falling rates of investment within the US, and the unique role of the US dollar, allowed the accumulation of huge trade deficits and foreign dollar holdings. A reciprocal opening of poorer countries and the form it took, of restricting domestic consumption and encouraging an export orientation, pushed several toward systematic surpluses. China's growth was the most spectacular. A globally more extensive form of accumulation, which China's rise epitomized, increased the demand for fuel and raw materials and, in the same liberalizing environment, enabled many oil-exporting countries to accumulate huge trade and dollar surpluses. Here again, the role of trade only makes sense as part of a wider process of economic restructuring and of institutional and financial reform. Trade mattered profoundly but its impact needs to be understood in its specific social and historical context.

11. Conclusions

At first sight the conclusions of this book might seem unsatisfying. There are problems with all the theories and much of the evidence is inconclusive. That is really the point, that a properly critical understanding of trade should not expect neat answers.

The evidence suggests that none of the most influential theories, from the beguiling elegance of comparative advantage through to ideas of monopoly and imperfect competition to the opposite pole of unequal exchange and the systematic disadvantage to poorer countries that it posits, provide much help in understanding the complexity of observed patterns of trade. There is evidence that trade is positively associated with growth, albeit neither the levels nor the statistical association warrant economists' general enthusiasm. Meanwhile, if there is a systematic disadvantage to poorer countries or to primary product exporters, or reciprocally if there is an advantage to rich countries or manufactured commodity exporters, this struggles to emerge from the evidence. At the very least, any such effects were being veiled, presumably by other, stronger economic forces.

The book was able to report some interesting and clearly positive results. For example, at least until the 2000s, trade deficits appear to have been conducive to faster national growth, indicating that a pervasive prejudice in favour of trade surpluses is misplaced. Countries do tend to trade, particularly to trade primary products, on the basis of their 'factor endowments' as predicted by the neo-classical Heckscher–Ohlin theorem. This result, of course, says nothing about how countries came to be land rich or labour poor. Nor, it was argued, does this association mean that countries' economies grow any faster as a result of trading according to their factor endowments. Turning to the within-country effects of trade on inequality and labour organization, the tests reported here cast doubt on the influential Stolper–Samuelson reading of income polarization in rich countries but confirmed that trade had significant, if as yet still imperfectly understood, impacts on inequality and industrial action.

Finally, it was argued that trade played an important role in generating the conditions that provoked the global financial and economic crisis of

2007–09. However, the development of global imbalances was understood in the context of wider processes of economic change and social struggle. Changing trade relations were inextricably connected to global money and finance, to the role of the dollar and to the opening of poorer countries to repay debts and in response to currency crises. They involved questions of power, cooperation and competition between leading rich-country states and relations between rich and poor countries, for example exercised and disputed through the World Trade Organization. They involved corporate interests in restructuring and relocating production and class struggles and political transformation within countries. The specifics of this recent history perhaps begin to make sense of what was often very ambiguous empirical evidence discussed in the earlier chapters. National economies were inserted into the global system in different ways, hard to reduce to their bare economic or demographic characteristics.

In many ways, the negatives of this book can only hope to provide a clearing of the ground for a more thoroughly critical political economy of trade. The simple formulae (and the sometimes convoluted mathematics) to which trade is too often reduced provide an inadequate starting point. Trade is itself a diverse and contested social process, inescapably linked to the broader political economy. Trade matters and often matters profoundly but it matters in different ways for different people and at different times and places. Chapter 5 developed a critique of putatively radical trade theories based on Marx's (1973) description of an 'obvious' ordering of political economy. Some of these themes seem worth briefly revisiting to appreciate the limits of trade theory more generally and to consider how something more adequate might be developed.

Both mainstream and critical theories typically accept a worldview close to that which scholars of international relations call 'Realist theory'. This sees a system of competing states, each constrained by the inter-state structure. For trade orthodoxy, the structure reflects 'factor endowments' determining countries' natural economic position in an international division of labour. For critics, the power structures and a division of labour are maintained by core states and this is perhaps not quite the much criticized 'billiard ball' model, because the interacting balls are of different sizes and those different sizes are vitally important. However, the vision remains one of discrete entities jockeying for position. Realist international relations scholarship offers important insights and elements of it have been embraced by Marxists, amongst others (Callinicos 2007). But it has been subjected to all sorts of criticisms, identifying how international structures are changeable social achievements. The numerous criticisms of Realism have hardly impinged on the trade debates and it is worth reflecting on how they might usefully do so.

This shared national orientation has both methodological and practical implications. Liberal trade theory typically extrapolates the logic of competitive individuals to that of nation states. This is an awkward jump for neo-classical economics, for which methodological individualism is almost always seen as essential to securing the basic economic models. It is individuals who perceive utility and whose choices drive economic processes (Jevons 1965). As Robinson wryly observes (1964: 58–9), the models insist:

> There is one equilibrium position in which each individual is doing the best for himself, so that no one has any incentive to move. (For groups to combine to better themselves collectively is strictly against the rules.) [...] Setting the whole thing out in algebra is a great help. The symmetrical relations between x and y seem smooth and amiable, entirely free from the associations of acrimony which are apt to be suggested by the relation between 'capital and labour'.

Trade theory clings to the amiability and freedom from acrimony (not to mention the algebra). But suddenly the individual disappears, superseded by the state as the vital agent. Liberal trade theory simply treats states as if they were rational individuals, with 'wants' and marginal utility. What is reckoned true of individuals is extrapolated to country welfare (Caves et al. 1993). Unfortunately, having a superordinate national structure undermines the individualism on which the economic models ultimately hang (Guzzini 1998). Few bother to reflect on the conceptual precipice over which they are jumping. Where an attempt is made to justify the approach, the presumptions can sit in considerable tension with the usual declarations of cosmopolitanism and mutual gains. Caves and his co-authors invoke a 'universal xenophobia' to explain countries' emotional states (Caves et al. 1993: 3), doing little to establish the good pedigree of universalism or 'the country as a solid unit' (Raffer 1987: 174).

Many critical writers are, if anything, less embarrassed by seeing states as the agents of change. Chang (2002) embraces List's phrase about 'kicking away the ladder', showing how rich states that got rich while restricting trade now seek to prevent others from following the same course. The implication is that to make trade relations more equitable, it is necessary to have more state intervention in trade by poorer-country governments. Faith in the invisible hand of the market is jettisoned for the benign hand of the state (Balogh 1976). Too often, in practice, the apparent radicalism conceals a rather naive nationalism (Kidron 1974). It is easy to imagine how, in practice, powerful sectional interests might conceal themselves behind 'national oppression' while shifting attention from class relations to the arena of trade competition. On both sides of the trade debate, much of the argument thus ends up sitting, more or less knowingly, in the tradition of state-centric political realism also in the sense of offering advice to rulers, whose concerns for other questions – for example, of poverty and inequality – are likely to be secondary at best.

This is not to downplay the practical importance of national political economies. Boundaries matter and policy is precisely carried out primarily at a national level. It is also appropriate to acknowledge here that with the best of intentions it is very hard to break with state-centric perspectives in discussing and analysing international trade. To a certain extent everybody becomes a prisoner of the statistics (literally state data) whereby we know in detail the level of border-crossing activity but usually much less about exchanges within borders. The empirical chapters here used conventional data. This risks reproducing state-centric ways of thinking but at the very least it is possible to acknowledge the limitations of what is being investigated and to worry about whether what should be challenged is instead being reinforced. This happens very seldom, with little reflection on taking nation states as the appropriate units of analysis. The object remains the wealth (or sometimes the poverty) of nations.

In practice, mainstream theorists, notably in the Heckscher–Ohlin and Stolper–Samuelson theorems, discussed in Chapters 7 and 8, have been at least as likely as the putatively radical dependency tradition to prise open the national economy, explaining why trade might be experienced differently by different groups within countries who might therefore either support or oppose it. This can be couched in terms of lamentable attempts to subvert the natural order of comparative advantage and the national interest but at least it provides some notion of agency and of how and why things can be different. The theories struggle to explain observed variations but rather than radicalizing and deepening their insights, critics too often revert to a vision that goes no further than international competition and exploitation. Most conspicuously, Emmanuel (1972), despite his Marxist background, rejects class analysis to focus on national exploitation. Few would go so far but there is a tendency to posit two distinct sets of relations, trade relations between countries and a quite other set of social relations within them. In principle, at least, border-crossing trade should be seen as only a sub-set of a broader set of economic exchange relations.

Exchange relations, in turn, are themselves only one aspect of the economy. Mainstream economics acknowledges that its object of enquiry is the distribution of scarce resources. This is a ridiculously limited question. It is rather like defining ornithology in terms of a discussion of the colour of birds' plumage, ruling questions of flight and feeding and breeding out of bounds. Exchange relations alone, whether fair exchanges or unequal exchanges, can tell us little about all sorts of vital processes, most obviously about where all the resources come from. And this view too is essentially shared by both sides of the trade debate, by free traders and by the mercantilists and dependency theorists. Both liberal and nationalist perspectives on trade conceive the fundamental issues as those of acquisition and distribution between countries, and so naturalize exchange relations as the essence of the problem and of discussions of welfare and common good. Marx memorably criticizes what he calls 'vulgar economics' for the priority it gives to exchange where everything appears a world of 'freedom, equality, property and Bentham' (1976: 280). He argues for an analysis that looked behind the veil of exchange relations to reveal the dynamics of exploitation in production. Brenner (1977) and Skocpol (1977) develop important criticisms of Wallerstein's world-systems theory in this vein. A focus on the transfer of value rather than production leads to a static, rather transhistorical view of the world that blurs the distinctive features of its specifically capitalist nature.

Of course, critics of the trade regime, including Marx himself, later Marxists, Keynes and the Keynesian tradition, have all pointed out that exchange relations need not be equitable. The US and the European Union (EU) have power in both formal and informal structures by means of which they can gain at the expense of poorer and weaker states. Giant corporations do not confront peasant suppliers as equals. Identifying these inequalities seems entirely proper and useful. However, what happens next for many critics is that the argument shifts back to trying to make these trade relations more equitable without challenging the exploitative dynamics in production that ultimately underlie them. Analysts identify the practical restrictions on trade introduced by powerful states like the farm subsidies in the US and the EU Common Agricultural Policy, but then demand their abolition and the effective implementation of free trade (Oxfam 2002; Birdsall 2006). At this point the critics and the mainstream trade theorists converge. None of this makes worrying about exchange illegitimate but it implies that exchange relations in general and trade relations in particular should be understood in the context of broader economic relations and particularly relations of production.

Moreover, trade is not just a narrowly economic process in either cause or effect and economic relations are themselves always only one aspect of broader social processes. Trade has major impacts on society, in its marketization, in how it is gendered and in terms of our relationship with the environment and so on. Where heterodox economists are usually keen to unpick the asocial character of mainstream economics, criticizing assumptions of rational, self-interested, utility-maximizing individuals, little of this surfaces in the radical trade theory. The neglect goes both ways and sociologists have had almost as little to say about international trade as trade theory about wider society, but more dialogue is needed not least to overcome the way economic categories are constructed. Just as the trade data reinforce national boundaries, so economic data in general reinforce notions of what counts as economic gain. All this accentuates the way both sides of the trade debate proceed with a set of assumptions that are asocialized, and that accept relations of production, states and the interstate system as more or less given.

Finally, I should acknowledge that writing a book like this involves a remarkable learning experience. One of the first and most important lessons is the sheer size of the literature and the impossibility of mastering it all. I hope I have not misrepresented anybody too egregiously but can only apologize to the numerous people whose work I have overlooked, and who may well be frustrated either because they have provided arguments or evidence contradicting what I have said or because they have already said something similar themselves. I hope they are not too many and hope at least that they are outnumbered by those encouraged to look again at trade and to look at trade more critically than has been the norm.

References

Acemoglu, D. (2003), 'Patterns of skill premia', *Review of Economic Studies*, **70**(2), 199–230.

Adler, P.S. (2004), 'Skill trends under capitalism and the socialisation of production', in C. Warhurst, I. Grugulis and E. Keep (eds), *The Skills that Matter*, Basingstoke: Palgrave Macmillan.

Akkermans, A. (2008), 'Union competition and strikes: the need for an analysis at the sectoral level', *Industrial and Labor Relations Review*, **61**(4), 445–59.

Allen, L. (2005), *The Global Economic System Since 1945*, London: Reaktion Books.

Amin, S. (1974), *Accumulation on a World Scale: A Critique of the Theory of Underdevelopment*, New York: Monthly Review Press.

Amin, S. (1976), *Unequal Development*, New York: Monthly Review Press.

Amsden A. (1992), *Asia's Next Giant: South Korea and Late Industrialization*, New York: Oxford University Press.

Anderson, E. (2005), 'Openness and inequality in developing countries: a review of theory and recent evidence', *World Development*, **33**(7), 1045–63.

Anderson, P. (1979), *Lineages of the Absolutist State*, London: Verso.

Archibugi, D. and J. Michie (1997), *Technology, Globalisation and Economic Performance*, Cambridge: Cambridge University Press.

Armstrong, P., A. Glyn and J. Harrison (1984), *Capitalism Since World War II*, London: Fontana.

Augelli, E. and C.N. Murphy, (1993), 'Gramsci and international relations: a general perspective with examples from recent US policy towards the Third World', in S. Gill (ed.), *Gramsci, Historical Materialism and International Relations*, Cambridge: Cambridge University Press.

Babones, S.J. (2010), 'Trade globalization, economic development and the importance of knowledge as education', *Journal of Sociology*, **46**(1), 45–61.

Babones, S.J. and D.C. Vonada (2009), 'Trade globalization and national income inequality – are they related?', *Journal of Sociology*, **45**(1), 5–30.

Baiman, R. (2006), 'Unequal exchange without a labor theory of prices: on the need for a global Marshall Plan and a solidarity trading regime', *Review of Radical Political Economics*, **38**(1), 71–89.

Baiman, R. (2010), 'The infeasibility of free trade in classical theory: Ricardo's comparative advantage parable has no solution', *Review of Political Economics*, **22**(3), 419–37.

Balaam, D.N. and M. Veseth (2001), *Introduction to International Political Economy*, Upper Saddle River, NJ: Prentice Hall.

Baldwin, R.E. (2008), *The Development and Testing of Heckscher–Ohlin Trade Models: A Review*, Cambridge, MA: MIT Press.

Balogh, T. (1976), 'Keynes and the International Monetary Fund', in Thirlwall, A.P. (ed.), *Keynes and International Monetary Relations*, London: Macmillan.

Banaji, J. (2011), *Theory as History*, Chicago, IL: Haymarket.

Baran, P. (1957), *The Political Economy of Growth*, New York: Monthly Review Press.

Baran, P.A. and P.M. Sweezy (1968), *Monopoly Capital*, Harmondsworth: Penguin.

Barnet, R.J. and J. Cavanagh (1994), *Global Dreams: Imperial Corporations and the New World Order*, New York: Touchstone.

Bell, D. (1974), *The Coming of Post-Industrial Society*, London: Heinemann Educational.

Bentley, J.H. (1993), *Old World Encounters*, New York: Oxford University Press.

Bettelheim, C. (1972), 'Appendix I: theoretical comments', comments contributed to A. Emmanuel, *Unequal Exchange: A Study of the Imperialism of Trade*, New York: Monthly Review Press.

Bhagwati, J. (ed.) (1987), *International Trade: Selected Readings*, 2nd edn, Cambridge, MA: MIT Press.

Bhagwati, J. (2002), *Free Trade Today*, Princeton, NJ: Princeton University Press.

Bhagwati, J. (2005), 'Reshaping the WTO', *Far Eastern Economic Review*, **168**(2) (Jan/Feb), 25–30.

Bieler, A. and A.D. Morton (2014), 'Uneven and combined development and unequal exchange: the second wind of neoliberal "free trade"?' *Globalizations*, **11**(1), 35–45.

Birdsall, N. (1998), 'Life is unfair: inequality in the world', *Foreign Policy*, **112** Summer, 76–83.

Birdsall, N. (2006), 'Stormy days on an open field: asymmetries in the global economy', Centre for Global Development working paper no. 81.

Blackburn, R. (1988), *The Overthrow of Colonial Slavery*, London, Verso.

Blackburn, R. (1997), *The Making of New World Slavery*, London, Verso.

Bloch, M. (1965), *Feudal Society*, London: Routledge and Kegan Paul.

Bordogna, L. and P.G. Cella (2002), 'Decline or transformation? Change in industrial conflict and its challenges', *Transfer*, **8**(4), 585–607.

Bourdieu, P. (1977), *Outline of a Theory of Practice*, London: Routledge.

Bourdieu, P. (1984), *Distinction: A Social Critique of the Judgement of Taste*, London: Routledge.

Bourdieu, P. (1998), *Acts of Resistance*, Cambridge: Polity.

Bowles, S. and R. Boyer (1990), 'A wage-led employment regime: income distribution, labour discipline, and aggregate demand in welfare capitalism', in S.A. Marglin and J.B. Schor (eds), *The Golden Age of Capitalism: Reinterpreting the Post-War Experience*, Oxford: Clarendon Press.

Bown, C. (2011), 'Developing countries and monitoring WTO commitments in response to the global economic crisis', in T. Cottier and M. Elsig (eds), *Governing the World Trade Organization*, Cambridge: Cambridge University Press.

Bracking, S. and G. Harrison (2003), 'Africa, Imperialism and new forms of accumulation', *Review of African Political Economy*, **95**(5), 5–10.

Braverman, H. (1974), *Labour and Monopoly Capital*, New York: Monthly Review.

Brenner, R. (1976), 'Agrarian class structure and economic development in pre-industrial Europe', *Past and Present*, **70**(1), 30–75.

Brenner, R. (1977), 'The origins of capitalist development: a critique of neo-Smithian Marxism', *New Left Review*, **104**, 25–92.

Brenner, R. (1998), *The Economics of Global Turbulence*, *New Left Review*, I/**229** (May–June), special issue.

Brenner, R. (2006), 'The origins of capitalism' transcript of the discussion with Chris Harman, London, 2004, *International Socialism*, **111**, 127–63.

Brewer, A. (1990), *Marxist Theories of Imperialism*, London: Routledge.

Brown, P. (1995), 'Cultural capital and social exclusion', *Work, Employment and Society*, **9**(1), 29–51.

Brolin, J. (2006), *The Bias of the World: Theories of Unequal Exchange in History*, Lund, Sweden: Lund University.

Buckman, G. (2005), *Global Trade: Past Mistakes, Future Choices*, Halifax, NS: Fernwood.

Bukharin, N. (1972), *Imperialism and World Economy*, London: Merlin.

Bunker, S.G. (1984), 'Modes of extraction, unequal exchange, and the progressive underdevelopment of an extreme periphery: the Brazilian Amazon, 1600-1980', *American Journal of Sociology*, **89**(5), 1017–64.

Burkett, P. and M. Hart-Landsberg (2000), *Development, Crisis, and Class Struggle*, New York: St. Martin's Press.

Bush, R. (2004), 'Undermining Africa', *Historical Materialism*, **12**(4), 173–201.

Callinicos, A. (2007), 'Does capitalism need the state system?', *Cambridge Review of International Affairs*, **20**(4), 533–49.

Callinicos, A. (2009), *Imperialism and the Global Political Economy*, Cambridge: Polity.

Cardoso, F.H. and E. Falleto (1979), *Dependency and Development in Latin America*, Berkeley, CA: University of California Press.

Castells, M. (2000), *The Information Age: Economy, Society and Culture, Volume 1*, Oxford: Blackwell.

Caves, R.E., J.A. Frankel and R.W. Jones (1993), *World Trade and Payments*, 6th edn, New York: HarperCollins.

Cerny, P. (1993), 'The deregulation and re-regulation of financial markets in a more open world', in P.G. Cerny (ed.), *Finance and World Politics: Markets, Regimes and States in the Post-hegemonic Era*, Aldershot and Brookfield, VT, USA: Edward Elgar.

Chakrabarti, A. (2000), 'Does trade cause inequality?', *Journal of Economic Development*, **25**(2), 1–21.

Chang, H.-J. (2002), *Kicking Away the Ladder: Policies and Institutions for Development in Historical Perspective*, London: Anthem Press.

Chang, H.-J. (2007), *Bad Samaritans: Rich Nations, Poor Policies and the Threat to the Developing World*, London: Random House.

Chusseau, N. and M. Dumont (2013), 'Growing income inequalities in advanced countries', in J. Hellier and N. Chusseau (eds), *Growing Income Inequalities: Economic Analyses*, Basingstoke: Palgrave Macmillan.

Chusseau, N. and J. Hellier (2013), 'Inequality in emerging countries', in J. Hellier and N. Chusseau (eds), *Growing Income Inequalities: Economic Analyses*, Basingstoke: Palgrave Macmillan.

COFER (2012), Currency Composition of Official Foreign Exchange Reserves. Available at: http://www.imf.org/external/np/sta/cofer/eng/ (accessed 1 July 2012).

Cohn, T.H. (2005), *Global Political Economy*, New York: Pearson.

Colen, L., M. Maertens and J. Swinnen (2008), 'Foreign direct investment as an engine for economic growth and human development: a review of the arguments and empirical evidence', Leuven Centre for Global Governance Studies, working paper no. 16.

Conca, K. (2000), 'The WTO and the undermining of global environmental governance', *Review of International Political Economy*, **7**(3), 484–94.

Cottier, T. and M. Elsig (2011), 'Introduction' in T. Cottier and M. Elsig (eds), *Governing the World Trade Organization*, Cambridge: Cambridge University Press.

Cox, R.W. (1981), 'Social forces, states and world orders', *Millennium: Journal of International Studies*, **10**(2), 126–55.

Crouzet, F. (1990), *Britain Ascendant*, Cambridge: Cambridge University Press.

Curtin, P.D. (1984), *Cross-cultural Trade in World History*, Cambridge: Cambridge University Press.

Cypher, J.M. and J.L. Dietz (1998), 'Static and dynamic comparative advantage: a multi-period analysis with declining terms of trade', *Journal of Economic Issues*, **32**(2), 305–14.

Darity, W. Jnr and L.S. Davis (2005), 'Growth, trade and uneven development', *Cambridge Journal of Economics*, **29**(1), 141–70

Darlington, R. (2009), 'Leadership and union militancy: the case of the RMT', *Capital and Class*, **98**, 3–32.

David, M. and S. Gollasch (2008), 'EU shipping in the dawn of managing the ballast water issue', *Marine Pollution Bulletin*, **56**(12), 1966–72.

Deraniyagala, S. (2005), 'Neoliberalism in international trade', in A. Saad-Fihlo and D. Johnston (eds), *Neoliberalism: A Critical Reader*, London: Pluto.

Deraniyagala, S. and B. Fine (2001), 'New trade theory versus old trade policy: a continuing enigma', *Cambridge Journal of Economics*, **25**(6), 809–25.

Dicken, P. (2003), *Global Shift*, London: Sage.

Dobb, M. (1963), *Studies in the Development of Capitalism*, New York: International Publishers.

Dollar, D. (1992), 'Outward-oriented developing countries really do grow more rapidly; evidence from 95 LDCs 1875–1985', *Economic Development and Cultural Change*, **40**(3), 523–44.

Dollar, D. and A. Kraay (2004), 'Trade, growth, and poverty', *The Economic Journal*, **114** (February), 22–49.

Dos Santos, T. (1970), 'The structure of dependence', *The American Economic Review*, **60**(2), 231–6.

Dreher, A. and N. Gaston (2006), 'Has globalisation increased inequality?' Econstor, working paper no. 140.

Dunkley, G. (2004), *Free Trade: Myth, Reality and Alternatives*, London: Zed.

Dunn, B. (2004a), 'Capital movements and the embeddedness of labour', *Global Society*, **18**(2), 127–43.

Dunn, B. (2004b), *Global Restructuring and the Power of Labour*, Basingstoke: Palgrave Macmillan.

Dunn, B. (2009), 'Myths of globalisation and the new economy', *International Socialism*, **121**, 75–97.

Dunn, B. (2014a), *The Political Economy of Global Capitalism and Crisis*, London: Routledge.

Dunn, B. (2014b), 'Skills, credentials and their unequal reward in a heterogeneous global political economy', *Journal of Sociology*, **50**(3), 349–67.

Edwards, S. (1998), 'Openness, productivity and growth: what do we really know?', *The Economic Journal*, **108**(447), 383–98.

Eichengreen, B. (1984), 'The tasks of economic history', *The Journal of Economic History*, **44**(2), 363-7.

Emmanuel, A. (1972), *Unequal Exchange: A Study of the Imperialism of Trade*, London: New Left Books.

Engels, F. (n.d.), 'Protection and free trade', in *K. Marx and F. Engles on Colonialism*, London: Lawrence and Wishart.

Erasmus, G. (2010), 'Accommodating developing countries in the WTO: from mega-debates to economic partnership agreements', in D.P. Steger (ed.), *Redesigning the World Trade Organization for the Twenty-first Century*, Ottawa, ON: Wilfrid Laurier University Press.

Evans, D. (1984), 'A critical assessment of some neo-Marxian trade theories', *The Journal of Development Studies*, **20**(2), 202–26.

Findlay, R. and K.H. O'Rourke (2007), *Power and Plenty: Trade, War, and the World Economy in the Second Millennium*, Princeton, NJ: Princeton University Press.

Fine, B. (2004), 'Examining the ideas of globalisation and development critically', *New Political Economy*, **9**(2), 213–31.

Fine, B. and L. Harris (1979), *Rereading Capital*, London: Macmillan.

Flam, H. and M.J. Flanders (1991), 'Introduction', in H. Flam and M.J. Flanders (eds), *Heckscher–Ohlin Trade Theory*, Cambridge, MA: MIT Press.

Forbes, D.K. (1984), *The Geography of Underdevelopment*, London: Croom Helm.

Foreman-Peck, J. (1983), *A History of the World Economy: International Economic Relations Since 1850*, Brighton: Wheatsheaf.

Foster, J.B. (2000), *Marx's Ecology*, New York: Monthly Review Press.

Foster, J.B. and R.W. McChesney (2012), *The Endless Crisis*, New York: Monthly Review Press.

Frank, A.G. (1970), 'The development of underdevelopment', in R.I. Rhodes (ed.), *Imperialism and Underdevelopment*, New York: Monthly Review.

Frank, A.G. (1978), *Dependent Accumulation and Under-Development*, London: Macmillan.

Frankel, J.A. and D. Romer (1999), 'Does trade cause growth?', *The American Economic Review*, **89**(3), 379–99.

Frieden, J.A. (1991), 'Invested interests: the politics of national economic policies in a world of global finance', *International Organization*, **45**(4), 425–51.

Friedman, M. (1962), *Capitalism and Freedom*, Chicago, IL: University of Chicago Press.

Friedman, T. (2000), *The Lexus and the Olive Tree*, London: Harper-Collins.

Fröbel, F., J. Heinrichs, and O. Kreye (1980), *The New International Division of Labour: Structural Unemployment in Industrial Countries and Industrialisation in Developing Countries*, Cambridge: Cambridge University Press.

Galbraith, J.K. and J.T. Hale (2009), 'The evolution of economic inequality in the United States, 1969–2007: evidence from data on inter-industrial earnings and inter-regional incomes', University of Texas Inequality Project working paper no. 57, 2 February.

Gallagher, J. and R. Robinson (1953), 'The imperialism of free trade', *Economic History Review*, **6**(1), 1–15.

Garrett, G. (2000), 'Shrinking states? Globalization and national autonomy', in N. Woods (ed.), *The Political Economy of Globalization*, Basingstoke: Macmillan.

Gereffi, G., J. Humphrey, and T. Sturgeon (2005), 'The governance of global value chains', *Review of International Political Economy*, **12**(1), 78–104.

Gibson, B. (1980), 'Unequal exchange: theoretical issues and empirical findings', *Review of Radical Political Economics*, **12**(3), 15–35.

Gilpin, R. (1987), *The Political Economy of International Relations*, Princeton, NJ: Princeton University Press.

Gilpin, R. (2001), *Global Political Economy*, Princeton, NJ: Princeton University Press.

Glyn, A. (2008), 'Explaining labor's declining share of national income', UNCTAD, Intergovernmental Group of Twenty Four, G-24, Policy Brief No. 4.

Goldfrank, W.L. (2000), 'Paradigm regained? The rules of Wallerstein's World-System Method', *Journal of World-System Research*, **6**(2), 150–95.

Gowan, P. (1999), *The Global Gamble*, London: Verso.

Graham, F.D. (1923), 'Aspects of protection further considered', *The Quarterly Journal of Economics*, **37**(2), 199–227.

Green, F. and Y. Zhu (2010), 'Overqualification, job dissatisfaction, and increasing dispersion in the returns to graduate education', *Oxford Economic Papers*, **62**, 740–63.

Greider, W. (1997), *One World, Ready or Not: The Manic Logic of Global Capitalism*, Harmondsworth: Penguin.

Guzzini, S. (1998), *Realism in International Relations and International Political Economy*, London: Routledge.

Hall, J.K. and L.E. Bass (2012), 'The effects of global interaction on poverty in developing countries, 1991-2005', *Journal of World-Systems Research*, **18**(2), 236-65.

Hamilton, A. (1792), *Report on the Subject of Manufactures*, Dublin: P. Byrne.

Harman, C. (1984), *Explaining the Crisis*, London: Bookmarks.

Harman, C. (1989), 'From feudalism to capitalism', *International Socialism*, **45**, 35–87.

Harvey, D. (1990), *The Condition of Postmodernity: An Enquiry into the Origins of Cultural Change*, Oxford: Blackwell.

Heaton, H. (1948), *Economic History of Europe*, New York: Harper & Brothers.

Heckscher, E. (1950), 'The effect of foreign trade on the distribution of income', in B.F. Haley (ed.), *Readings in the Theory of International Trade*, London: George Allen and Unwin.

Heckscher, E. (1955a), *Mercantilism, Vol. I*, London: George Allen and Unwin.

Heckscher, E. (1955b), *Mercantilism, Vol. II*, London: George Allen and Unwin.

Heilbroner, R. (1997), *Teachings from the Worldly Philosophers*, New York: Norton.

Held, D., A. McGrew, D. Goldblatt and J. Perraton (1999), *Global Transformations*, Cambridge: Polity.

Heller, H. (2011), *The Birth of Capitalism*, London: Pluto.

Helleiner, E. (1993), 'American hegemony and global economic structure: from closed to open financial relations in the postwar world', thesis submitted for the PhD Degree, LSE, University of London.

Helleiner, E. (1994), *States and the Reemergence of Global Finance*, Ithaca, NY: Cornell University Press.

Hellier, J. (2013), 'The North–South HOS model, inequality and globalization', in J. Hellier and N. Chusseau (eds), *Growing Income Inequalities: Economic Analyses*, Basingstoke: Palgrave Macmillan.

Helpman, E. (1981), 'International trade in the presence of product differentiation, economies of scale and monopolistic competition', *Journal of International Economics*, **11**(3), 305–40.

Henderson, W.O. (1983), 'Editor's introduction' to F. List, *The Natural System of Political Economy*, London: Frank Cass.

Hicks, J.R. (1953), 'An inaugural lecture', *Oxford Economic Papers*, **5**(2), 117–35.

Higgot, R. (1998), 'The Asian economic crisis', *New Political Economy*, **3**(3), 333–56.

Hilferding, R. (1981), *Finance Capital*, London: Routledge & Kegan Paul.

Hilton R. (1985), 'A crisis of feudalism', in T.H. Aston and C.H.E. Philpin (eds), *The Brenner Debate*, Cambridge: Cambridge University Press.

Hirschman, A.O. (1958), *The Strategy of Economic Development*, New Haven, CT: Yale University Press.

Hirschman, A.O. (1989), 'How the Keynesian revolution was exported from the United States, and other comments', in P. Hall (ed.), *The Political Power of Economic Ideas: Keynesianism Across Nations*, Princeton, NJ: Princeton University Press.

Hirst, P. and G. Thompson (1999), *Globalization in Question*, 2nd edn, Cambridge: Polity.

Hobsbawm, E.J. (1969), *Industry and Empire*, Harmondsworth: Penguin

Hobson, J.A. (2007), *Imperialism, A Study*. Available at: http://www.marxists.org/archive/hobson/1902/imperialism/ (accessed 21 March 2007).

Holloway, J. (1995), 'Capital moves', *Capital and Class*, **57**, 137–44.

Hornborg, A. (1998), 'Towards an ecological theory of unequal exchange', *Ecological Economics*, **25**(1), 127–36.

Horvat B. (1999), *The Theory of International Trade: An Alternative Approach*, Basingstoke: Palgrave Macmillan.

Hudson, M. (2003), *Super Imperialism*, London: Pluto.

Hummels, D.L. and R.M. Stern (1994), 'Evolving patterns of North American merchandise trade and foreign direct investment, 1960-1990', *The World Economy*, **17**(1), 5–29.

Husted, S. and M. Melvin (1990), *International Economics*, New York: Harper & Row.

Hutton, W. (1995), *The State We're In*, London: Jonathan Cape.

Hyman, R. (1999), 'Imagined solidarities: can trade unions resist globalization?' in P. Leisink (ed.), *Globalization and Labour Relations*, Northampton, MA, USA and Cheltenham, UK: Edward Elgar.

ILO (1997), *World Labour Report: Industrial Relations, Democracy and Social Stability, 1997–98*, Geneva: International Labour Office.

ILO (2008), *Global Wage Report 2008/9*, Geneva: International Labour Office

ILO (2010), 'Laborsta Internet'. Available at: http://laborsta.ilo.org/ (data accessed June–August 2010).

IMF (2011), 'World economic outlook: tensions from the two-speed recovery', April 2011. Available at: https://www.imf.org/external/pubs/ft/weo/2011/01/ (accessed 15 November 2014).

IMF (2014), 'International financial statistics'. Available at: http://elibrary-data.imf.org.ezproxy2.library.usyd.edu.au/ViewData.aspx?qb=f435527289a0b3f97f495481e7e366ce (accessed 23 May 2014).

InflationData (2014), data from InflationData.com. Available at: http://www.inflationdata.com/ (accessed 15 September 2014).

Janvry, A. de and F. Kramer (1979), 'The limits of unequal exchange', *Review of Radical Political Economics*, **11**(3), 3–15.

Jevons, H.S. (1965), *The Theory of Political Economy*, 5th edn, New York: Augustus M. Kelley.

Jomo, K.S. and E.S. Reinert (2005), 'Introduction', in K.S. Jomo and E.S. Reinert (eds), *The Origins of Development Economics*, London: Zed.

Jones, R.W. (2006), 'Protection and real wages: the history of an idea', *Japanese Economic Review*, **57**(4), 457–66.

Kaldor, N. (1940), 'A note on tariffs and the terms of trade', *Economica*, **7**(28), 377–80.

Kaldor, N. (1989), *Further Essays on Economic Theory and Policy*, F. Targetti and A.P. Thirlwall (eds), London: Duckworth.

Keesing, D.B. and D.R. Sherk (1971), 'Density in patterns of trade and development', *American Economic Review*, **61**(5), 956–61.

Keller, R.P., J.M. Drake, M.B. Drew and D.M. Lodge (2011), 'Linking environmental conditions and ship movements to estimate invasive species transport across the global shipping network', *Diversity and Distribution: A Journal of Conservation Biogeography*, **17**(1), 93–102.

Kelly, J. (1998), *Rethinking Industrial Relations: Mobilization, Collectivism and Long Waves*, London: Routledge.

Kenwood, A.G. and A.L. Lougheed (1992), *The Growth of the International Economy: 1820–1990*, London: Routledge.

Keynes, J.M. (1973), *The General Theory of Employment, Interest and Money*, London: Macmillan.

Kho, B.-C., R.M. Stulz and F.E. Warnock (2006), 'Financial globalisation, governance and the evolution of the home bias', Bank for International Settlements working paper no. 220.

Kidron, M. (1974), *Capitalism and Theory*, London: Pluto.

Kincaid, J. (2001), 'Marxist political economy and the crises in Japan and East Asia', *Historical Materialism*, **8**(1), 433–41.

Kindleberger, C. (1956), *Terms of Trade: A European Case Study*, New York: Wiley.

Kindleberger, C.P. (1973), *The World in Depression 1929–39*, London: Allen Lane, the Penguin Press.

Kolm, S.-C. (1968), 'Review: Léon Walras' correspondence and related papers', *The American Economic Review*, **58**(5), 1330–41.

Kovel, J. (2002), *The Enemy of Nature*, Halifax, NS: Fernwood.

Krasner, S.D. (1976), 'State power and the structure of international trade', *World Politics*, **28**(3), 317–47.

Krippner, G.A. (2011), *Capitalizing on Crisis: the Political Origins of the Rise of Finance*, Cambridge, MA: Harvard University Press.

Krugman, P.R. (1979), 'Increasing returns, monopolistic competition, and international trade', *Journal of International Economics*, **9**, 469–79.

Krugman, P.R. (1989), 'Industrial Organization and International Trade', in R. Schmalenss and R.D. Willig (eds), *Handbook of Industrial Organization*, Amsterdam: Elsevier.

Krugman, P.R. (1990), *Rethinking International Trade*, Cambridge, MA: MIT Press.

Krugman, P.R. (1991), 'Increasing returns and economic geography', *Journal of Political Economy*, **99**(3), 483–99.

Krugman, P.R. (1993), *Geography and Trade*, Leuven, Belgium: Leuven University Press

Krugman, P.R. (1994) 'The myth of Asia's miracle', *Foreign Affairs*, **6**(73), 62–78.

Krugman, P.R. (1995), 'Growing world trade: causes and consequences', *Brookings Papers on Economic Activity*, **1**(Spring), 327–77.

Krugman, P.R. (2008), 'Trade and wages, reconsidered', *Brookings Papers on Economic Activity*, Spring, 103–54.

Krugman, P.R. and M. Obstfeld (2003), *International Economics: Theory and Policy*, 6th edn, Boston, MA: Addison-Wesley.

Kuznets, S. (1953), *Economic Change: Selected Essays in Business Cycles, National Income, and Economic Growth*, New York: Norton.

Laibson, D. and J. Mollerstrom (2010), 'Capital flows, consumption booms and asset bubbles: a behavioral alternative to the savings glut hypothesis', *Economic Journal*, **120**(544), 354–74.

Lapides, K. (1992), 'Henryk Grossman and the debate on the theoretical status of Marx's *Capital*', *Science and Society*, **56**(2), 133–62.

Lawrence, R.Z. (2008), 'Comment' on Krugman, P.R. (2008) 'Trade and wages, reconsidered', *Brookings Papers on Economic Activity*, Spring, 103–54; Lawrence's comments appear in same issue, pp. 149–53.

Leamer, E.E. (2012), *The Craft of Economics: Lessons from the Heckscher–Ohlin Framework*, Cambridge, MA, MIT Press.

Leamer, E.E. and J. Levinson (1994), 'International trade theory: the evidence', National Bureau for Economic Research working paper series no. 4940.

Lenin, V.I. (1975), *Imperialism, the Highest Stage of Capitalism*, Beijing: Foreign Languages Press.

Leontief, W. (1953), 'Production and foreign trade: the American capital position re-examined', *Proceedings of the American Philosphical Society*, **97**(4), 332–49.

Leys, C. (1996), *The Rise & Fall of Development Theory*, Nairobi, Kenya: EAEP.

List, F. (1885), *The National System of Political Economy*, London: Longmans, Green and Co.

List, F. (1983), *The Natural System of Political Economy*, London: Frank Cass.

Lowe, J. (2000), 'International examinations: the new credentialism and reproduction of advantage in a globalising world', *Assessment in Education*, **7**(3), 363–77.

Lukes, S. (1974), *Power: A Radical View*, London: Macmillan.

Luxemburg, R. (1963), *The Accumulation of Capital*, London: Routledge & Kegan Paul.

MacLean, J. (2000), 'Philosophical roots of globalization and philosophical routes to globalization', in R.D. Germain (ed.), *Globalization and its Critics*, Basingstoke: Macmillan.

Maddison, A. (2003), *The World Economy: Historical Statistics*, Paris: OECD.

Maddison, A. (2007), *Contours of the World Economy 1-2030 AD: Essays in Macro-Economic History*, Oxford: Oxford University Press.

Magdoff, H. (1969), *The Age of Imperialism*, New York: Monthly Review Press.

Mann, M. (1986), *The Sources of Social Power*, Cambridge: Cambridge University Press.

Markussen, J.R., J.R. Melvin, W.H. Kaempfer and K.E. Maskus (1995), *International Trade: Theory And Evidence*, New York: McGraw-Hill.

Marshall, A. (2009), *Principles of Economics*, 8th edn, New York: Cosimo.

Marx, K. (1973), *Grundrisse*, New York: Random House.

Marx, K. (1974), *The First International and After*, New York: Vintage.

Marx, K. (1976), *Capital: A Critique of Political Economy: Volume I*, Harmondsworth: Penguin.

Marx, K. (1977), *Selected Writings*, (ed.) D. McLellan, Oxford: Oxford University Press.

Marx, K. (1981), *Capital: A Critique of Political Economy: Volume III*, Harmondsworth: Penguin.

Marx, K. (2006), 'Draft of an article on Friedrich List's book: *Das Nationale System der Politischen Oekonomie*'. Available at: https://marxists.anu.edu.au/archive/marx/works/1845/03/list.htm on (accessed 26 June 2006).

Marx, K. and F. Engels (1965), *Manifesto of the Communist Party*, Beijing: Foreign Languages Press.

Matsushita, M., T.J. Schoenbaum and P.C. Mavroidis (2006), *The World Trade Organization: Law, Practice, and Policy*, 2nd edn, Oxford: Oxford University Press.

Meschi, E. and M. Vivarelli (2009), 'Trade and income inequality in developing countries', *World Development*, **37**(2), 287–302.

Metcalfe, J.S. and I. Steedman (1974), 'A note on the gain from trade', *Economic Record*, **50**(132), 581–95.

Milberg, W. and D. Winkler (2010), 'Financialisation and the dynamics of offshoring in the USA', *Cambridge Journal of Economics*, **34**, 275–93.

Mill, J.S. (1994), *Principles of Political Economy*, Oxford: Oxford University Press.

Mishel, L., J. Bernstein and S. Allegretto (2007), *The State of Working America, 2006/7*, Ithaca, NY: ILR Press.

Moody, K. (1997), *Workers in a Lean World*, London: Verso.

Mun, T. (1959), *England's Treasure by Foreign Trade*, Oxford: Basil Blackwell.

Narlikar, A. (2003), *International Trade and Developing Countries: Bargaining Coalitions in the GATT and WTO*, London: Routledge.

Narlikar, A. (2006), 'Fairness in international trade negotiations: developing countries in the GATT and WTO', *The World Economy*, **29**(8), 1005–29.

Naude, W. and T. Gries (2009), 'Explaining regional export performance in a developing country: the role of geography and relative factor endowments', *Regional Studies*, **43**(7), 967–79.

Navarro, V. (2000), 'Are pro-welfare state and full-employment policies possible in the era of globalization', *International Journal of Health Services*, **30**(2), 231–51.

O'Brien R. and M. Williams (2004), *Global Political Economy*, Basingstoke: Palgrave Macmillan.

Ocampo, J.A. and M. Parra-Lancourt (2010), 'The terms of trade for commodities since the mid-19th century', *Revista de Historia Econmmica/Journal of Iberian and Latin American History*, **28**(1), 11–43.

O'Connor, J. (1988), 'Capitalism, nature, socialism: a theoretical introduction', *Capitalism, Nature, Socialism*, **1**(1), 11–38.

OECD (Organisation for Economic Co-ordination and Development) (2010), data available from OECD.StatExtracts http://stats.oecd.org/ (data extracted 21 June 2010).

OECD (2014), data from OECD.StatExtracts, available at http://stats.oecd.org/ (accessed 15 September 2014).

Ohlin, B. (1991), 'The theory of trade', in H. Flam and M.J. Flanders (eds), *Heckscher–Ohlin Trade Theory*, Cambridge, MA: MIT Press.

Oxfam (2002), *Rigged Rules and Double Standards*. Available at: http://policy-practice.oxfam.org.uk/publications/rigged-rules-and-double-standards-trade-globalisation-and-the-fight-against-pov-112391 (accessed 2 March 2007).

Oxford English Dictionary (OED) (1982), *The Concise Oxford English*, Oxford: Clarendon.

Pareti, L. (ed.) (1965), *History of Mankind: Cultural and Scientific Development, Vol II*, London: George Allen and Unwin.

Pasinetti, L.L. and R. Scazzieri (1987), 'Capital theory: paradoxes', in J. Eatwell, M. Milgate and P. Newman (eds), *The New Palgrave: A Dictionary of Economics*, Palgrave: London.

Peterson, E.W.F. and S.R.K. Valluru (2000), 'Agricultural comparative advantage and government policy interventions', *Journal of Agricultural Economics*, **51**(3), 371–87.

Piazza, J.A. (2005), 'Globalizing quiescence: globalization, union density and strikes in 15 industrialized countries', *Economic and Industrial Democracy*, **26**(2), 289–314.

Polanyi, K. (2001), *The Great Transformation*, Boston, MA: Beacon Press.

Prebisch, R. (1950), *The Economic Development of Latin America and its Principal Problems*, New York: United Nations.

Prebisch, R. (1959), 'Commercial policy in the underdeveloped countries', *American Economic Review*, **49**(2), 251–73.

Prebisch, R. (1971), *Change and Development – Latin America's Great Task*, New York: Praeger.

Radice, H. (2000), 'Responses to globalisation: a critique of progressive nationalism', *New Political Economy*, **5**(1), 5–19.

Raffer, K. (1987), *Unequal Exchange and the Evolution of the World System: Reconsidering the Impact of Trade on North-South Relations*, New York: St Martin's Press.

Rangarajan, L. (1984) 'The politics of international trade', in S. Strange (ed.), *Paths to International Political Economy*, London: George Allen & Unwin.

Reich, R.B. (1991), *The Work of Nations*, London: Simon & Schuster.

Reinert, E.S. and S.A. Reinert (2005), 'Mercantilism and economic development', in K.S. Jomo and E.S. Reinert, *The Origins of Development Economics*, London: Zed.

Reuveny, R. and Q. Li (2003), 'Economic openness, democracy, and income inequality: and empirical analysis', *Comparative Political Studies*, **36**(5), 575-601.

Ricardo, D. (1951), *On the Principles of Political Economy and Taxation*, Cambridge: Cambridge University Press

Robinson, J. (1964), *Economic Philosophy*, Harmondsworth: Pelican.

Robinson, J. (1979), *Aspects of Development and Underdevelopment*, Cambridge: Cambridge University Press.

Rodney, W. (1974), *How Europe Underdeveloped Africa*, Washington, DC: Howard University.

Rodriguez, F. and D. Rodrik (2000), 'Trade policy and economic growth', working paper 9912. Available at: https://ideas.repec.org/h/nbr/nberch/11058.html (accessed 15 November 2014).

Rodrik, D. (1997), 'Has globalization gone too far?', Washington, DC: Institute for International Economics.

Rodrik, D. (1998), 'Globalisation, social conflict and economic growth', *The World Economy*, **21**(2), 143–58.

Rodrik, D. (2001), 'The global governance of trade: as if development really mattered', United Nations Development Programme.

Rodrik, D. (2003), 'Growth strategies', NBER working paper series 10050. Available at: http://www.nber.org/papers/w10050 (accessed 14 November 2014).

Rodrik, D. (2007), 'How to save globalization from its cheerleaders', *The Journal of International Trade and Diplomacy*, **1**(2), 1–33.

Rogowski, R. (1989), *Commerce and Coalitions: How Trade Affects Domestic Political Alignments*, Princeton, NJ: Princeton University Press.

Ros, J. (1987), 'Growth and international trade', in J. Eatwell, M. Milgate and P. Newman (eds), *The New Palgrave: A Dictionary of Economics*, London: Macmillan.

Rosdolsky, R. (1977), *The Making of Marx's Capital*, London: Pluto.

Rosenberg, J. (1994), *The Empire of Civil Society*, London: Verso.

Rosenberg, J. (2006), 'Why is there no international historical sociology?', *European Journal of International Relations* **12**(3), 307–40.

Rosenberg, J. (2008), in A. Callinicos and J. Rosenberg, 'Uneven and combined development: the social-relational substratum of 'the international'? An exchange of letters', *Cambridge Review of International Affairs*, **21**(1), 77–112.

Rosenberg, J. (2009), 'Basic problems in the theory of uneven and combined development: a reply to the CRIA forum', *Cambridge Review of International Affairs* **22**(1), 107–110.

Rosenberg, J. (2010), 'Basic problems in the theory of uneven and combined development. Part II: unevenness and political multiplicity', *Cambridge Review of International Affairs*, **23**(1), 165–89.

Ross, M.L. (1999), 'The political economy of the resource curse', *World Politics*, **51**(2), 297–322.

Roxborough, I. (1979), *Theories of Underdevelopment*, Basingstoke: Macmillan.

Sachs, J.D. and A. Warner (1995a), 'Economic reform and the process of global integration', *Brookings Papers on Economic Activity*, **1995**(1), 25th Anniversary Issue, 1–95.

Sachs, J.D. and A.M. Warner (1995b), 'Natural resource abundance and economic growth', NBER working paper 5398.

Samuelson, P.A. (1948), 'International trade and the equalisation of factor prices', *The Economic Journal*, **58**(230), 163–84.

Samuelson, P.A. (1966), 'A summing up', *Quarterly Journal of Economics*, **80**(4), 568–83.

Samuelson, P.A. (2004), 'Where Ricardo and Mill rebut and confirm arguments of mainstream economists supporting globalization', *Journal of Economic Perspectives*, **18**(3), 135–46.

Sau, R. (1978), *Unequal Exchange, Imperialism and Underdevelopment*, Kolkata, India: Oxford University Press.

Scheuer, S. (2006), 'A novel calculus? Institutional change, globalization and industrial conflict in Europe', *European Journal of Industrial Relations*, **21**(2), 143–64.

Scholte, J.A. (2000), *Globalization: A Critical Introduction*, Basingstoke: Palgrave Macmillan.

Schumpeter, J.A. (1986), *History of Economic Analysis*, London: Routledge.

Sell, S.K. (2000), 'Big business and the new trade agreements', in R. Stubbs and G.R.D. Underhill (eds), *Political Economy and the Changing Global Order*, Oxford: Oxford University Press.

Selwyn, B. (2009), 'An historical materialist appraisal of Friedrich List and his Modern-Day followers', *New Political Economy*, **14**(2), 57–80.

Selwyn, B. (2011), 'Beyond firm-centrism: re-integrating labour and capitalism into global commodity chain analysis', *Journal of Economic Geography*, **12**(1), 205–26.

Shaikh, A. (1979), 'Foreign trade and the law of value: part 1', *Science and Society*, **43**(3), 281–302.

Shaikh, A. (1980), 'Foreign trade and the law of value: part II', *Science and Society*, **44**(1), 27–57.

Shaikh, A. (2007), 'Globalization and the myth of free trade', in A. Shaikh (ed.), *Globalization and the Myths of Free Trade*, London: Routledge.

Sheppard, E. (2005), 'Constructing free trade: from Manchester boosterism to global management', *Transactions of the Institute of British Geographers*, **30**(2), 151–72.

Sheppard, E. (2012), 'Trade, globalization and uneven development: entanglements of geographical political economy', *Progress in Human Geography*, **36**(1), 44–71.

Sikka, P. and H. Willmott (2010), 'The dark side of transfer pricing: its role in tax avoidance and wealth retentiveness', Colchester: University of Essex Business School.

Silver, B. J. (2003), *Forces of Labor: Workers' Movements and Globalization Since 1870*, New York: Cambridge University Press.

Singer, H.W. (1950), 'The distribution of gains between investing and borrowing countries', *The American Economic Review*, **40**(2), 473–85.

Skocpol, T. (1977), 'Wallerstein's World Capitalist System: a theoretical and historical critique', *American Journal of Sociology*, **82**(5), 1075–90.

Sloman, J. and K. Norris, (1999), *Economics*, Sydney, NSW: Prentice Hall.

Smith, A. (1997), *The Wealth of Nations, Books I–III*, London: Penguin.

Smith, A. (1999), *The Wealth of Nations, Books IV–V*, London: Penguin.

Solow, B.L. and S.L. Engerman (eds) (1987), *British Capitalism and Caribbean Slavery*, New York: Cambridge University Press.

Solt, F. (2013), The Standardized World Income Inequality Database. Available at: http://myweb.uiowa.edu/fsolt/papers/Solt2014/ (accessed 14 November 2014).

Steedman, I. and J.S. Metcalfe (1977), 'Reswitching, primary inputs and the Heckscher–Ohlin–Samuelson theory of trade', *Journal of International Economics*, **7**(2), 201–208.

Stiglitz, J. and A. Charlton (2005), *Fair Trade for All*, Oxford: Oxford University Press.

Stolper, W.F. and P.A. Samuelson (1941), 'Protection and real wages', *Review of Economic Studies*, **9**(1), 58–73.

Strange, S. (1996), *The Retreat of the State: Diffusion of Power in the World Economy*, Cambridge: Cambridge University Press.

Strange, S. (1998), 'Globalony?', *Review of International Political Economy*, **5**(4), 704–711.

Sweezy, P. (1976) 'A critique', in R. Hilton (ed.), *The Transition from Feudalism to Capitalism*, London: NLB.

Tabb, W.K. (1999), *Reconstructing Political Economy*, London: Routledge.

Thomas, K.P. (1997), *Capital Beyond Borders: States, and Firms in the Auto Industry, 1960–1994*, Basingstoke: Macmillan.

Todaro, M.P. and S.C. Smith (2009), *Economic Development*, 10th edn, Harlow: Addison-Wesley.

Trefler, D. (1993), 'International factor price differences: Leontief was right!', *Journal of Political Economy*, **101**(6), 961–87.

United Nations (UN) (1962), International Trade Statistics: 1900–1960. Available at: http://unstats.un.org/unsd/trade/imts/historical_data.htm (accessed 5 February 2013).

UN (1993), *1992 International Trade Statistics Yearbook: Volume 1, Trade by Country*, New York: United Nations.

UN (2007), *Human Development Report 2007/2008*, New York: United Nations Development Programme.

UN (2011), *2010 International Trade Statistics Yearbook: Volume 1, Trade by Country*, New York: United Nations.

UN (2012), *Trade and Development Report*, Geneva: United Nations.

United Nations Educational, Scientific and Cultural Organization (UNESCO) (2011), 'Education: gross enrolment ratio by level of education', data available at: http://stats.uis.unesco.org/unesco/Report Folders/ReportFolders.aspx?IF_ActivePath=P,50&IF_Language=eng (accessed 14 November 2014).

Office of the United States Trade Representative (USTR) (2014), Free Trade Agreements. Available at: http://www.ustr.gov/trade-agreements/ free-trade-agreements (accessed 21 May 2014).

Vandaale, K. (2011), 'Sustaining or abandoning "social peace"?, Strike developments and trends in Europe since the 1990s', ETUI working paper 2011.05, Brussels.

Viner, J. (1965), *Studies in the Theory of International Trade*, New York: Augustus M. Kelley.

Wacziarg, R. and K. Horn Welch (2008), 'Trade liberalization and growth: new evidence', *The World Bank Economic Review*, **22**(2), 187–231.

Wade, R. (1990), *Governing the Market*, Princeton, NJ: Princeton University Press.

Wade, R. (2003), 'What strategies are viable for developing countries today? The World Trade Organization and the shrinking of "development space"', *Review of International Political Economy*, **10**(4), 621–44.

Wade, R. (2009), 'The global slump: deeper causes and harder lessons', *Challenge*, **52**(5), 5–13.

Walker, R.A. (1999), 'Putting capital in its place: globalization and the prospects for labor', *Geoforum*, **30**(3), 263–84.

Wallerstein, I. (1974), *The Modern World-System: Capitalist Agriculture and the Origins of the European World-Economy in the Sixteenth Century*, New York: Academic Press.

World Bank (WB) (1993), *The East Asian Miracle*, Oxford: Oxford University Press.

WB (2012), data, available at http://databank.worldbank.org/ddp/home.do (accessed on various dates 2014).

WB (2014), Explore. Create. Share: Development Data. Available at: http://databank.worldbank.org/ddp/home.do (accessed on various dates 2014).

Webber, M.J. and D.L. Rigby (1996), *The Golden Age Illusion: Rethinking Postwar Capitalism*, New York: The Guilford Press.

Weiss, L. (1998), *The Myth of the Powerless State*, Ithaca, NY: Cornell University Press.

Weiss, L. (1999), 'Managed openness: beyond neoliberal globalism', *New Left Review*, **238**, 126–40.

Weiss, L. (2005), 'Global governance, national strategies: how industrialized states make room to move under the WTO', *Review of International Political Economy*, **12**(5), 723–49.

Williams, E.E. (1964), *Capitalism and Slavery*, London: Deutsch.

Winters, L.A. (2004), 'Trade liberalisation and economic performance: an overview', *The Economic Journal* **114**(493), 4–21.

World Investment Report (WIR) (2011), 'World Investment Report 2011: non-equity modes on international production and development'. Available at: http://unctad.org/en/pages/PublicationWebflyer.aspx?publication id=84 (accessed 15 September 2014).

Williamson, J. (1990), What Washington means by policy reform', in J. Williamson (ed.), *Latin American Adjustment: How Much Has Happened?*, Peterson Institute for International Economics. Available at: https://edisk.fandm.edu/min/IST-325-Ecuador/What-Washington-Means-by-Policy-Reform.pdf (accessed 15 September 2014).

Wolf, M. (2005), *Why Globalization Works*, New Haven, CT: Yale Nota Bene.

Wolf, M. (2010), *Fixing Global Finance*, expanded and updated edition, New Haven, CT: Yale University Press.

Wolfe, R. (2004), 'Crossing the river by feeling the stones: where the WTO is going after Seattle, Doha and Cancun', *Review of International Political Economy*, **11**(3), 574–96.

Womack, J.P., D.T. Jones and D. Roos (1990), *The Machine That Changed the World: The Story of Lean Production*, New York: Rawson Associates.

Wood, A. (1994), *North–South Trade, Employment and Inequality: Changing Fortunes in a Skill-Driven World*, Oxford: Clarendon, Oxford University Press.

Wood, A. (1998), 'Globalisation and the rise in labour market inequalities', *The Economic Journal*, **108**(450), 1463–82.

Wood, A. and K. Berge (1997), 'Exporting manufactures: human resources, natural resources, and trade policy', *The Journal of Development Studies*, **34**(1), 35–59.

Wood, A. and J. Mayer (2001), 'Africa's export structure in a comparative perspective', *Cambridge Journal of Economics*, **25**(3), 369–94.

Wood, E.M. (2002), *The Origin of Capitalism: A Longer View*, London: Verso.

Woolley, L. (1963) 'The beginnings of civilization', in J. Hawkes and L. Woolley, *History of Mankind: Cultural and Scientific Development, Vol I*, London: George Allen and Unwin.

Wray L.R. (2008), 'The commodities market bubble: money manager capitalism and the financialization of commodities', The Levy Economics Institute of Bard College Public Policy Brief No. 96.

World Trade Organization (WTO) (2014), What is the World Trade Organization? Available at: http://www.wto.org/english/thewto_e/what is_e/tif_e/fact1_e.htm (accessed 18 May 2014).

Yanikkaya, H. (2003), 'Trade openness and economic growth: a cross-country empirical investigation', *Journal of Development Economics*, **72**(1), 57–89.

Index